MULTIMEDIA DESIGN AND PRODUCTION FOR STUDENTS AND TEACHERS

EDWARD L. COUNTS, JR.
University of Tennessee

PEARSON

Boston ■ New York ■ San Francisco
Mexico City ■ Montreal ■ Toronto ■ London ■ Madrid ■ Munich ■ Paris
Hong Kong ■ Singapore ■ Tokyo ■ Cape Town ■ Sydney

Series Editor: *Arnis Burvikovs*
Series Editorial Assistant: *Christine Lyons*
Marketing Manager: *Tara Whorf*
Production Administrator: *Michael Granger*
Editorial-Production Service: *Omegatype Typography, Inc.*
Composition and Prepress Buyer: *Linda Cox*
Manufacturing Buyer: *Andrew Turso*
Cover Administrator: *Kristina Mose-Libon*
Electronic Composition: *Omegatype Typography, Inc.*

Library of Congress Cataloging-in-Publication Data

Counts, Edward L.
    Multimedia design and production for students and teachers / Edward L. Counts, Jr.
      p. cm.
    Includes bibliographical references and index.
    ISBN 0-205-34387-2 (alk. paper)
    1. Multimedia systems. 2. System design. I. Title.

  QA76.575 .C684 2004
  006.7—dc21

                                      2002038506

Printed in the United States of America

10 9 8 7 6 5 4 3 2 1   08 07 06 05 04 03

CONTENTS

Preface   vii

CHAPTER ONE

Freed from the Boundaries of Time and Space: Working with Multimedia Technologies   1

ALTERNATIVE ASPECTS OF INSTRUCTIONAL TECHNOLOGY   2

WHO THIS BOOK IS FOR   5

MULTIMEDIA GOES TO SCHOOL: SOME ASSUMPTIONS
AND STATEMENTS   6

SUMMARY: USING THIS BOOK   9

THOUGHT PROVOKERS   10

REFERENCES   10

CHAPTER TWO

Creating Fresh Perceptions of the World: A Brief History of Multimedia   11

MULTIMEDIA: A FRAMEWORK   12

EXPLAINING THE WORLD: THE POWER OF THE DOCUMENTARY   13
> BOX 2.1   The Continuing Power
> of the Documentary: *9/11*   20

ANIMATION FROM Z TO A: ZOETROPES TO ANIME   21

AUDIOVISUAL TOOLS ENTER THE SCHOOLS   28

SUMMARY: FROM GERTIE TO GIGABYTES   30

THOUGHT PROVOKERS   30
> BOX 2.2   Sources of Sometimes "Hard-to-Find" Titles   31

REFERENCES   32

CHAPTER THREE

A Multimedia Starter Kit: Motivation, Tools, Skills   33

THE MULTIPLES IN MEDIA: SOME THINGS TO THINK
ABOUT BEFORE STARTING   34

PLANNING   36

FAIR USE GUIDELINES   40

MULTIMEDIA, MULTIPLE MEDIUMS: SOFTWARE "WARHORSES"   42

BASIC DESIGN 101   47

SUMMARY: MAKING MULTIMEDIA   49

THOUGHT PROVOKERS   49

REFERENCES   49

CHAPTER FOUR

Digital Stills: Revealing the World with a Digital Gallery   51

A PHOTOGRAPHIC HISTORY AND AESTHETIC   52

MAKING AN ONLINE GALLERY   53

BOX 4.1   Digital Cameras in the Second Language Classroom
by Amy Kelly   54

SUMMARY: THE EVOLVING GALLERY   63

THOUGHT PROVOKERS   63

REFERENCES   64

CHAPTER FIVE

The Mechanical Eye Becomes the Digital Eye: Revealing the World with Video   65

THE CLASSIC STEPS: PREPRODUCTION,
PRODUCTION, POSTPRODUCTION   66

MAKING DIGITAL MOVIES: SKILLS AND CONCEPTS   67

DIGITAL VIDEO EXERCISES   90

**A CULMINATING VIDEO PROJECT: DOING THE HUMANITIES
WITH DIGITAL VIDEO   108**

> **BOX 5.1**   Using Video to Create Portraits: Team Building
> with Special Needs Kids   *by Dr. Kathryn Dipietro*   110

SUMMARY: MOVIEMAKING REFLECTIONS AND TIPS   115

THOUGHT PROVOKER   116

REFERENCES   116

CHAPTER SIX

Living Pixels: Digital Animation   117

**THEORIES AND METHODS OF ANIMATED MOTION:
HOW IT WORKS AND HOW TO MAKE IT WORK   118**

> **BOX 6.1**   Neighborhood Stories: A Case Study in Claymation
> *by Ron Schildknecht and Ruben Moreno*   127

DRAWING ON THE COMPUTER   137

ANIMATION EXERCISES AND PROJECTS   144

INFORMATION SOURCES AND IDEAS FOR LEARNING ABOUT ANIMATION   193

SUMMARY: HAPPY ANIMATING   195

THOUGHT PROVOKERS   196

REFERENCES   196

CHAPTER SEVEN

A Final Project and Vertov Revisited   198

CONSTRUCTING MULTIMEDIA MOUNTAINS   199

VERTOV REVISITED   201

THOUGHT AND PROJECT PROVOKERS: MULTIMEDIA IDEAS   202

Index   203

In 1982, *Time* magazine selected the personal computer as its "person of the year." At that time, the microcomputer was making its way into classrooms all over the world. Educators and students were encouraged to become computer-literate as they learned how to operate microcomputers and how to program in BASIC. As schools from kindergarten through university level installed computer labs and placed computers in classrooms, preservice and in-service teachers were encouraged and often required to learn to use technology. Instructional technology became a staple of teacher education curriculum. As computer hardware became less expensive and easier to use and the software became more sophisticated and engaging, educators snapped up this technology. The hardware and software were in place, yet educators and teachers were still without guidelines or best practices for using these resources to enhance or even improve instruction. Further, this revolution was not without its critics. Clifford Stoll in *High-Tech Heretic* (1999), for example, made a strong case against the use of computers in education. No technophobe, Stoll argued convincingly that computers in schools had not improved education in the almost twenty years since their introduction. Social critics, researchers, and investigators pointed out the inequity of access to computers based on gender and economics, often referred to as the digital divide.

As more and more schools have connected to the Internet and the World Wide Web, the technological complexities have increased as has the search for meaningful instructional uses. With the flourishing of the Internet and the development of supporting digital technologies, the educational possibilities have multiplied. The concept of multimedia has refocused educators' interest in technology: the computer is now not only a deliverer of information but also a self-directed learning tool. Digital multimedia tools offer teachers and students the potential to engage technology in creative and expressive ways that enhance teaching and learning. This book makes a case for the use of instructional media and technology in schools as a creative, educational, learner-controlled media production resource that students and teachers can use in many creative ways—from composing simple digital "slide shows" to producing sophisticated digital videos and animated movies.

The emergence of the computer and related digital technologies is often referred to as revolutionary. That may be true, but there was a prior revolution. In 1923, the documentary filmmaker Dziga Vertov wrote:

> I'm an eye. A mechanical eye. I, the machine, show you a world the way only I can see it. I free myself for today and forever from human immobility. I'm in constant movement. I approach and pull away from objects. I creep under them. I move alongside a running horse's mouth. I fall and rise with the falling and rising bodies.

This is I, the machine, manoeuvering in the chaotic movements, recording one movement after another in the most complex combinations.

Freed from the boundaries of time and space, I coordinate any and all points of the universe, wherever I want them to be. My way leads towards the creation of a fresh perception of the world. Thus I explain in new ways the world unknown to you. (Berger, 1972)

That quote, in fact, summarizes the theoretical foundation for the projects in this book—using multimedia tools, as Vertov used his "mechanical eye," to reveal the world in new ways. (There is more about Vertov in Chapter 2.) Chapter 1, Freed from the Boundaries of Time and Space: Working with Multimedia Technologies, provides a conceptual framework for the use of this book. Chapter 2, Creating Fresh Perceptions of the World: A Brief History of Multimedia, examines the historical perspectives that influence contemporary multimedia design and production. Chapter 3, A Multimedia Starter Kit: Motivation, Tools, Skills, contains some ideas, perspectives, attitudes, and philosophical notions for potential multimedia producers to consider. This chapter also describes systematic planning for multimedia productions, including storyboarding, and summarizes the concept of the fair use of various elements of multimedia production. Chapter 4, Digital Stills: Revealing the World with a Digital Gallery, presents the educational and creative power of digital still photography. Chapter 5, The Mechanical Eye Becomes the Digital Eye: Revealing the World with Video, describes some step-by-step ideas and methods for using the tools of digital video production creatively and expressively. Chapter 6, Living Pixels: Digital Animation, presents an overview of animation as an art form and describes how contemporary digital production tools can be used to engage learners in a number of creative animation projects. Chapter 7, A Final Project and Vertov Revisited, describes a culminating activity based on the skills and ideas presented in previous chapters plus some final suggestions for multimedia projects.

The ideas, projects, and exercises in this book can be adapted to many teaching and learning situations. It is hoped that this book will also address, at least in some small way, the simple question that so many educators ask: "How can we use this stuff?"

Warning! Learning to use this vast and stimulating array of multimedia tools can be fun and addictive—even life changing!

E.L.C.

ACKNOWLEDGMENTS

For many years, I have had the pleasure and privilege of working with many teachers, artists, media producers, and most of all students—from elementary schoolchildren to doctoral candidates. I especially want to acknowledge those hundreds of students for providing the inspiration for this book. I have never been disappointed in the freshness and originality of their work and their eagerness to learn. In particular, two of those I knew as students are now cherished colleagues and creative collaborators: Ron Schildknecht of the University of Louisville and Kathryn Dipietro of Lehigh University. Another colleague, John Ray of the University of Tennessee, provided the support and motivation to undertake this project.

Many thanks to the reviewers of this edition for their helpful comments and suggestions: Dr. Mac Adkins, Troy State University Montgomery; Dr. Kimberly Fatata-Hall, Nova University; Jean Morrow, Emporia State University; and Sandra Sutherland, Carlsbad Unified School District.

Finally, I acknowledge the encouragement and suggestions provided by my wife Janice.

REFERENCES

Berger, John. (1972). *Ways of Seeing: A Book Made by John Berger and Others*. London: British Broadcasting Corporation.

Stoll, Clifford. (1999). *High-Tech Heretic: Reflections of a Computer Contrarian*. New York: Doubleday.

■ ■ ■ ■ ■

CHAPTER ONE

FREED FROM THE BOUNDARIES OF TIME AND SPACE

Working with Multimedia Technologies

TOPIC OUTLINE

ALTERNATIVE ASPECTS OF INSTRUCTIONAL TECHNOLOGY

This section describes some perspectives of instructional technology in a digital era.

WHO THIS BOOK IS FOR

Listed here are potential school audiences that may benefit from the activities, ideas, and projects in this book.

MULTIMEDIA GOES TO SCHOOL: SOME ASSUMPTIONS AND STATEMENTS

This section describes some ideas and presumptions to consider when learning to use contemporary multimedia tools.

SUMMARY: USING THIS BOOK

Suggestions are provided for teachers and students to help them successfully implement the multimedia projects and exercises contained in this book.

THOUGHT PROVOKERS

These are suggestions for personal reflections on the nature of instructional technology and multimedia.

OBJECTIVES

After reading, reflecting on, and discussing the topics in this chapter, the reader will be able to:

■ Describe the constructivist conceptual framework for the use of the tools and processes of instructional technology in general and multimedia technology in particular.

■ Describe multimedia skills before selecting projects and activities described in this book.

- Understand some common assumptions about the nature of learning about and using multimedia resources.
- Understand that the projects and skills in this book can be adapted to unique needs, interests, and circumstances.

ALTERNATIVE ASPECTS OF INSTRUCTIONAL TECHNOLOGY

This book exists at the convergence of education, technology, culture, and art. Its primary purpose is practical in that it describes ideas and techniques that will bring life, expression, and learning to the application of various multimedia tools. The author's perspective on the nature of instructional technology is the result of his education in the visual arts, his work as an independent media artist, his study of the theoretical nature of teaching and learning, and his many years of working with teachers and students from the primary grades through graduate school.

Historically, the dominant theoretical foundation for what has come to be referred to as *instructional technology* has been the psychology of behaviorism. That is, the design and use of a variety of nonprint media has been and often still is based on the specification of measurable and observable behavioral objectives. Behaviorism had its origins in the experimental studies of animal behavior by researchers such as E. L. Thorndike and B. F. Skinner, who proposed that the modification or control of behavior in people, as well as in animals, was based on the theory of operant conditioning. Simply stated, operant conditioning means that a swift reward to desirable behavior reinforces that behavior. Behaviorism (far more complex than can be stated here) has become one of the most influential theoretical foundations for the design and evaluation of instruction. Another common influence on the use of instructional media has been the assumption that it should serve as an aid to conventional teacher-centered instruction, that is, "audiovisual aids." This approach sees instructional media or audiovisuals as a supplement to or support of the traditional teacher-centered lecture. Another influential and widely used model for the planning and use of instructional media has been Edgar Dale's "Cone of Experience." Dale argued that communication exists on a concrete-to-abstract continuum with verbal symbols of language being abstract and direct experience being concrete. Based on this perspective, Dale suggested that the less abstract the instruction, the better.

The behavioral, audiovisual, and abstract-to-concrete models can be practical and useful if used thoughtfully or, better, creatively. However, these approaches tend to be teacher and material centered. Thus, one may observe that much contemporary instructional computer software that directs learners to "interact" in specified ways is merely a continuation of conventional classroom instruction. The computer and its software direct the instruction, exactly as it is programmed and distributed by the software designer. Again, for some objectives such as drill and practice, for example, that use may even be the best choice. However, the emergence of a new generation of digital media tools allows the computer to be used not only for instruction but also for construction. In other words, the role of technology in the classroom can be expanded from computer-delivered instruction to user-directed construction.

A Technology of Instruction

What was once known as "audiovisual education" and later as "instructional communications," "educational media," or "instructional media" is now known as *instructional technology.* This term conjures several meanings depending on whom one asks to define it. Some see instructional technology as consisting only of computers and related hardware and software. Others may include a whole range of instructional devices ranging from computers, slide projectors, camcorders and VCRs, to overhead projectors. From another theoretical perspective, that of instructional technologists and instructional designers, instructional technology does not refer to machines or devices at all but rather to what is often described as systematic instruction. A comprehensive definition of instructional technology does exist, however. In 1994 the Association for Educational Communications and Technology (AECT), the oldest learned society devoted to the study, support, and advocacy of instructional technology, proposed a comprehensive definition of the domain of instructional technology.

> Instructional Technology is the theory and practice of design, development, utilization, management, and evaluation of processes and resources for learning.

Thus, one can see that by this definition, the concept of instructional technology includes a very wide range of theories and applications from research to support. Though this book, as previously noted, exists at the convergence of education, technology, culture, and art, its activities fit squarely within the AECT definition, in particular as a "resource for learning."

Instruction

The history of the tools and devices of instructional technology parallels and often intersects the history of media such as the motion picture, television, and interactive computer-based multimedia. As the motion picture evolved as an entertainment and documentary medium, for example, educators adopted it for use in schools. Other media were developed specifically for educational purposes, including the filmstrip projector, lantern slide projector, and overhead projector. Media such as color photography and audio recordings were and are used throughout society, including in education.

As these tools were invented and adopted, theories for their effective application to teaching and learning evolved. As noted in the previous sections, these theories are often presented as models that guide the planning, producing, using, and assessing of instruction that uses various instructional media. The primary characteristic shared by most of these instructional models is the emphasis on precisely stated goals and objectives that result in observable and measurable results. In other words, the effectiveness of the instruction is based on the learner's ability to perform, demonstrate, or provide observable evidence that the objective was achieved, often using computers as in Figure 1.1.

FIGURE 1.1   Technology as Instructor. Learners responding to preprogrammed instruction delivered via computers.

This process, referred to as instructional design, has practical advantages because of its emphasis on precision. Thus, for some objectives and some learners, the instructional design concept works very well. For that reason, the concepts of instructional design, or systematic instruction, are fundamental to the study of instructional technology. In particular, the instructional design concept is a practical way to plan training and instruction that integrates technology in support of the specified objectives of teacher, school, state, or corporate training.

Construction

Although acknowledging the crucial role of instructional design in the evolution of a technology of instruction, the perspective of this book is the idea that the primary driving force of multimedia is constructivist in nature. Though technology provides powerful tools for delivering information, technology also enables students and teachers to create a wide range of media for various uses. That is, students and teachers are looking for ways to use multimedia technologies to construct and direct their own learning rather than to provide preprogrammed sequences of instruction.

The conceptual framework of this book is based on the concepts and theories of media production as developed by the creators of an art or language of media production. The rationale for this perspective is that what is often referred to as "multimedia" is the dynamic combination of elements and ideas pioneered by the diverse interests and theories of educators, communications theorists, media producers, animation artists, software designers, and others. The obvious effectiveness of presenting information and ideas via a range of media formats has been adapted to all levels of education and instruction. Most important though is the fact that multimedia in all its manifestations is a phenomenon of possibilities. The most potent of these possibilities are the creative production tools in the hands of students and teachers as shown in Figure 1.2.

The focus and responsibility is on the creator to use these tools to experiment, to try, to retry, and to create. These tools, by their very nature, are learner centered and learner directed. Ideas are of paramount importance and these tools exist to express ideas. Whereas conventional computer-centered tutorials provide direct instruction based on precisely defined objectives, the creation of multimedia products depends on the users' willingness to deal with the ambiguities and unpredictability of the creative process. Teachers who understand the open-ended possibilities of multimedia tools can coach or guide their students as they engage the diversity and power of multimedia tools and processes. This book provides concepts and ideas that will help teachers and students do just that.

WHO THIS BOOK IS FOR

In keeping with that spirit of construction, this book is designed for teachers and students. Teachers can refer to the activities, projects, and ideas to prepare lessons on the creative use of multimedia technologies, or they can make and use multimedia tools in support of assignments and units. Further, students can use these descriptions as guides for multimedia projects. Though the projects are described in detail, each one can be adapted to meet specific and unique needs. In particular, these projects are designed to work for teachers and students with limited resources, experiences, and technical skills who

- Want to learn some fundamental skills to build on
- Want to use technology creatively and expressively
- May not have access to large quantities of expensive tools
- May not have the support of an instructional technologist or media specialist

The projects in this book are not intended for experts, even though experienced digital media producers may learn from them. These projects can be followed step-by-step, or they can be modified and interpreted to match particular purposes.

FIGURE 1.2   Technology as Construction. Modern
multimedia tools provide creative and expressive
capabilities for students and teachers.

Finally, one of the most important aspects of this book is that the ideas and
projects can be useful for teachers and students at all levels. For example, a simple
animation method using inexpensive software on a common desktop or laptop
computer can be stimulating for adults and children, teachers and students, in
many learning contexts, for many purposes.

MULTIMEDIA GOES TO SCHOOL: SOME
ASSUMPTIONS AND STATEMENTS

The core assumption of this book is that students and teachers can learn to use
multimedia tools, theories, and skills to create original, inventive, and expressive

works of high technical quality. This does *not* include recording book reports, plays, sports, news reports, and so on. Although those are very important applications, this book will focus, again, on creativity, originality, inventiveness, and expressiveness.

There are students and teachers who want to *make* media, not just *watch* and *interact* with commercially produced products. Indeed, digital multimedia technologies are based on the assumption that users are also creators. Consider the tools: digital movies and video, digital still photography, and an infinite and growing selection of software for drawing, painting, moviemaking, recording, editing, animating, writing, printing, and showing. This book explores the unlimited educational–creative potential of combining the newer digital media and technologies with the expressive powers of traditional media production as pioneered by those described in Chapter 2.

The following chapters will concentrate on activities and projects that students and teachers can use to make media products that are stimulating, creative, expressive, and educationally valuable to the maker and user. The described methods, projects, and activities are based on resources and tools that are relatively inexpensive and frequently found in school classrooms, computer labs, homes, and library media centers. Most important, though, is that these projects are described conceptually and step-by-step. References to software types and tools are included, but the projects are based on the assumption that many skills and software titles exist that can be used to design and create effective and dynamic multimedia works. That is, various software packages may be used to do the same things. Therefore, the step-by-step descriptions are presented in such a way that they may be adapted to available resources.

The creative tools of technology will evolve; some will become bigger, some will become smaller, but all will become faster. Software will become more plentiful and more sophisticated, and creative opportunities for teachers and their students will increase. So, what can teachers and students do with these rapidly evolving resources to teach, to create, and to examine the world around them? To use these tools thoughtfully and educationally in ways that benefit teachers and learners requires much more than knowing how the computer and software work. That is only the first step. Knowledge and appreciation of the origins, theories, techniques, and materials of almost one hundred years of all types of media production can nourish and enrich the use of contemporary computer-based multimedia tools. Therefore, the media production activities described in this book have been developed with the following assumptions in mind.

The More Things Change, the More They Stay the Same

An understanding of many age-old principles, theories, and practices will continue to be fundamental to the design of effective and expressive media works. For example, juxtaposing a series of images or shots in a sequence that tells a story, makes assertions, leads the viewers to make inferences, or reveals a plot is based on practices that editors have been using for many years. In other words, editing is based on an understanding of storytelling, whether one is cutting strips of film, dropping slides in a tray, designing web sites, or using the latest digital editing software. The success and effectiveness of any media product ultimately depends on ideas. The hardware and software provide creative potential and may even affect how the final production is perceived because of the strong connection between medium and content. One affects the other as Marshall McLuhan pointed out in his book *Understanding Media.* Nonetheless, the creative powers of a user's tools are of little use without the ideas, knowledge, and skills to exploit them successfully.

The Evolution of Communications Technology Is Additive

Communications technologies combine and complement one another technically, artistically, and historically. Older media become the ingredients of newer media. To cite a contemporary example, consider the elements of the World Wide Web—text, photographs, illustrations, graphics, animation, movies, music, radio and television broadcasts, instructional modules, among others. These elements are not new; the novelty of the Web lies in the technologies that allow us to combine them in interactive, dynamic, and worldly ways. Creative potential exists in everything from pencils and crayons to the latest digital tools. Therefore, the activities described in this book include techniques and ideas for using everything from felt-tipped pens and index cards to digital animation.

Version 1, V. 1.1, V. 2, V. 2.4, V. 3, 3.05, V. 4, V. 5, V. 6, V. 7, . . .

Whereas the simple technologies of felt-tipped pens, pencils, and index cards will not change significantly, the technicalities of digital hardware and software will change at a furious pace. The computer-based activities in this book will be covered in conceptual yet practical and specific ways. The focus will be on creativity, ideas, and execution of those ideas that can be adapted to the resources, versions, and upgrades one has access to.

Diffusion of Technology

With contemporary technologies, virtually anyone can be a moviemaker. We no longer have to depend on television networks, movie studios, and a host of commercial production companies. Even more revolutionary than simply making our own movies, we can distribute them to the world via the World Wide Web. However, having the tools and knowing how to manipulate them is not enough to produce quality, lively works. The producers who understand the expressive possibilities of various media and learn some basic planning and polishing techniques will make successful and effective products that people will enjoy seeing. The guidelines, information, and activities described in this book will provide a start for doing just that.

Concepts and Skills

Learning to use the growing number of multimedia tools available is a complex and never-ending endeavor. Many of these tools require hours of experimentation, manual reading, tutorial taking, consultation, trying, and retrying. New versions and changing hardware requirements add to the complexities of skills one must acquire. Unfortunately, if one wishes to use multimedia tools creatively, there is no way to avoid the many hours that it takes to learn to use them. Most often, however, the time spent pays off in successful and sometimes even spectacular results. Therefore, the activities in this book are based on concepts and ideas that come into play *after* learning the basics of specified software. This book is not a tutorial or guide for learning specific software, but it will help learners to master concepts and principles that they can apply to a variety of multimedia tools.

For example, when studying the concept of "editing," the learner must understand that editing is a process of arranging images, sounds, scenes, shots, and other elements in ways that make assertions, persuade, inform, teach, move, touch, scare, and lead viewers to make inferences. That is a concept. The multimedia tools one chooses to do the work of editing can be anything from simple *PowerPoint* shows to *Flash* projects, but the effective use of any of the applications requires an understanding of the concept. The activities in the following chapters will be based on concepts and ideas for teaching, learning, using, and combining these tools and processes in creative ways.

Finally, the Most Important Assumption

Although we are bombarded with elaborate and often spectacular media products and events produced by major commercial studios, the most vital and vivid use of contemporary digital tools is often the work of individual media artists and producers in schools or homes. Although one must acknowledge the impressive accomplishments of the high-end media producers of video games and feature movies, there is no doubt that the work created by teachers and students using off-the-shelf tools with little or no budget can have vitality, originality, and energy.

SUMMARY: USING THIS BOOK

This chapter presented a conceptual framework that provides insight about and perspective on the activities in the following chapters. The activities and projects represent a diverse set of concepts and skills. They have all been field-tested with appropriate audiences and settings.

Teachers may want to use this book as a manual or set of guidelines, principles, and methods to assist their students. In particular, teachers may adapt these ideas to fit specific objectives or to prepare lessons and activities that emphasize the creative uses of multimedia tools and resources.

Students in grade levels from elementary to high school and even college should be able to replicate, modify, and adapt the projects. The projects may be simplified or made more complex depending on such variables as age, skill levels, and availability of resources.

Though anyone interested in instructional technology should be able to learn something from this book, it is not designed for experts. As stated previously, the projects are designed primarily for teachers and students who have limited resources, want to learn basic production skills, are looking for production ideas, or do not have support from a media production specialist.

THOUGHT PROVOKERS

1. Before attempting any of the projects in the following chapters, write definitions of the terms *instructional technology* and *multimedia*. Be personal and original and use your own words.

2. Based on your own experiences as a student and/or a teacher, write a rationale for the value of multimedia as an educational and creative tool. Include an example of a particularly effective use of multimedia in a class that you have had. Interpret multimedia to include the wide range of so-called "nonprint" materials from simple overheads to state-of-the-art computer-based methods.

REFERENCES

Ely, Donald P., & Plomp, Tjeerd. (1996). *Classic Writings on Instructional Technology*. Englewood, CO: Libraries Unlimited.

Jonassen, David H., Peck, Kyle L., & Wilson, B. G. (1999). *Learning with Technology: A Constructivist Perspective*. Upper Saddle River, NJ: Merrill.

McLuhan, Marshall. (1964). *Understanding Media: The Extensions of Man*. New York: McGraw-Hill.

Seels, Barbara B. (1995). *Instructional Design Fundamentals: A Reconsideration*. Englewood Cliffs, NJ: Educational Technology Publications.

CHAPTER TWO

CREATING FRESH PERCEPTIONS OF THE WORLD

A Brief History of Multimedia

T O P I C   O U T L I N E

MULTIMEDIA: A FRAMEWORK
This section offers an explanation of the theoretical and historical foundations of the concept known as "multimedia."

EXPLAINING THE WORLD: THE POWER OF THE DOCUMENTARY
The origins and continuation of the classical concept of the documentary film are traced in the history of media design and production.

BOX 2.1: THE CONTINUING POWER OF THE DOCUMENTARY: *9/11*
This describes the documentary *9/11* by filmmakers Gedeon and Jules Naudet.

ANIMATION FROM Z TO A: ZOETROPES TO ANIME
This section describes the origins of animation as a highly expressive and popular media production method from the pre–motion picture era to its use online.

AUDIOVISUAL TOOLS ENTER THE SCHOOLS
Here is a brief summary of the emergence of nonprint media and processes as instructional tools.

SUMMARY: FROM GERTIE TO GIGABYTES
This summarizes the concept of multimedia as an often complex, yet highly creative phenomenon that has emerged from a long history of media production for education, art, and entertainment.

THOUGHT PROVOKERS
These questions and activities encourage the reader to reflect on the influences of living in an extremely media-rich culture.

BOX 2.2: SOURCES OF SOMETIMES "HARD-TO-FIND" TITLES
This provides some sources in which to look for the many media titles referred to in this book.

OBJECTIVES

After reading, reflecting on, and discussing the topics in this chapter, the reader will be able to:

- Articulate an expanded notion of multimedia.
- Define the "classical" concept of the documentary by pointing out filmmakers and films that exemplify that concept.
- Trace the origins and history of animation as a media production process by offering contrasting definitions and pointing out historically significant animators, studios, and animated movies.
- Describe some early "audiovisual" tools used in education, and describe an early model used to guide teachers in using instructional media.
- Formulate and articulate a personal vision of multimedia based on specific and original experiences with a wide range of media tools, programs, and processes.

The creative and expressive power of contemporary multimedia production tools is nearly unlimited. However, this power is not a new development. Many years ago, filmmakers, artists, photographers, teachers, and others experimented with the many elements of communication and artistic media. What they learned and what they did influence how contemporary tools are used and how audiences interpret the products made with them. Insight derived from a basic understanding of the rich history of multimedia production can enhance and nourish the use of modern multimedia resources. This chapter presents an overview of some of the people, events, ideas, and inventions that have contributed to our media-rich environment and provides a starting point for the multimedia projects and activities described in subsequent chapters.

MULTIMEDIA: A FRAMEWORK

The conventional notion of multimedia usually refers to a mixture of interactive computer products and processes. For the purpose of this book, the conventional definition is expanded to refer to the dynamic combinations of a variety of nonprint, or audiovisual, media ranging from still photography to computer-based media products. In this sense, the term *multimedia* refers to the digital tools of filmmaking, video production, and animation, as well as related skills, technologies, and concepts.

An understanding of the metaphorical language of multimedia is a vital tool in the creative repertoire of every media producer, whether in elementary school or in Hollywood. Merely having some skills in operating tools and devices cannot compensate for a lack of vision, imagination, motivation, passion, and above all, a point of view. The ability to use multimedia to express a point of view compellingly can be nourished by understanding the wide range of media production styles and genres that have been developed by media producers over the last one hundred years. The purpose of this chapter is to provide an overview of just that and thus establish a conceptual context for the activities and projects described in subsequent chapters.

The following section describes the inventions, media producers, and concepts that laid the foundations for what would eventually be described as multimedia. The section begins with the evolution of the documentary film as a powerful tool for revealing, persuading, and informing, and the next section continues with a chronicle of the origin and history of animated filmmaking. Note that the history of the narrative feature film is not included. The methods and ideas developed by the Hollywood-style feature filmmakers have had and continue to have an enormous influence on the study of media production. This is, of course, a massive and fascinating history. However, for the purposes of this book, the emphasis is on the history and evolution of documentary and animated filmmaking, both of which have contributed more directly to the contemporary notion of multimedia design and production as educational, artistic, and informative. The last section describes a brief history of the use of audiovisuals and instructional technology in schools.

The innovators, ideas, theories, and inventions chronicled in this chapter are drawn from a large number of potential examples. They have been selected because of their influence on contemporary media producers. A knowledge and understanding of these historical influences should make a qualitative difference in the reader's ability to create a wide range of multimedia products. Figure 2.1 (pages 14–15) charts the parallel developments of the documentary film, animation, and educational media and technology. The chart's purpose is to illustrate graphically some ideas and inventions that have contributed to the contemporary notion of multimedia. Of course, this history is much more complex and could include hundreds of additional titles, yet the chart does represent the conceptual framework on which the activities in this book are based.

EXPLAINING THE WORLD: THE POWER OF THE DOCUMENTARY

The term *documentary film* conjures various meanings and images. Perhaps the most common notion is of an objective, nonfiction film or even a category of educational film. Another much more dynamic notion of the documentary film or video is that it need not be objective at all, but may present a subjective and even pointed perspective on social, cultural, or political issues or controversies. The points of view frequently presented in documentaries give voice to the underrepresented. Historically, that is the dominant concept of the classic documentary form. As with the genre of animation, the documentary tradition began in the very early twentieth century, pioneered by Robert Flaherty and others. The documentary tradition is still a strong, persuasive tool. As with animation, this genre has been expanded by contemporary media production tools. An early visionary of the motion picture machine as an observer and documenter was the revolutionary Soviet filmmaker Dziga Vertov.

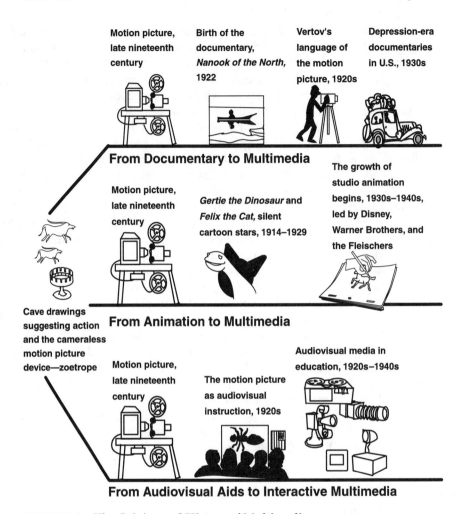

FIGURE 2.1 The Origins and History of Multimedia

Vertov's Fresh Perceptions of the World

Dziga Vertov, reflecting on the emerging technology of moviemaking in 1923, wrote the following (also included in the Preface):

> I'm an eye. A mechanical eye. I, the machine, show you a world the way only I can see it. I free myself for today and forever from human immobility. I'm in constant movement. I approach and pull away from objects. I creep under them. I move alongside a running horse's mouth. I fall and rise with the falling and rising bodies. This is I, the machine, manoeuvring in the chaotic movements, recording one movement after another in the most complex combinations.

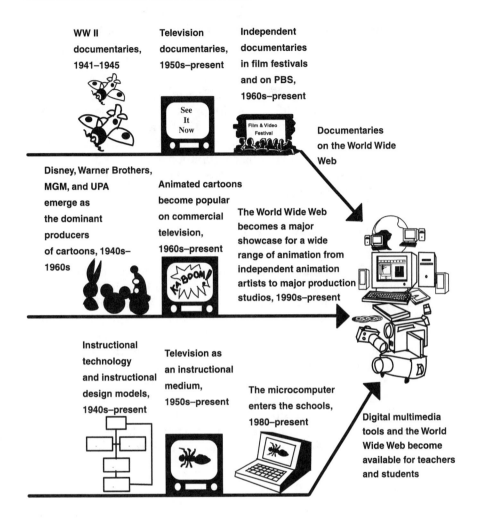

Freed from the boundaries of time and space, I coordinate any and all points of the universe, wherever I want them to be. My way leads towards the creation of a fresh perception of the world. Thus I explain in new ways the world unknown to you. (Berger, 1972)

In Vertov's time the new technology of the motion picture was beginning to create fresh perceptions of the world, as it continues to do. Many and varied digital technologies are explaining "in new ways the world unknown" to us just as film was doing in the 1920s. One important difference, though, is that the contemporary technologies are pervasive throughout our culture. Virtually everyone can use these powerful tools to express, teach, explain, and create individual and fresh perceptions of the world.

Vertov's real name was Denis Kaufmann. Deeply engaged with the emerging theories of moviemaking, he changed his name to Dziga Vertov, or "spinning top." His classic work, *Man with a Movie Camera,* is a frenetically paced sequence of images recording daily life in revolutionary Kiev. The viewer is always aware of the presence of the camera, as Vertov worked extensively with early special effects. *Man with a Movie Camera* is an energetic and at times surrealistic documentation of everyday reality. Vertov's lasting contribution to the evolution of the documentary film was his vision and demonstration of the motion genre as vital, expressive, and even celebratory of everyday life.

A "Language" Emerges

Vertov's ideas and visions suggested that there is a language and grammar of film. When watching a movie, most viewers can follow the narrative or plot because they are "visually literate," that is, they are used to seeing stories told with images and sounds. In a metaphorical sense, they have learned the "language" of media production. They know how to interpret sequences of images and understand relationships between the many elements that media producers use to make assertions and tell stories. Scenes and shots, glued, spliced, inserted, placed, and juxtaposed are how the filmmaker, editor, and storyteller make assertions and thus touch, teach, persuade, entertain, inform, or frighten viewers. Of course, there is much more to the language of media production. Media producers use composition, transitions, lighting, and sound to support the story, plot, and message. This basic theory of storytelling with multiple media applies to the simplicity of a flip book just as it does to the complexities of modern multimedia works.

The Classical View of Documentaries

The first uses of the motion picture camera were to document. Louis Luminere in France and Thomas Edison in the United States made short movies documenting everything from French village life to Native American dances. In the early 1920s, Robert Flaherty documented the struggle for survival in the harsh environment of northern Ontario in *Nanook of the North.* The classic approach to documentary filmmaking quickly evolved out of this purely documentary impulse in an approach that emphasized the viewpoint or perspective of the filmmaker. This perspective, in the classical sense, was often an unconventional, even personal statement by the producer about a social issue. Often, strong documentary works present the visions of underrepresented social groups as did Flaherty in *Nanook of the North.* The classical analytical approach to often divisive issues in documentary film is often criticized as biased and nonobjective. Traditionally, media producers and artists are labeled as predisposed or biased if they use their art forms to examine and present alternative perspectives that may challenge the beliefs of the majority. However, the distinctiveness of perspective is what gives the genre its power and vitality. The motives of a passionate documentary filmmaker go beyond commercial gain or profit. Perhaps because of their controversial, independent perspectives, documentaries are unfortunately rarely seen on commercial network television. Some cable channels show documentary work and the Public Broadcasting System occasionally shows strong independent works. Further, certain film festivals are dedicated to the exposure of independent media productions, many of which are documentaries. Also, the Academy of Motion Picture Arts and Sciences awards two Oscars per year to documentary filmmakers, one for a short work and one for a feature-length work. And that is about it. Possibly because of the sometimes controversial nature of strong documentaries and the lack of name recognition associated with them (directors, actors, and the various celebrities associated with commercial work), independent documentary work is rarely seen.

Whereas another perspective on the documentary exists in the journalistic, news reporting, or informational approach, the classical approach appeals to the notion of using the tools of media production not only to inform but also to challenge widely held assumptions and perspectives. Digital video technology puts the power to challenge prevailing views in the hands of virtually anyone with a message or perspective to share. Understanding the history and origins of the classical approach to documentary is vital for appreciating the potential of these new technologies.

Flaherty and Nanook: The "Documentary" Is Born

In the late nineteenth and early twentieth centuries, inventors Louis Luminere in France and Thomas Edison in the United States used their motion picture cameras to record and document aspects of everyday life photographically. Yet it was Robert Flaherty in 1922 who produced what is often described as the film that launched the documentary as a vital and important genre. Flaherty, a geologist-turned-filmmaker, shot his film under the difficult circumstances and harshness of northern Ontario. By the time *Nanook* was released in commercial theaters, the silent narrative, or Hollywood-style feature, was well established, although the theoretical and stylistic conventions of the art form were still evolving. American D. W. Griffith and Russian Sergei Eisenstein were incorporating and expanding the motion picture as an art form in its own right, not just a continuation or variation of live theater. Flaherty adapted these evolving ideas in making *Nanook of the North* by applying the storytelling and cinematic methods of composition and editing that were pioneered in narrative theatrical films to the work of documenting a distinctive reality.

Flaherty never considered himself to be a documentary filmmaker, though he is often described as the "Father of Documentary." His wife, Frances Hubbard Flaherty, reinforced that description in a 1960 chapbook. She wrote, "he was the first to fashion his films from real life and real people." She went on to describe the "documentary movement" as consisting of films made from "preconceived plans and perspectives." Her husband's films, though consisting of "real life" and "real people," were not preconceived. In fact, when *Nanook* was released, the term *documentary* had not even been used to describe a motion picture. That would come several years later when Scottish documentary filmmaker John Grierson used the term while reviewing Flaherty's second film, *Moana*. Because of Grierson's lifetime of making and promoting the documentary genre, Frances Flaherty considers him to have "fathered" the documentary movement. Nonetheless, whether Flaherty was a documentary filmmaker, one cannot avoid addressing his work in the context of documentary film. The important point is that Flaherty's contribution to moviemaking is undisputed.

The story of the production of *Nanook of the North* is one of the most fascinating accounts in the history of filmmaking. While on geological expeditions to northern Ontario, Flaherty became interested in the lives of the native people of that region; he was fascinated by their struggle to survive in such harsh conditions. Led by Nanook, Flaherty shot and processed thousands of feet of film over several years under very harsh conditions. Although by the 1920s, the region's people were hunting with motorboats and rifles, Nanook (see Figure 2.2) and Flaherty reenacted traditional survival events such as the very dangerous task of hunting walrus with a harpoon. Most of Flaherty's footage for the first version perished in a fire that injured him seriously. (In those days, film stock was made of nitrate and Flaherty was known as an avid cigar smoker.) Undeterred, he returned and refilmed all of it. The result was a beautiful feature-length film documenting what Flaherty saw as a dying culture. Flaherty's empathy and respect for his subjects meant that he did far more than simply film or record whatever his camera viewed. The film demonstrated that the motion picture could be used to enlighten, to persuade, to touch, to educate, and to stimulate, as well as simply to record. Documentary filmmakers were inspired by the work of Flaherty and Nanook. In the late 1970s, *Nanook of the North* was restored, a new score was written and added, and the film was rereleased to match its 1922 appearance. No original versions remained of the 1922 print; thus, the restoration was an educated guess as to how it may have appeared. Flaherty continued to make feature films of real life with real people, most of which are regarded as masterpieces of the documentary genre. *Man of Aran* and *Louisiana Story* are two examples.

With the advent of sound motion pictures accompanied with other technological developments in filmmaking such as color film and portability, the documentary genre grew more powerful and influential. In Germany in 1934, Leni Riefenstahl created her masterpiece, *Triumph of the Will*, and in 1936 *Olympia*. She never admitted to promoting the politics of the Nazi party, insisting that she was only an artist working in her medium of filmmaking. In the United States, Depression-era filmmakers such as Pare Lorentz produced documentaries promoting New Deal programs. *The Plow that Broke the Plains* and *The River*—both about the uncontrolled exploitation of the country's resources—received much contemporary attention. *The Plow that Broke the Plains* exposed the greedy and wasteful farming practices that led to the dust bowl years of the Depression. *The River* justified the reasons for the establishment of the Tennessee Valley Authority. Another important documentary about urban expansion was *The City*, written by Louis Mumford and filmed by Willard Van Dyke.

The need for training and propaganda in support of the United States in World War II caused a great surge in documentary filmmaking. Hollywood's film-

FIGURE 2.2   Nanook from Robert Flaherty's *Nanook of the North*

makers were drafted to create documentaries in support of the war effort. Notable among this work was Frank Capra's heavily propagandistic *Why We Fight* series promoting and explaining U.S. involvement in a foreign war to a largely isolationist population of the early 1940s. William Wyler's *Memphis Belle* was shot under actual air combat missions. Elia Kazan's epic *The True Glory* followed the Allies' progress from the Normandy invasion to the capture of Berlin. John Huston contributed *The Battle of San Pietro,* ironically with a strong pacifist message. There were many others.

After the war, documentary filmmakers gained access to millions of homes through another technological revolution: television. Many of these documentary filmmakers focused their cameras on cultural and social issues. Remarkable among these was Edward R. Murrow's *See It Now* series. On Thanksgiving eve in 1960, Murrow's classic TV documentary, *Harvest of Shame,* revealed the shameless exploitation of migrant farmworkers in the United States. As television evolved into a commercial entertainment medium, documentary work was deemphasized by the commercial networks. The year 2002 brought a stunning exception. Box 2.1 describes the work of two courageous French documentary filmmakers during the terrorist attacks on the World Trade Center on September 11, 2001.

■ ■ ■ ■ ■ ▬

BOX 2.1

THE CONTINUING POWER OF THE DOCUMENTARY: *9/11*

Media producers often use the documentary genre to address human tragedy and conflict. Keep in mind that the most often accepted concept of the documentary is distinctly different than the supposedly objective or neutral journalistic or news-gathering concept. In the year 2002 the power of the documentary returned to commercial television for one evening in March.

New York University–educated French filmmakers Gedeon and Jules Naudet, at great personal risk, filmed the September 11, 2001, World Trade Center terrorist attack as it unfolded and the resulting shock and heroism of New York City firefighters and citizens. The Naudets had set out to document the coming-of-age of rookie firefighters when the tragedy occurred. Immediately, they accompanied one of the first units to respond, the lower Manhattan firefighters of Engine 7, Ladder 1. Aired on CBS Television in March 2002 with limited interruptions, the resulting uncensored and candid work *9/11* was a milestone in network television broadcasting. Unlike conventional journalistic coverage, the Naudets' *9/11* is personal and spontaneous. The firefighters were totally unaware of the camera because they were exclusively focused on the gravity and unpredictability of their mission. Viewers travel with the firefighters from the moment they enter the building till they reconvene at the station many hours later. Through accident, or fate, these two filmmakers were there at the right time to document the shock and horror of that day in a way no news-gathering journalists could have. *9/11* is real. It is a simple, unsentimental, and moving statement about the firefighters and their deadly mission. *9/11* no doubt will take its place in the long history of the powerful genre of the documentary.

In the 1960s and 1970s, improvements in filmmaking technology, accompanied by social and political upheavals, stimulated independent documentary work. Near the end of the Vietnam War in 1974, Peter Davis released a devastating account of U.S. intervention in that war, the rarely seen yet enormously powerful *Hearts and Minds.* Later, in 1976, Barbara Kopple documented a labor strike in the mountains of eastern Kentucky in the Academy Award–winning *Harlan County, U.S.A.* In the early 1980s, Bill Moyers of CBS Television produced a documentary about the rising homelessness in the United States entitled *People Like Us.* The message and tone of this work moved the Reagan administration to label the revealing work as propaganda.

Many other outstanding examples of documentary filmmaking can be found. Independent documentary filmmakers take on subjects and issues that the more mainstream media avoid. Notable among these have been Michael Moore's *Roger and Me,* an often ironic and humorous yet serious treatment of corporate indifference to the social and economic consequences of closing a community's long-established factories. Moore has continued to address volatile social and culture issues. His documentary about the American gun culture, entitled *Bowling for Columbine* and released in 2002, was one of the highest-profile films at the Cannes Film Festival. Documentaries are rarely screened at Cannes.

The continuing growth of television via cable and satellite has created important outlets for the work of documentary filmmakers. Paralleling and often interacting with that development has been the growth of the World Wide Web. Via this resource, independent documentary filmmakers can bypass distributors and television networks and present their work directly to virtually anybody in the world who wants to see it.

Thus, this tradition initiated by Flaherty and Nanook in the 1920s flourishes due in part to the powerful and accessible technologies of the twenty-first century. The best examples of documentary film, based on the preceding history, are not objective. That is, the best documentary work is often driven by the passion of its producer to reveal new or alternative perspectives on social issues. This expressive impulse sparks the vitality of the genre. The new tools of digital video and editing and accompanying resources enhance the classic documentary tradition by putting inexpensive, off-the-shelf tools into the hands of anyone who has something to say or a point of view to share. Thus, the concept of the documentary has grown and expanded into a democratic, grassroots, and thus more alive genre—"real people in real life." That is of vital importance to understanding the history and origins of the documentary—the spirit of independence associated with the best works in this genre.

ANIMATION FROM Z TO A: ZOETROPES TO ANIME

The genre of animation is so vast that a single definition is inadequate or maybe even impossible. According to former Disney animator and animation director, Don Bluth, the producer of numerous animated features, Walt Disney used the term to mean "life." That is, for Disney, the purpose of animation was to create a convincing illusion of life in all its manifestations so that audiences could see characters as living and breathing personalities. He wanted his characters to display emotion, to think, to fear, to breathe, to laugh, and to cry. He was not concerned with impressing audiences with the classical refinement of the animation. He saw animation as the way for audiences to suspend belief in the real world and to care about, empathize with, and sometimes even fear his characters. This was the philosophical foundation on which Disney was able to create some of the greatest animated films ever produced. On the other hand, in the era of digital media, the term *animation* is also used to describe moving or manipulated elements such as graphics, artwork, and objects. Disney and his animators probably would not accept moving graphics as animation, yet this concept is a fundamental one in the production of digital multimedia works. The concept of moving graphics may refer to simple graphical interchange format (GIF) animations on web pages to highly complex graphics and movements created with state-of-the-art software.

The suggestion of motion in still images goes all the way back to the cave paintings of the Paleolithic or Old Stone Age, over 15,000 years ago. Hoping for good fortune in hunting, hunters drew motions and gestures in their depiction of the animals that were their prey. The caves in Lascaux, France, contain such examples. Many centuries later, Egyptian, Greek, and Roman paintings often depicted subjects in action. Well into the nineteenth century, artists and illustrators had to be content with merely suggesting motion, gesture, and action in their illustrations and paintings. One particular master of gesture was the French artist, satirist, and social critic Honore Damuier (1808–1879.)

By the nineteenth century, simple, cameraless gadgets had been invented that could play a series of images in such a way as to make them appear to move. With such strange names as the thaumatrope, the phenakistoscope, the praxinoscope, and the zoetrope, these contraptions worked with images from either drawings or photographs. Though these simple machines were considered to be toys or novelties, they were very effective and successful in making objects appear to move. One of the more popular ones was the zoetrope, French for "wheel of life." In fact, zoetropes are easy and fun to make with a computer and are therefore still popular. Chapter 6 has a zoetrope production project with detailed descriptions and illustrations.

In 1906, J. Stewart Blackton used a movie camera to make *Humorous Phases of Funny Faces.* Each shot was manipulated or changed before the frame was exposed, thus creating what is often considered to be the first animated movie. At about the same time, the pioneer French animator Emil Cohl successfully created a series of animated movies. By the early twentieth century, the technique of film animation had been amply demonstrated. The efforts of those two pioneers paved the way for what became a milestone film in the history of the animated movie and, in fact, in the history of the motion picture in general.

Gertie Is Born

In 1914, newspaper cartoonist Winsor McCay released his magnificent cartoon *Gertie the Dinosaur.* His talent as a cartoonist was widely known in the early twentieth century, but he was also interested in developing ways to make cartoons come to life. As mentioned previously, by the late nineteenth century, the techniques and basic theories for making crude animated movies had been demonstrated. McCay's vision was to expand the methods to bring life to the animated movie. In this respect, he anticipated the potential of film animation that Walt Disney later exploited.

The little cartoon *Gertie the Dinosaur* is considered by most film scholars and historians to be the first animated motion picture that has a character with dimension, realistic anatomy, personality, emotion, and above all life (Figure 2.3). In the years before his production of *Gertie the Dinosaur,* McCay adapted his drawing to the creation of animated movies. His early films, such as *Little Nemo,* were mostly experimental, yet they did show that McCay could create moving characters with dimension, depth, and character. These experimental works were characterized by linear precision, exceptionally strong draftsmanship, and highly accurate renderings of shapes in motion in space. Though these brief films were beautiful and revolutionary, it was not until McCay created *Gertie the Dinosaur* that he applied what he had learned about animation to a complete cartoon intended for theatrical distribution. *Gertie the Dinosaur* was interactive as well. McCay stood on vaudeville stages in front of the projected cartoon and directed Gertie as she performed tricks.

FIGURE 2.3   Winsor McCay's *Gertie*

This short movie consisted of thousands of hand-drawn ink images on white cards. McCay was one of the filmmakers and artists who anticipated how highly expressive moving images would add life, action, insight, and emotion to all aspects of our culture from entertainment, to art, to education.

After *Gertie*, McCay continued to develop the art form of animation. One of his most fascinating works was an animated version of the sinking of the *Lusitania*. This was not a cartoon in the conventional entertaining sense, but was actually an animated newsreel based on eyewitness accounts. The animated drawings render a strangely realistic and effective visual interpretation of the tragic sinking, in a vein similar to the use of contemporary computer simulations. Viewing this work makes one wonder what means McCay would choose to create simulations if he had access to all the tools of the digital era.

In spite of McCay's technical and artistic successes, the commercial possibilities and entertainment popularity of animation were not realized until Felix the Cat became the first cartoon superstar several years after *Gertie*. What Winsor McCay did with the elegant simplicity of ink and paper to make *Gertie* live is a conceptual ancestor to the gigabytes of creativity of modern multimedia tools.

A Silent Felix

Two of the great stars of the silent era of motion pictures were Charlie Chaplin and Felix the Cat, the first cartoon star. Created by animator Otto Messmer for producer

Pat Sullivan, Felix, whose comedic style was compared to Chaplin's, established the animated cartoon as a popular art form.

He was a somewhat misbehaved and raunchy character, drawn in a hard-edged and linear graphics style. As an animated Chaplin, Felix would sometimes use his tail as a cane to imitate the great living silent star. In *Felix in Hollywood,* an animated Chaplin character appeared with Felix. Sullivan's studio produced Felix cartoons throughout the 1920s. Sadly, Felix did not make the transition to sound successfully and soon faded away as a force in animation. Although he reappeared several times with various studios and distributors, he never achieved his former popularity. His style and success were dependent on the crude but energetic silent film.

Animation's Golden Age: Walt Disney

While *Felix the Cat* was dominating the silent era, young artists such as Walt Disney and Max Fleischer were learning the art and craft of animation and laying the foundation for the greatest era in studio animation, although their early silent cartoons did not achieve the popularity of Felix. Disney headed for the West Coast where he pioneered such innovations as sound cartoons, the color process, the multiplane animation camera, and feature-length cartoons. In 1932 he was awarded an Oscar for "Flowers and Trees," the first cartoon to receive this award. Probably his most important accomplishments in advancing animation as a serious art form were his early feature animated movies, beginning with *Snow White and the Seven Dwarfs* in 1938. Though this film was not the first feature-length animated film (in 1923–1926, German animator Lotte Reiniger had produced the animated feature *The Adventures of Prince Achmed*), it was the first one to demonstrate that feature-length cartoons could attract large audiences. Skeptical colleagues warned Disney not to take such a risk, yet *Snow White and the Seven Dwarfs* continues even now as a profit maker for Walt Disney Studios, as each new generation discovers it. Encouraged by the success of *Snow White and the Seven Dwarfs,* Disney followed with *Pinocchio* in 1940, *Fantasia* in 1940, and *Bambi* in 1942. *Fantasia,* conceptually ahead of its time, was too unconventional to enjoy great commercial success. In fact, Disney himself is said not to have liked it very much, although it continues to draw much critical and artistic interest.

The Disney tradition of innovative animated features continues in the twenty-first century. In the year 2000, for example, Disney Studios released *Fantasia 2000* featuring a wide range of animation methods from computer based to traditional (including *The Sorcerer's Apprentice* from the original). *Fantasia 2000* was produced exclusively for the enormous screen size, fast projection speed, and high-fidelity surround sound of the Imax system. Seeing *Fantasia 2000* in an Imax theater is the ultimate animation-viewing experience.

Animation's Golden Age on the Other Coast: Max and Dave Fleischer

At the same time Disney was establishing himself on the West Coast, brothers Max and Dave Fleischer settled in New York City where they likewise pursued innovations such as three-dimensional backgrounds and an inventive artistic and story-telling style. Whereas Disney's work was technically perfect, wholesome, highly polished, and big budgeted, the Fleischers' work was economical, unpredictable, unconventional, surrealistic, and edgy, perhaps reflecting the Great Depression–era urban environment from which it came.

In 1934, a significant event in motion picture history occurred, one that especially affected the Fleischer Studios. Due in part to the public criticism of the content of theatrical motion pictures, the self-censoring Motion Picture code was adopted by the industry. Prior to the enactment of the code, cartoons were full of sexual innuendo, violence, and abusive, mean-spirited characters. Even Mickey Mouse was known to spend time teasing barnyard animals and flipping Minnie with her own panties. The plots of a number of Fleischer cartoons were based on the sexual seduction of Betty Boop, who was drawn with a very, very short skirt that did not cover all of her anatomy. The effect of the code, at least initially, was to drain some of the energy from the Fleischer cartoons. Betty Boop's skirt grew longer and her roles became much more tame.

However, Max and his brother Dave adapted to the new atmosphere and continued to create some of the most original and remarkable cartoons ever. One high point was their own version of the Grimm Brothers' fairy tale, "Snow White and the Seven Dwarfs." This seven-minute cartoon designed for theaters with Betty Boop as "Snow White" was released in 1935, three years before Disney's version. The title was simply "Snow White." Betty Boop was accompanied by two Fleischer brothers' characters, Koko the Clown and Bimbo.

After the success of Disney's *Snow White and the Seven Dwarfs*, the Fleischer Studios released its own feature-length cartoon. *Gulliver's Travels*, while it flopped commercially, displayed some unique visual effects. One of these was a process called rotoscoping, which Disney had also used. It involved filming an actor in live action and tracing the individual frames as cartoon images. The process was very effective for the creation of Gulliver. However, the Lilliputians were created in conventional cartoon style and thus appear somewhat out of sync visually with the extremely realistic Gulliver. Further, the Fleischer Studios did not have the rights to use the newly developed Technicolor process that made the Disney films so visually striking.

After the commercial failure of *Gulliver's Travels*, Max and Dave Fleischer concluded that their forte was the short film, although they did produce a few excellent one-reel Popeye cartoons of about twenty minutes in length. Despite the fact that they did not have the resources of Disney, the Fleischer brothers and their imaginative and unique cartoons played a major role in defining and shaping the art of animation.

Animation's Golden Age: Warner Brothers

Just as distinctive and influential as the productions of Disney and the Fleischers were the cartoons produced at Warner Brothers. On the back lot at Warner Brothers, animators turned out hundreds of cartoons, initially in the early black-and-white series of *Looney Tunes* and later in the color series of *Merrie Melodies*. Directors and animators such as Chuck Jones and Bob Clampett and talents such as the composer

Carl Stallings and the voice characterization specialist Mel Blanc created a distinct cartoon style based on fast-paced rhythm, dynamic scoring, and sometimes irreverent and violent gags. The characters they created had distinct and diverse personalities, from the street-smart Bugs Bunny to the gullible though blustering Daffy Duck and many others. One could make a case that the Warner Brothers cartoons are the best and most popular ever. The popular fascination with the Warner Brothers cartoons continues as strong as ever, though the last of the original series was made in 1964.

Although many notable cartoons and characters were produced at Warner Brothers, some stand out in the history of cartoon making. In *A Wild Hare* made in 1940, a character invented by Tex Avery debuted—Bugs Bunny. Over sixty years later, Bugs is as popular as ever. In 1943, Bugs appeared with Porky Pig and Elmer Fudd in a hilarious spoof of Disney's *Fantasia,* entitled *Corny Concerto.* Much later in his career, in 1957, Bugs appeared in one of the greatest cartoons ever made, *What's Opera Doc?*

The Golden Age: Metro Goldwyn Mayer

Produced by major talents such as Tex Avery, who had also worked at Warner Brothers, and Preston Blair, Metro Goldwyn Mayer (MGM) cartoons were known for their very high production values, their solid artistic quality, and Avery's eye-popping exaggeration. One of MGM's most notable works was *Red Hot Riding Hood.* This cartoon challenged the production code with its sexually suggestive images and plot. The fast-paced action and the bizarre gags were typical of Avery's work. Although many of MGM's cartoons of the early 1940s were, and still are, aired on television, *Red Hot Riding Hood* was not one of them, probably because of its perceived adult content. However, for the 1989 feature *Who Framed Roger Rabbit?,* animation director Richard Williams chose an MGM/Preston Blair/Tex Avery style. In particular, the character Jessica Rabbit is modeled after Preston Blair's *Red Hot Riding Hood.*

During the early 1940s, many Americans were opposed to participating in the foreign wars raging overseas. One of the popular cultural expressions of that isolationist perspective was MGM's cartoon *Peace on Earth.* This visually stunning pacifist work used typical cartoon forest animals to reveal barbaric human tendencies. *Peace on Earth* was very popular and was included on theater marquees along with feature film titles. Though it was beautifully produced, its major contribution was to demonstrate that an animated cartoon can effectively and seriously address a crucial issue and deliver a powerful message. In the mid-1950s, *Peace on Earth* was reproduced as a cinemascope movie and rereleased in theaters.

A New Age Begins: UPA

In 1943, partly as the result of a labor strike at Disney, a group of former animators formed United Productions of America, or UPA. The primary leadership came from former Disney animator, Stephen Bosustow. The animation style of UPA was a radical departure from the highly polished three-dimensional and artistically confining

Disney style. UPA artists embraced the bold colors, shapes, and flat figure–ground compositions of modern art. The bold new style was fresh and stimulating; one of the UPA films, *Gerald McBoing Boing*, was awarded an Oscar in 1951. UPA's most recognized character was Mr. Magoo, who appeared in 1949. The radical stylistic departure pioneered by UPA animators, along with the growing popularity and influence of television, prompted major changes in the art form of animation in the 1960s.

Television Animation

Although the studios continued to produce some excellent animation during the 1950s, television brought new challenges to animators. As theaters discontinued showing cartoons before features, the made-for-television cartoon arrived in force with shows such as *Rough and Ready, Huckleberry Hound,* and *Underdog.* Possibly the most innovative of these was Jay Ward's *Rocky and Bullwinkle,* produced by animators consuming unlimited quantities of popcorn, KitKat bars, and Coca-Cola. Restored *Rocky and Bullwinkle* shows remain popular because of their double entendres, bad puns, and pointed satire. In 1960, Hanna and Barbera released the first episode of *The Flintstones,* the first prime-time animated situation comedy, followed shortly by *The Jetsons.* Another notable televised animated show was *A Charlie Brown Christmas,* which aired in 1964. The success of Bill Melendez's show encouraged the creation of numerous animated Christmas classics, one of the more popular being Chuck Jones and Dr. Seuss's *How the Grinch Stole Christmas.*

A common criticism of made-for-television animation was that its artwork and motion were flat and jerky because of the production demand for weekly programming. To keep up with the production schedules, studios often cut the amount of artwork in half, thus reducing the smoothness and subtleties of the traditional theatrical cartoons.

Cartoons and animated shows continue to be popular television programming. Though most are aimed at children and are aired at times they can watch, some, such as *South Park, The Simpsons,* and *King of the Hill,* take on adult topics and controversial themes. The future of made-for-television animation is promising because of technological improvements in production processes.

Independent and International Animation

The work of independent artists and animators around the world was a vital force in the advancement of animation as an art form. International animation artists explored the use of all sorts of materials and processes. In Canada, the National Film Board of Canada supported and distributed innovative works by independent animation artists. Norman McLaren in particular became a giant figure in animation, and his works comprise some of the best animation of the twentieth century. Though entertaining, his work was most distinguished by the use of many unusual materials and processes and of animation to address a number of issues. Zagreb, Yugoslavia, has become a center of animation production and annually hosts one of the world's most highly respected animation festivals.

One of the most important film animation movements of the late twentieth and early twenty-first centuries began in Japan with the epic animated feature *Akira.* Japanese animation, known by the abbreviated "Anime," includes a large body of animated works, often consisting of complex plots, social criticism, and science-fiction themes. Anime is a mainstream popular art form that appeals both to children with such series as *Pokémon* and to adults with such features as *Ghost in the Shell.* The origins of Anime can be traced from ancient Japanese art to contemporary Japanese comic books. Anime is popular worldwide and is one of the most important animation advances in this contemporary art form.

The World Wide Web

The miniaturization of electronics and the coming of the digital era have simultaneously enhanced traditional animation and expanded animation as a powerful tool. Likewise, the term *animation* has expanded to include a growing number of computer-based effects for television graphics, music videos, instructional simulations, and motion picture effects.

As the Internet has become more and more accessible, the World Wide Web has become a channel for displaying independent animated works. There are web sites that deal with theory and history and sites that display or provide showcases for animated works. Many of these works are simply digitized versions of traditional animation forms, but others are made specifically for presentation on the World Wide Web. Online animation venues provide a place for independent filmmakers to present their creations. The largest source is *iFilm,* a site that contains thousands of independent works from live action to animation, representing many categories.

From *Gertie the Dinosaur* to the gigabytes of the digital age, animation in all its styles, processes, and perspectives is as popular as ever. Young multimedia designers using the latest software and computers are for all practical purposes driven by the same artistic and expressive passions that drove early animators. In March 2002, the Academy of Motion Picture Arts and Sciences established feature-length animation as a new award category. The winner was *Shrek.*

AUDIOVISUAL TOOLS ENTER THE SCHOOLS

Several years after the invention and perfection of the motion picture, Thomas Edison predicted that it would replace textbooks. In 1925 in his diary, he wrote:

> Now let us take the class in geography. It seems to me that motion pictures offer here a rather astonishing substitute for the colorless, standardized lessons of the textbooks—not only an opportunity to teach directly from a busy world at work but with all of the atmosphere of adventure, romance, achievement. (Edison, 1948)

Although the motion picture became primarily an entertainment medium, schools did adopt the new medium despite the fact that the projectors were heavy and bulky and the nitrate film stock of the era highly flammable. Eventually, smaller projectors and safer 16mm film made the use of motion pictures more practical in classrooms. In fact, a severely watered-down 16mm short version of *Nanook of the North* was distributed for use in schools.

As new communications and teaching tools became available, teachers and educators looked for ways to use them to enhance teaching and learning. In the 1920s and 1930s, media such as filmstrips, lantern slides, and 16mm film became available for classroom use. In the 1940s, in response to wartime training needs, overhead transparencies and audio recordings were used by military trainers. After the war, both were adapted for use in regular kindergarten through twelfth-grade classrooms.

In searching for a systematic process for the effective use of these tools, Professor Edgar Dale proposed his "Cone of Experience." This early pedagogical model organized instructional materials and processes in a concrete-to-abstract continuum. The emphasis in this model was on the physical properties of the materials rather than on learning objectives based on the needs of learners. Thus, according to Dale's model, the more realistic the media or materials were, the more likely that learning would occur. As media and technology became more sophisticated, so did the theoretical rationale for their use. Out of the theoretical discussion arose the notion of designing instruction based on learner analysis, needs assessments, specification of objectives, assessment, and revision—and many variations thereof. Also conceived as a systematic approach to instruction, the essence of the instructional design approach was not on the simulation of reality, but rather on specifying learning outcomes and designing instruction to achieve those outcomes.

The Electronic Surround

In the early 1960s, communications theorist and author Marshall McLuhan prophetically pointed out in *The Medium Is the Massage*:

> The medium, or progress, of our time—electric technology—is reshaping and restructuring patterns of social interdependence and every aspect of our personal life. It is forcing us to reconsider and re-evaluate practically every thought, every action, and every institution formerly taken for granted. Everything is changing— you, your family, your neighborhood, your education, your job, your government, your relation to "the others." And they're changing dramatically.

This technological change in social institutions first entered schools via educational television and computers. Initially, the products for these media were produced and distributed by vendors specializing in educational media and technology and were used mostly to deliver information and in some cases to facilitate some user interaction. The arrival of the Internet accompanied by the World Wide Web in educational institutions stimulated interest in the creative powers of multimedia. Though the Internet is a vast resource of information, it also provides a platform for creating and sharing a variety of multimedia products produced by students, teachers, artists, writers, and many others.

SUMMARY: FROM GERTIE TO GIGABYTES

This book is about multimedia projects, ideas, and exercises that can be adapted to many age and skill levels. An appreciation of the origins and precursors of modern media production is indispensable whether one is designing educational products or creating art. McCay, Edison, Flaherty, Vertov, Disney, McLuhan, and others were not educators, at least not by training, but what they learned and what they did has helped create a lively and media-rich world that educators can and should take advantage of. Contemporary multimedia tools—hardware and software—are simply a continuation or, even better, an expansion of ideas, inventions, and processes that have been evolving for over one hundred years. Box 2.2 gives information on some possible sources for obtaining a variety of historically significant and hard-to-find titles.

THOUGHT PROVOKERS

1. Reflect on your educational experience as a student or teacher at any level, and describe an example of how a teacher or professor used media—movies, computers, photographs, recordings, or any nonprint media—to explain, teach, or persuade you.

2. Select a documentary film that made a special impact on you, and describe the elements, qualities, production methods, and other characteristics that contributed to that impact.

3. Review the section on Robert Flaherty. Suggest some aspect of your community that may be changing or even disappearing, and describe how you would document it. What would you have an audience learn about it?

4. Select an animated film—a cartoon, a series of cartoons, an animated TV series, an animated feature—that has had a special impact on you, and describe the elements, qualities, production methods, and other characteristics that contributed to that impact.

5. List examples of electronic communications media that surround you in everyday life and describe the messages or information they are delivering.

6. Describe some multimedia projects you have created and/or participated in that you found stimulating and effective, and tell why. Also list some multimedia skills that you want to learn to use—for example, creating interactive movies, shooting and editing live-action video, or creating animated cartoons.

7. Antonio Gaudi (1852–1926), the Spanish architect who created radical new architectural forms, mostly in Barcelona, was quoted as saying, "To be original is to go back to the origins." Describe some ways that multimedia artists using digital technologies "go back to the origins" of media production.

8. Using the ideas listed in Box 2.2, locate at least one of the movies mentioned in this book. Watch it with a group, and discuss all aspects of it from production methods to audience reaction. If possible, do the same things with additional movies. List some qualities of the production that you would like to learn to incorporate into your own work.

BOX 2.2

SOURCES OF SOMETIMES "HARD-TO-FIND" TITLES

Titles of selected media productions are cited throughout this book. Fledging multimedia producers can learn a lot by watching and analyzing these works. Finding and evaluating some of these titles requires some searching, but the effort may pay off by making a qualitative difference in your own multimedia works. Some sources include the following.

- *Public libraries.* Many public libraries circulate videos—VHS and DVD. Some of the titles may be classical and historical documentaries, or titles from such sources as the National Film Board of Canada, PBS, and commercial distributors specializing in historical and classical works.
- *College and university audiovisual and nonprint collections.* Many higher education institutions maintain collections of media titles that support coursework and study in media theory, history, or production. These collections often contain a variety of media from film to common video formats.
- *The World Wide Web.* Not surprisingly, the Internet is a vast source of information about all forms of media production. Using a common search engine, a user may locate titles for purchase or loan. In some cases, one may be able to view clips and/or in some cases entire works via downloaded or streaming movies. Modern browsers have movie plug-ins such as *Real Media Player, QuickTime Player,* or *Windows Media Player.* Movie player plug-ins may also be downloaded.
- *Selective television viewing.* The proliferation of cable television provides another source for viewing historical and hard-to-find titles. In particular, PBS often airs the work of independent documentary filmmakers, for example, its *P.O.V.* (point-of-view) series. Even commercial channels occasionally air some historical or rarely seen works. The Cartoon Network, for example, devotes some time to works of the National Film Board of Canada. The Cartoon Network also occasionally presents historical specials, such as its one-hour program about animated films produced during World War II in support of the war effort. The *Biography* series on the Discovery Channel aired a biography of Betty Boop. The same channel also aired a two-hour special on the Fleischer Studios hosted by Leonard Maltin, author of *Of Mice and Magic,* one of the most important and influential scholarly works about American studio animation.
- *Purchase inexpensively.* Used book and video stores may also have an occasional rare title. One example is the Fleischer Studios' *Gulliver's Travels.* Though marketed as a children's program, shoppers who are aware of the historical significance of *Gulliver's Travels* may find a used or even new copy at a very low price. Large discount stores often have new videos for sale at very low prices. Digging through these may result in discovering a rare title; for example, the *Why We Fight* series of documentaries produced by Frank Capra during World War II are often marketed at greatly discounted prices.

Popular culture is driven by name recognition. The vast majority of consumers are looking for familiar and highly promoted titles and producers. For that reason, even in our media-rich culture, certain titles are often difficult to find. However, searching for them may be a learning experience in itself.

9. Log on to the Internet. Select a search engine such as Yahoo! or Google. In the Search box type "Nanook of the North." Try it with and without the quotes. Examine the search results and select some interesting sites. See what you can learn about this famous documentary and its maker, Robert Flaherty. Select some other titles mentioned in this chapter and see what you can learn.

10. Carefully examine the chart in Figure 2.1. Based on your own experiences and studies, expand or modify the chart to exclude items and/or include ones that you believe would better represent the concept of multimedia production. Use computer graphics, make or acquire illustrations, and make it in color. Also, when you learn some interactive software such as *Macromedia Flash,* make your chart interactive.

REFERENCES

Barnow, Erik. (1974). *Documentary: A History of Non-Fiction Film.* London: Oxford University Press.

Berger, John. (1972). *Ways of Seeing.* London: British Broadcasting Corporation.

Dale, Edgar. (1954). *Audio-Visual Methods in Teaching.* New York: Dryden Press.

Edison, Thomas A. (1948). *The Diary and Sundry Observations of Thomas Alva Edison.* Dagobert D. Runes (Ed.). New York: Philosophical Library.

Flaherty, Frances Hubbard. (1960). *The Odyssey of a Film-Maker: Robert Flaherty's Story.* Urbana, IL: Beta Phi Mu.

Maltin, Leonard. (1987). *Of Mice and Magic.* New York: Penguin Books.

McLuhan, Marshall. (1967). *The Medium Is the Massage.* New York: Bantam Books.

Napier, Susan. (2001). *ANIME: Akira to Princess Mononoke.* New York: Palgrave.

Runes, Dagobert D. (1948). *The Diary and Sundry Observations of Thomas Alva Edison.* New York: Philosophical Library.

Saettler, Paul. (1990). *The Evolution of American Educational Technology.* Englewood, CO: Libraries Unlimited.

- - - - - -

CHAPTER THREE

A MULTIMEDIA STARTER KIT
Motivation, Tools, Skills

TOPIC OUTLINE

THE MULTIPLES IN MEDIA: SOME THINGS TO THINK ABOUT BEFORE STARTING
This section presents some motivational ideas to consider before jumping into
multimedia production.

PLANNING
Here is a description of a simple model that can be used for planning a multimedia
production.

FAIR USE GUIDELINES
This section summarizes the concept of fair use.

MULTIMEDIA, MULTIPLE MEDIUMS: SOFTWARE "WARHORSES"
This describes a selection of software fundamental to multimedia production.

BASIC DESIGN 101
Here are suggestions of some fundamental visual design principles for multimedia.

SUMMARY: MAKING MULTIMEDIA
This summarizes the steps to take before beginning a multimedia project.

THOUGHT PROVOKERS
These questions and exercises are related to the design and production of multimedia
projects.

OBJECTIVES

After reading, reflecting on, and/or discussing the topics in this chapter, the reader will
be able to:

- Understand and implement some vital motivational ideas about learning to create
  multimedia productions.
- Apply sound planning concepts and methods to the production process.
- Respect creative and intellectual properties and adhere to fair use guidelines.
- Recognize and describe some major multimedia production software titles.

The activities and projects in this book are designed to empower, enable, and motivate. To that end they are intended to stimulate ideas and processes that will encourage teachers and students to tackle the often mystifying and complex tools of multimedia confidently. The accompanying web site for this book is updated frequently with interesting developments, news, and multimedia products. Further, it is a showplace for online multimedia projects made by students and teachers in a variety of settings. This chapter describes some multimedia basics including motivation, planning, and software.

THE MULTIPLES IN MEDIA: SOME THINGS TO THINK ABOUT BEFORE STARTING

There is no way to avoid dedicating hours to learn multimedia software. However, multimedia software is not difficult to learn, just time-consuming. No one individual could possibly know everything about every software package. Often, an effective way to learn a piece of complex software is to start with a simple idea. For example, "How can I use *Flash* to make a circle evolve or morph into a square?" Manuals, web sites, *Flash* books, teachers, tutorials, or friends can provide help with such simple tasks. Accomplishing a variety of simple tasks will assist one in learning the software. Those skills will provide a solid foundation as projects become more complex and challenging.

Be Yourself

Be original. To do less is to defeat the power of the concepts and tools of multimedia technology. Of course, do not reinvent the wheel, but learn from the work of others. Look for inspiration and ideas that will trigger your own creative energy. In particular, look at and analyze the work of independent media producers. Some of this work may be pretty bad; some may be highly original and well executed. Look for inspiration in diverse, even unusual sources in all media, print included. Do not try to emulate or imitate big-time media. Instead, ask yourself what *you* have to say and how you want to say it. Then ask yourself how you can say it with style, energy, and originality. Again, to do less is really not to use multimedia tools to their fullest.

Try, Retry, and Try Again

There is no such thing as user-friendly software and hardware. Expect problems. Expect frustrations and be willing to solve problems. The results will prove to be worth the effort when you see your work come to life, especially when you know that others are learning from and enjoying what you have created. The habit of persistence is crucial to being a successful multimedia creator.

Assume that digital tools will need troubleshooting. Try to solve problems on your own before you seek help. Be independent. You cannot expect someone else to solve your digital difficulties automatically, though the expertise of hardware and software experts is crucial at times. Realize that there is no substitute for the time it takes to learn.

Enjoy the Voyage of Discovery

Assuming that one must know all the features of a production package before using it is simply too overwhelming. Learn a little at a time. Soon, this approach becomes almost intuitive and before you know it, you are making sophisticated multimedia events and actions. As you develop some knowledge and confidence, you will find yourself discovering numerous features, tricks, and ideas. In particular, with software such as *Flash,* there is no end to the ways its many features and creative capabilities can be combined and exploited in creative and often unpredictable ways. Take time to play and experiment. You will learn something new every time you do!

Choose a Limited Objective for Starters

As mentioned previously, the exercises in this book are only starting points. Expand them, modify them, and adapt them to particular tasks whether instructional or purely creative. Multimedia skills are numerous, if not unlimited. As a beginner, select or write a limited objective—make a character "walk" across the screen, for example—then seek out and learn the features of a particular hardware and software tool that make that possible.

Do the Best You Can with What You Have

Realize that creativity is not dependent on having the most expensive or trendy items. Effective and successful projects can be created with common and simple software such as *AppleWorks* or *PowerPoint.* Conversely, using software such as *Flash* does not guarantee a high-quality result. It is not the software, but the way it is used, that determines the quality of the product.

Work for Simplicity and Elegance

For many multimedia design problems, the best solution is often the simplest one. When learning new software that has many new features, a designer is tempted to use all of them. This leads to cluttered, crowded products that may be difficult for users to read and operate. Elegant simplicity is not easily achieved. Ask any graphics artist who routinely organizes complex visual materials into attractive and comprehensible designs. Common multimedia design flaws include distracting backgrounds, hard-to-read typefaces, overuse of animation and sounds, and fragmented compositions. Use multimedia elements judiciously and thoughtfully. Not only are simplicity and elegance aesthetically pleasing, but they are also practical considering the time required for a user to download an online project, for example.

Know That You ARE Creative

Do not assume "I am not creative." You can be if you choose to work at it. Most often, creativity simply needs cultivation and practice. That, too, is one of the great appeals of multimedia as a concept. Creativity need not mean an ability to draw polished images. Instead creativity in multimedia production has more to do with using the software to combine elements—photos, text, movies, sounds, color, drawings—in ways that teach or communicate. In many cases people who considered themselves to be uncreative have discovered their creative possibilities through the use of multimedia tools.

The Designer Is the Learner

Producing educational or instructional media may be a more vital learning experience for the maker than for the viewer. Of course, this is just common sense. Effective instruction, no matter the manner of delivery, requires research and inquiry. In order to develop a subject logically in a multimedia program, the producer must plan carefully and systematically with a clear goal or purpose. In fact, students themselves may benefit more as producers of media than as consumers of commercially produced products.

PLANNING

A successful media production, whether a multimillion-dollar blockbuster or a multimedia program made in a school, requires some sort of planning. This may require a storyboard or a more detailed plan. Even in the case of the unpredictability of documentary or artistically expressive works, some sort of plan is usually needed. That is, the planning method chosen depends on the nature of the proposed project. One cannot expect to produce a successful product by accident. A multimedia program that has a specific educational purpose, for example, usually requires a fairly detailed plan. On the other hand, a more expressive or even artistic work may sort of evolve as the producer creates it. In both cases, however, the producer must have a vision in order to make appropriate media production choices.

The steps in media creation are generally categorized into preproduction, production, and postproduction phases. The preproduction phase may consist of bringing together many elements and resources such as budgets, scripts, talents, locations, and storyboards. What is required varies with the nature of the project. A feature motion picture, for example, may require years of preproduction. An educational or instructional work requires careful attention to purpose, content, and topic development. The production phase includes, for example, traveling to locations to shoot digital video or, in the case of an animated work, creating the artwork. During the postproduction phase, all of the above come together into a final product. This includes editing, sound design, special effects, and finishing in the desired medium. Obviously, these steps are logical and for very simple, quick works may not take long. However, having a map or guide to follow will keep the producer focused on the desired results. Projects in subsequent chapters follow the preproduction, production, and postproduction sequence. The following sections describe two conventional, time-tested preproduction devices—a planning document and the storyboard.

A Planning Model

The media production design model in Figure 3.1 contains elements and content that can be used to plan educational multimedia productions. Many variations of this model exist, and many media producers develop their own approach to design. Again, successful production does not happen by accident. The form or layout of one's plan is not the most important thing; the important thing is simply to have one. A plan for a media production is often called a treatment, which is simply an outline of the proposed production. The plan in Figure 3.1 is designed for students and teachers to guide their planning of media projects. The plan is generic and serves only as a starting point. As novice multimedia producers gain more experience, they usually devise processes that fit their own working styles.

The structure of this model is based on three major components—preproduction, production, and postproduction. Each one of those, in turn contains elements and ideas to be considered during the planning or development phase. Although this is a generic or synthesized model, it contains the major elements that are included in most media design models. Refer to Figure 3.1 while reviewing the following items.

Preproduction

Statement of Purpose.   The statement of purpose of a proposed project explains what the producer intends to accomplish—to touch, to convince, to amuse, to persuade, to scare. The statement of purpose answers these questions: Why is this being produced? What might viewers or users expect to learn from it? In the case of an educational goal or objective, what are viewers expected to know and/or be able to do as a result of the project?

Genre.   Which genre is the best match for the purpose of the proposed product? Documentary? Educational/instructional? Narrative? Animation? Online interactive? Artistic or expressive?

Media and Materials.   The term *media* refers to a gigantic body of resources from pencils to the latest Internet software. In the context of this book, the term refers to the tools of multimedia production. Many variables affect media selection: What is available? Is a budget needed? How is the program to be delivered—stand alone for group presentation or online?

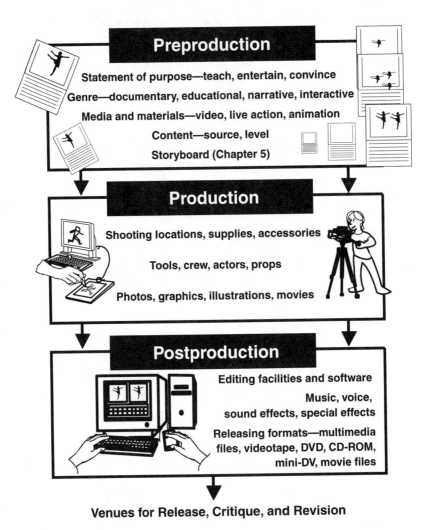

FIGURE 3.1   A Multimedia Design Model. This is a generic model that may be helpful in planning a multimedia production.

Content.   To accomplish that purpose or goal, what content, subjects, and information need to be included in the project? What are the sources of that content? Experts? Printed material? Personal experience? Original or archival material? Films and videos? Stories? Scripts? Locations? Interviews? Others? Determining content, of course, is a crucial step because one cannot expect to succeed by making the content up as one goes along. Of course, the planning of content needs to be flexible; changes are often necessary during the course of creating the product.

Script and Storyboard.   Once again, successful products do not just happen. Due to the many working styles of producers and the differences in genres, what happens at this step varies greatly. For example, some subjects of a media production may need to be developed logically and in detail in a fixed sequence. If so, completion of a detailed storyboard will be necessary to achieve that result. Others may not be linear or sequential but random and interactive. Plans for such projects may look quite different.

Storyboards may be homemade and informal or they may follow a particular format. Some are drawn or printed as multiple frames on a sheet and some are free-standing. Often, a storyboard is derived from a script. (Chapter 5 describes a storyboard exercise in detail. Though the exercise is included in the chapter on video production, the storyboard is a common preproduction tool whatever the medium.) Some scripts actually provide the essence of a production. A script may be written for recording voice-over narration or may simply be a sequential or branching description of a project. In the case of a narrative, or dramatic, storytelling work, the script contains all the dialogue, sequences, and actions necessary to tell the story. In fact, it is not unusual for a script to be the primary guiding document for a production instead of a storyboard. Some producers prefer a very thorough and detailed plan to use as a guideline before beginning a production. On the other hand, and again depending on the purpose and genre, a more open-ended or even unpreconceived approach may be the best choice; for example, for a documentary shot in a variety of locations that the producer may discover during the production phase. Nonetheless, any project, from a spontaneous art piece to an instructional work with specific objectives, will benefit from at least an outline, often described as a treatment outline. A treatment outline minimally provides a conceptual framework that can serve as an agenda and guide for the production team.

Production
Planning documents often contain information concerning the resources that will be needed for a media production. These resources can be as simple as a desktop computer and software to a full video production crew. The production step often includes location descriptions, lists of props, costumes, equipment, tools, actors, studios, or anything that will be needed to actually make the item. In movies and videos, this planning step is often called production design.

Postproduction
This step describes the tools and resources to complete the project. The most important postproduction resources are the editing facilities appropriate for the product's medium or format. For example, for a digital video production, a computer with digital editing software is essential. For another example, an interactive multimedia production designed for posting online requires software that allows the final version to be exported as a number of formats such as Hyper Text Markup Language (HTML), Shockwave, or a variety of movie files. Postproduction also includes music editing, sound effects editing, transitional effects, and a variety of special effects. This varies with the medium because production and postproduction are

more or less simultaneous when working with computer-based multimedia. Conversely, the postproduction step in digital video is a distinctly different task from the production step.

Venues for Release, Critique, and Revision

This simply refers to the process of assessing the project usually through field-testing with the targeted users. Revisions of the project can be made based on the results of this assessment. Digital media productions are made for many purposes and in a great variety of formats and genres. An interactive, instructional program, for example, will have clearly stated, measurable objectives. The assessment, therefore, will be to determine whether the users successfully achieve those objectives. Conversely, an artistic or expressive piece may be presented in online and offline media festivals, submitted to juried competitions, or even reviewed in print. Then again, a teacher may critique and grade a student's digital media production according to a range of criteria from technical considerations to originality. No matter which of those or other methods is used, the point is that media producers who are concerned about the quality of their work seek some sort of evaluation.

There is no one system to plan a proposed multimedia project. The model described in this section is an adaptable format that is representative of a basic process. Actually it is a generic form that is a synthesis of other models and media production planning methods. Planning is also a personal preference. Some designers may prefer a more formative approach, that is, developing the concepts and ideas and how to express them as the project is being created. Likewise, certain designers prefer a much more systematic process. Either way, keep in mind that a multimedia project probably will not be successful by accident no matter its purpose—expressive or educational.

FAIR USE GUIDELINES

All multimedia producers and users—students, teachers, instructional technologists, or artists—have an obligation to respect the work of others. This is an ethical as well as a legal expectation. The often expressed belief that copyrighted materials can be used in any manner desired for "educational purposes" is mistaken. There are ways to use or adapt copyrighted items in part or in whole according to a widely agreed on set of fair use guidelines. All educational users and producers should be aware of these fair use guidelines and adhere to them.

The Copyright Act of 1976 allows educators to use copyrighted materials according to the concept of "fair use." In 1976, of course, the Internet was not easily accessible by schools and consumers. Digital media production tools were either in their infancy or nonexistent. As media production and media delivery technologies became more sophisticated, the fair use principles of the 1976 Copyright Act became much more difficult to interpret.

In order to address the questions and uncertainties of fair use in a geometrically expanding era of digital media, in the mid-1990s, the Consortium of College and University Media Centers established a committee to propose fair use guidelines. The voluntary guidelines that this committee proposed were adopted by the Subcommittee on Courts and Intellectual Property Committee on the Judiciary, U.S. House of Representatives, on September 27, 1996, and related to Fair Use Guidelines for Educational Multimedia. The guidelines were endorsed by the Association of American Publishers, the Information Industry Association, the Software Publishers Association, and the Creative Incentive Coalition. The endorsing institutions and organizations include the Motion Picture Association of America, Inc., Microsoft Corporation, Time Warner, Inc., U.S. National Endowment for the Arts, U.S. Copyright Office, American Library Association, National School Boards Association, and the Public Broadcasting System among many others.

Some of the guidelines' key statements related to the production and use of multimedia works include:

> Section 2.1: Students may incorporate portions of lawfully acquired copyrighted works when producing their own educational multimedia projects for a specific course.

And,

> Section 2.2: Educators may incorporate portions of lawfully acquired copyrighted works when producing their own educational multimedia programs for their own teaching tools in support of curriculum-based instructional activities at educational institutions.

Other sections of the guidelines specify time limitations for use of multimedia works containing copyrighted items and portion limitations for fair use of motion media, text, music, lyrics, music video, illustrations and photographs, and numerical data sets. These fair use guidelines should be a crucial part of any multimedia producer's repertoire of knowledge. The full text of the fair use guidelines are available at www.indiana.edu/~ccumc/mmfumas. As you delve into the complexities of multimedia production, always be aware of the fair use guidelines. Copies for quick reference are readily available on several web sites.

In summary, as a producer and user of multimedia, one has an ethical obligation to follow the fair use guidelines. These are very detailed and specific as to what may be used, by whom, and for what purpose. Therefore, it is highly recommended that multimedia producers at any level adhere to these guidelines. In fact, most media festivals, online and offline, require the submitting producer to verify that all material in the submitted work be either original or permissible. To be on the safe side, it is wise to try to make or create as many of the elements as possible in one's multimedia products. This approach is not only fair but also a more challenging and creative production experience. Further, creating original elements, such as original music and artwork, is a valuable approach because it requires the producer to collaborate with others such as composers and artists.

MULTIMEDIA, MULTIPLE MEDIUMS:
SOFTWARE "WARHORSES"

At the risk of stating the obvious, the essence of multimedia is in the prefix *multi*. In contemporary multimedia production, several software packages are usually required to make one multimedia production; most projects combine several elements produced by different software. For example, a fairly complex online multimedia product may have required *Macromedia Flash, Adobe Photoshop, QuickTime Pro, iMovie* or *Final Cut Pro, Painter,* and maybe even some line coding such as Javascript. On the other hand, a versatile product such as *Flash* can handle most everything from sound editing to frame-by-frame animation to illustrations to text.

A list of all the software available for multimedia production or support would be virtually unlimited, with more being released all the time. The following section describes some multimedia warhorses: solid, time-tested software that can help accomplish one's purposes. Either in combination with one another, or in some cases standing alone, these may be all that is needed to create a range of products from very simple to highly complex and interactive. Further, all of the applications described have been around long enough to establish themselves as fundamental to multimedia production, in educational and business settings as well as in professional media production houses. They are also likely to be available in upgraded versions for many years.

Image Editing and Creation

Software that provides the designer or artist the means to manipulate still images is often described as image editing software. Still images—photos and illustrations—are a staple of multimedia production. Designers need to be able to manipulate still images—crop, resize, filter, and convert them to various file types. Contemporary multimedia software makes this possible. In fact, it works so well that designers and artists can create images and illusions that appear real—but are not.

Adobe Photoshop

Although other photo editing software exists, *Adobe Photoshop* has set the standard for a long time. One might think of *Photoshop* as a dark room or graphics lab in one's computer, but it offers even more than a digital darkroom. Among other things, it can filter images to make them appear as though they were drawn in charcoal or painted impressionistically. *Photoshop* is one of the most important tools in a designer's box, whether for manipulating images in preparation for use in other software or for creating stand-alone works. Learning *Photoshop* takes time; in fact, most experienced users do not know everything that it does. Upgrades are frequent, although older versions remain useful for several years, even without the latest features. *Adobe Photoshop* is widely available, and although not inexpensive, its many features make it more than worth its price.

Adobe Illustrator

Adobe Illustrator, or *Illustrator,* as it is popularly known, is a very sophisticated package used for creating images for a wide range of applications from desktop publishing to multimedia productions. Though *Illustrator* is a professional-level package, it is also used in educational and business settings. It is available for both the Macintosh and Windows systems.

Corel Painter

Corel Painter mimics a vast selection of artistic materials from felt-tipped pens to airbrushes. *Painter* also allows users to mimic surfaces from watercolor paper to a rough canvas and provides a wide range of creative choices for creating art for multimedia productions. It works especially well with digital graphics tablets such as those produced by *Wacom.*

Digital Video Editing

Video editing is no longer the exclusive domain of professionals with expensive hardware. Digital video technology is readily available to schools, businesses, and independent media artists. There are several choices for digitally editing video that is either shot on a digital format, such as mini-DV, or converted from an analog format such as VHS. Edited video can then be exported, converted, or rendered to any video format from VHS to DVD. Keep in mind that having good software is essential. Yet no matter how sophisticated the software is, the essence of editing is juxtaposing shots and scenes in ways that develop a topic, make a document, or tell a story. The editor, not the software, makes those choices.

Adobe Premiere

Adobe Premiere, often called simply *Premiere,* is one of the real veterans of digital editing. *Premiere* is available for both the Apple Macintosh and Windows operating systems. Its major advantage is its versatility: *Premiere* is used to edit everything from short movies for use on web sites to highly sophisticated professional productions. Further, it provides a large selection of postproduction effects ranging from transitions to sound design and sound editing. A computer equipped with *Premiere* becomes a powerful and expressive editing tool.

iMovie and Final Cut Pro

Both of these (at the time of the writing of this book) are designed only for the Macintosh operating system. *iMovie* is a very popular entry-level editing system that contains some transition effects such as dissolves and wipes; image filters, such as conversion to sepia tone or black and white; titling capabilities; and sound editing. Depending on the needs of a media producer, whether novice or professional, *iMovie* may be all that is needed to make clean, simple edits in order to tell a story or develop a topic. *iMovie* is inexpensive and comes already installed on many Macintosh computers. This depends on the philosophy or style of editing desired. In fact, professional editors tend toward simplicity, using special transitions and effects only sparingly yet creatively. *Final Cut Pro,* on the other hand, is a professional-level package with enormous creative potential. It offers more effects and flexibility but, not surprisingly, takes longer to learn. In that sense, *Final Cut Pro* is similar to *Premiere* because both are used to edit professional-level media productions.

Video Wave and *Studio Deluxe*

Two other Windows/PC-based digital video editing packages are Roxio's *Video Wave* and Pinnacle Systems' *Studio Deluxe.* They are not highly complex systems such as *Final Cut Pro* or *Adobe Premiere,* yet they offer a wide range of features for a reasonable price. In that sense, they are similar to *iMovie* and thus are excellent resources for students and teachers. Both support creation in formats such as DVD, VHS, CD-ROM, and web movies.

Multimedia Presentation Packages

There are multiple advantages in using multimedia tools to present information and concepts clearly, logically, and comprehensively. A major disadvantage of using multimedia in that manner is the time required actually to create the multimedia presentation. Some packages, however, can help alleviate that situation by offering quick and easy-to-learn features that yield very high-quality results.

Microsoft PowerPoint

PowerPoint has been around since the late 1980s. Since its introduction, it has improved greatly and is now one of the most, if not the most, widely used packages of its type. *PowerPoint* comes as part of the *Microsoft Office* series of software that is available for both of the leading operating systems, Windows and Macintosh.

Like many modern multimedia packages, *PowerPoint* may be used to produce simple yet visually interesting and professional-looking presentations quickly. But it can also be used to develop highly sophisticated and interactive works for individual use as well as group presentation. The essence of *PowerPoint* is in the choices it gives the user. These include background designs, clip art, sounds, animation, linking capabilities, and some image editing, to name only a few. Indeed, there are so many presentation features quickly available to the user, that they are too often overused and thus may be annoying to viewers.

HyperStudio

HyperStudio is a descendant of *Hypercard* from the mid-1980s. This software's primary use is in educational settings from early childhood to graduate school. Like *PowerPoint, HyperStudio* has a vast range of possibilities from relatively simple to very complex, sophisticated, and highly interactive, and it provides ready-made elements such as clip art. In some ways, it is similar to *PowerPoint,* yet due to the nature of its features, it is a little more complex. *HyperStudio* does provide a great deal of flexibility in laying out and presenting concepts and topics. Its major strength is in its ability to support highly interactive designs.

Getting Very Serious with Multimedia

The previously described software works well for many purposes from individual instruction to group presentation to creative expression. This section describes some multimedia software that greatly expands the creative and interactive possibilities.

Macromedia Flash

Macromedia Flash is one of the most versatile packages for producing multimedia products ranging from interactive web pages to sophisticated movies. This accounts for its popularity as one of the most used products for creating a wide range of works. One could make the case that *Flash* revolutionized the way inter-active products are made for the World Wide Web. *Flash* has a rather long, yet not difficult learning curve. It also has one of the better tutorials of any multimedia production software. For good reason, many potential users of multimedia soft-ware do not want to wade through awkward and sometimes confusing instruc-tions that accompany much software. However, *Macromedia Flash*'s built-in lessons are actually fun to use and, more important, very effective. The technical advan-tage of *Flash* is that through its special way of handling graphics, called vector graphics, it allows full-screen images of high resolution, fast operation, and high interaction with very small, even tiny file sizes. Further, *Flash* can be used to make simple web pages, to make animated movies, and to create highly interactive instruction for online learning. Media producers from independent animators to kindergarten through twelfth-grade teachers to corporate trainers have embraced this powerful software. For obvious reasons, every multimedia producer should be able to use *Flash*. Its versatility is unlimited. Some may use it exclusively to make animated movies and cartoons whereas others may use it just to create highly interactive and complex web sites. *Flash* also works well with most other multimedia software. Though not inexpensive, *Flash*'s capabilities make it more than worth its cost for use in schools to professional settings. Chapter 6 describes *Flash* in more detail with emphasis on its powerful creative possibilities. *Adobe GoLive* is similar in nature to *Flash* and can make Shockwave files (an interactive movie file) to be used with *Flash*. Both are available for Macintosh and Windows.

Macromedia Director and Macromedia Authorware

Macromedia Director and *Macromedia Authorware* were pioneers of what has come to be described as multimedia. They are used to create everything from instruc-tional CD-ROMs to online interactive instruction. *Director*'s strength is its movie-making powers, whereas *Authorware* is a highly sophisticated package for designing interactive instruction. Although these tools are powerful, the newer generation of software such as *Flash* can perform many of the same functions with only a fraction of the file size.

Macromedia Dreamweaver

Although this and other Web designing software can be categorized as "multi-media," it is more accurately described as "what you see is what you get" web page software. Though often used as a stand-alone package for interactive web site construction, *Dreamweaver* is also an excellent platform for the delivery and display of multimedia productions made with *Flash,* for example. Similar products are *Adobe GoLive* and *Microsoft Front Page.*

Adobe AfterEffects

AfterEffects is often thought of as the *Photoshop* for motion and animation. This software provides two- and three-dimensional features for designing and creating effects for use in other multimedia software.

Animation and Movies

One of the most appealing aspects of contemporary multimedia production is moviemaking, whether live action or animation. Although the multimedia titles previously described provide possibilities for creating everything from web pages to animated movies, some popular software is dedicated to moviemaking—live action and animation. One of the most popular animation tools for use on the World Wide Web is the animated GIF and two of the most popular movie editing and presentation packages are *QuickTime* and *Real Media.*

GIF Animation

The World Wide Web is full of short movies and animated cycles that can be produced in various ways. Most of the animated cycles that come in clip art are animated GIFs. However, the most popular way to create animated GIFs is with software designed to do so. This software is referred to as GIF-building software, and hundreds of titles are available. A Web search will yield many titles of GIF builders from freeware to shareware to commercial products. A very popular and inexpensive one designed for Windows is *Ulead GIF Animator.* This versatile product provides numerous effects. It is ideal for use in schools because, though quite sophisticated, it can be learned quickly and students can be turning out little movies immediately. Software packages such as the previously described *Photoshop* and *Flash* allow users to make movies and export them as animated GIFs.

Live-Action Movie Software

Two popular movie editing and projection titles are *QuickTime* and *Real Media.* Both of these plug-ins are already installed in Web browsers, or the player versions may be downloaded free. Both also provide movie editing and production versions that can also be downloaded for a fee from QuickTime or RealNetworks. Both offer many possibilities for editing, sound recording, and converting and exporting to a variety of file types—from simple animated GIFs to digital video streaming for use in digital video editing software. With both, a lot of creative potential is available for a very small price, thus making them ideal for school use.

QuickTime VR

QuickTime VR is a virtual reality package offered by QuickTime. This software creates 360-degree panoramic views or 360-degree rotation views of objects, and it can also zoom in or out on user-selected portions of a scene. The use of *QuickTime VR* requires a digital camera and a good-quality, sturdy tripod.

Line Coding

Multimedia works designed for posting to the World Wide Web are often created with a variety of software such as those mentioned previously. In some cases, however, designers use line coding to create web pages. Popular languages for creating web pages are Hyper Text Markup Language (HTML), Java, and Javascript. Software such as *Flash* provides line coding called *Actionscript,* which allows the designer to incorporate an even wider range of effects. Learning to use these coding tools does take time, but they provide a measure of control and precision that appeals to professional or experienced designers.

Software Summary

There are many other excellent choices of software and many more on the way. The applications described, however, represent a wide range of multimedia production capabilities. They have established themselves as fundamental tools for the creation of multimedia for teaching and learning, creating and expressing. Every multimedia producer develops a personal working style over time and selects software that fits his or her working style. For instance, some designers may prefer to learn to line code whereas others may prefer manipulating and experimenting with the features of assorted multimedia software. In that sense, the choice of software becomes a personal preference that matches each producer's unique needs and purposes. Choosing one's style and software requires experimentation, a willingness to learn from mistakes, and persistence.

BASIC DESIGN 101

Knowledge of fundamental design and layout principles is crucial to the success of multimedia products. The essence of multimedia production is communication, and communication requires clarity, legibility, and structure. When these elements are combined with a sense of creative and expressive design, the results are usually attractive, comprehensible, and effective. Although no absolutes exist for design and layout, there are some criteria to be aware of at least in the beginning. It is not unusual though for an especially effective solution to a design problem to be radical or even rule breaking.

Graphic artists tend not to conform strictly to rules or guidelines. It is OK to color outside the lines to achieve effective results, but successful graphic artists are guided by concepts that provide a basis for successful design that balances clarity, comprehensibility, and interactivity with creativity. The following sections will describe some principles to keep in mind while designing multimedia products. Again, these are not rules that inhibit creativity, but they do suggest some design principles to consider.

Design Basics

The temptation to overuse the numerous effects and features of multimedia software is hard to resist, especially for beginners. The early infatuation with the sounds, transition effects, and artistic tools the software provides may be overwhelming. That is not necessarily bad because learning to use multimedia software requires motivation and enthusiastic experimentation. The next step, however, is learn how to use all these resources effectively, guided by some principles all based, more or less, on common sense.

Typeface Legibility

Because the purpose of multimedia is communication, one basic principle is that the viewer must be able to read the text easily. Modern software offers thousands of typefaces. Some are elegant. Some are feisty. Some are decorative. Some are simple. Simple typefaces are the most legible for most multimedia readers. Also, in general, mixed uppercase and lowercase are easier to read than all caps. Capital letters should not be strung together to form words and sentences. Font size is also crucial. Obviously, text that is too small is hard to read. Finally, for a given project, select a typeface and stick with it. The stylistic variations among one typeface are numerous and include bold, italic, color, and size.

Color

Color presents extremely complex design issues. The best and most effective uses of color tend to be simple. There are many philosophies of how to do so and which colors to use. The relationship of text color to background color is also a legibility concept. By all means select colors that are pleasant to look at—but not at the expense of legibility. Although some combinations may be pretty or they may be the personal preferences of the media designer, they may also be unreadable. As a designer, always consider the needs of the viewers.

Layout

Much design is intuitive and instinctive, yet professional graphic designers spend years learning their art. Often what they learn is simplicity and unity. Simplicity is not simple to achieve, especially when laying out multiple items. The trick is to achieve a layout of multiple elements that is visually unified, attractive, stylish, and easy to read. The best graphic designers are in fact artists who are able to be creative and innovative yet achieve a design that serves a communications purpose. For nonprofessionals, the key concept again is simplicity. Avoid the visually busy backgrounds that compete with the key communications elements.

Graphic design is crucial to successful multimedia production. For multimedia producers who are not graphic designers, the previously described elements will provide some ideas to consider. As with all multimedia production tasks, improvement comes with observation, experimentation, experience, and practice.

SUMMARY: MAKING MULTIMEDIA

Designing and creating a variety of multimedia works can be challenging and complex. This chapter provided some ideas to consider before taking on this fascinating endeavor. These included some motivational considerations, a planning method, a review of fair use guidelines, descriptions of major multimedia software, and design principles. All of this is only a starting point. The ultimate success of any multimedia production experience depends on the willingness of the producer to be patient, to solve problems, to try and retry, to adapt, to plan, and most of all to be innovative and creative.

THOUGHT PROVOKERS

When reading and or implementing these activities, keep notes or a journal about how you can adapt and/or improve on them. Apply those ideas as you work and consider the following:

1. If you could create a multimedia project right now, what would it be? What would it look like? Whom would it be for? And why would you pick this topic?

2. Design a storyboard format and use it to tell a little story. Include simple drawings and script. Think of a short joke that you know that has a beginning, middle, and end, and storyboard it as though you were going to make a little movie. Have your friends read it and see if they understand it. Improve it based on their reactions.

3. Find a copy of the fair use guidelines. For example, look at www.indiana.edu/~ccumc/mmfumas/sld013.htm. Review the guidelines to get an idea of their purpose. Then tell in your own words why producers of multimedia works should respect the work of other artists, musicians, teachers, writers, and moviemakers.

4. Locate and try out some of the titles covered as multimedia warhorses in this chapter. Keep notes of which ones you used and describe your impressions of them. Look for other software packages that could have or even should have been included in that section.

REFERENCES

Adobe. (2002). *AfterEffects* [Computer Software]. San Jose, CA: Author.
Adobe. (2002). *GoLive* [Computer Software]. San Jose, CA: Author.
Adobe. (2002). *Illustrator* [Computer Software]. San Jose, CA: Author.
Adobe. (2002). *Photoshop* [Computer Software]. San Jose, CA: Author.
Adobe. (2002). *Premiere* [Computer Software]. San Jose, CA: Author.
Alessi, S. M., & Trollip, S. R. (2001). *Multimedia for Learning: Methods and Development*. Boston: Allyn & Bacon.
Apple Computer. (2002). *Final Cut Pro* [Computer Software]. Cupertino, CA: Author.

Apple Computer. (2002). *QuickTime VR* [Computer Software]. Cupertino, CA: Author.

Apple Computer. (2001). *iMovie* [Computer Software]. Cupertino, CA: Author.

Apple Computer. (2001). *QuickTime Pro* [Computer Software]. Cupertino, CA: Author.

Consortium of College and University Media Centers. (2001). *Fair Use Guidelines for Educational Multimedia* (www.indiana.edu/~ccumc/mmfumas).

Corel. (1999). *Corel Draw* [Computer Software]. Ottawa, Ontario, Canada: Author.

Corel. (1999). *Painter* [Computer Software]. Ottawa, Ontario, Canada: Author.

Macromedia. (2002). *Flash* [Computer Software]. San Francisco: Author.

Macromedia. (2001). *Director* [Computer Software]. San Francisco: Author.

Macromedia. (2001). *Dreamweaver* [Computer Software]. San Francisco: Author.

Microsoft. (2002). *Front Page* [Computer Software]. Redmond, WA: Author.

Microsoft. (2002). *PowerPoint* [Computer Software]. Redmond, WA: Author.

Pinnacle Systems. (2001). *Studio Deluxe* [Computer Software]. Mountain View, CA: Author.

RealNetworks. (2001). *RealPlayer Plus* [Computer Software]. Seattle, WA: Author.

Roxio Software. (2002). *Video Wave* [Computer Software]. Santa Clara, CA: Author.

Sunburst Technologies. (2000). *HyperStudio* [Computer Software]. Geneva, IL: Author.

Ulead Systems. (2002). *Ulead GIF Animator* [Computer Software]. Torrance, CA: Author.

■ ■ ■ ■ ■ ■

CHAPTER FOUR

DIGITAL STILLS
Revealing the World with a Digital Gallery

TOPIC OUTLINE

A PHOTOGRAPHIC HISTORY AND AESTHETIC
Here is a brief history of the still photograph as a medium of expression and communication.

MAKING AN ONLINE GALLERY
This section describes a step-by-step progression in designing and producing an online still photo gallery.

BOX 4.1: DIGITAL CAMERAS IN THE SECOND LANGUAGE CLASSROOM
This describes a creative use for photography in classrooms.

SUMMARY: THE EVOLVING GALLERY
This summarizes the online gallery project and looks further ahead.

THOUGHT PROVOKERS
These activities encourage further explorations in photography.

OBJECTIVES

After reading the topics in this chapter and following the directions, the reader will be able to:

- Conceptualize a theme or motif for creating an online still photo gallery and select and/or create photos that express that theme.
- Use selected multimedia tools to construct the design proposed in the first objective.

The technology of making still pictures and images continues to multiply and advance. Humans' intimate relationship with still images has lasted from the time of cave drawings to the digital age. New photographic processes and tools are becoming faster and less expensive. Chemical-dependent darkrooms disappear as digital "darkrooms" in the form of computers, software, and printers replace them. Though one can hardly imagine Ansel Adams using a digital camera, digital photography enriches rather than replaces the very old and venerable traditions of the art of photography. In spite of the increasing technical and practical potential of digital still photography, one key element remains: the sensitivity of the image's creator.

A PHOTOGRAPHIC HISTORY AND AESTHETIC

Photography was invented in the early nineteenth century and by the time of the American Civil War was a rather advanced art form. George Eastman brought this medium to the masses later that century with his Brownie camera. In the early twentieth century, photography emerged as a modern art form through the work of photographers such as Man Ray. During the Great Depression of the 1930s, photographers working for the Farm Security Agency documented the plight of the urban and rural poor and dispossessed. Notable among these were Dorthea Lange, Doris Ulman, and Walker Evans, who collaborated with James Agee on *Now Let Us Praise Famous Men*. Other milestones in the evolution of still photography included the documentation of World War II. In 1955, the most famous exhibition of photography up to that point, *The Family of Man*, consisted of black-and-white prints by the world's greatest photographers. American photographer Edward Steichen provided the leadership and vision for this exhibit, which opened at the Museum of Modern Art in New York. Subsequently, *The Family of Man* was exhibited in thirty-eight countries. Photography had arrived as a universal artistic language. Throughout all of those years, *Life* magazine grew into one of the most influential showplaces of the world's best photographers and their work.

Historically, photography required the use of chemicals such as developers, acid stop baths, fixers, and washes. Traditional photography required darkrooms and specialized and expensive resources such as enlargers, photographic paper, reels, trays, and dryers. Access to large volumes of running water was necessary and temperature control was crucial. When done properly, chemical-based photography can be extraordinarily beautiful and of the highest quality, accuracy, and resolution. From photographic prints to transparent slides, chemical-based photography remains an important image-making resource. However, the emergence and continuing improvement of digital photography, stimulated by the growth of the World Wide Web, has established its own tradition.

In everyday contemporary life the photograph is taken for granted. Still photography is an educational tool, an artist's medium, a journalistic resource, and a component of advertising. Though movies and video have sound and motion and action, the still photograph's lack of those elements is its strength. An outstanding photograph invites contemplation and reflection on a moment frozen for all time by a sensitive and observant photographer. There is no motion. There is no sound. There is only a motionless composition inviting interpretation and response. Viewing and responding to a great photograph is often a personal experience. Although a still photograph may be described as real or objective, it may actually be just the opposite. Most viewers simply take for granted or assume or are conditioned to interpret the image as realistic unless the photographer or artist obviously or intentionally distorted the subject for expressive effect. More accurately, a photo is a two-dimensional representation of a specific time and place in which the photographer made many choices. Although photography can create an accurate illusion of reality, photos are a result of many subjective choices on the part of the picture taker, including cropping and composing, point of view, camera angle, use of light, visual emphasis, focus, lens choice, and most of all the subject. One of the continuing appeals of black-and-white photographs, for example, is the unique and expressive aesthetic quality that attracts sensitive photographers and viewers. The abstractness or the unreal mood created by a powerful black-and-white photo is alluring. Some photographers want to photograph the picturesque, such as a fall landscape, and others choose to search out and photograph the unusual, the surrealistic, or even the disturbing. Whatever the subject, the result is a two-dimensional representation of a three-dimensional scene or subject. In that sense, the image is abstract.

The still photographic image is one of the most versatile and useful media ever devised by humankind—see Box 4.1 for a creative use of photography in the classroom. Some photographers document the passage of time and history, and others use photographs as a means of personal expression. Still photographic images have helped define and shape our notions about history, society, culture, nature, or anything that can be photographed.

Perhaps the most monumental use of still photography ever was in documenting the terrorist attack on the World Trade Center in New York City on September 11, 2001. This tragic event and its aftermath were photographed by amateurs using consumer cameras and by professional photojournalists. Their pictures were displayed side-by-side in books and exhibits. One cannot imagine a more sensitive, heartfelt, shocking, and spontaneous collection of images. In November 2001, Time Inc. published *In the Land of the Free: September 11—And After.* Notwithstanding the stunning video images that were shot, the still images included in that volume capture and convey the tragedy in special and personal ways that no other medium can.

MAKING AN ONLINE GALLERY

Photographers representing many specialties have embraced the World Wide Web. The meshing of the traditions and science of still photography with the newer technological phenomenon of the Internet expands the opportunities to experience photography in new and unique ways. For this project, a web site containing a gallery of photographs will be created. The photographs will be either original digital photos or scanned prints. The World Wide Web contains literally millions of photographs mostly as components of web page design. However, in this project a gallery will be created that contains a display of photographs each of which is a self-contained and freestanding work in its own right. The gallery may be a one-person show, a group show, or even a thematic show. The design and layout of this gallery can vary greatly depending on many variables.

■ ■ ■ ■ ■ ▬▬▬▬▬▬▬▬▬▬▬▬▬▬▬▬▬▬▬▬▬▬▬▬▬▬▬▬▬▬▬▬▬▬

BOX 4.1

DIGITAL CAMERAS IN THE SECOND LANGUAGE CLASSROOM

Amy Kelly

VOCABULARY PRACTICE

In a second language class, taking notes for vocabulary can be especially dull, especially the ensuing study of those vocabulary notes. As we and our introductory language students began our study of the vocabulary of the body, we looked for an alternative way for us to take those notes so they would not be as "cumbersome" to use and study. This is what came out of that desire to avoid tedium.

If we took a little piece of all of us, preferably the best piece, could we put all the parts together to make a perfect person? Well, not exactly. Nevertheless, that's what we set out to do with expectantly far from perfect results in my second language classroom. The ensuing activities masked the physical "quality" of the results.

We took digital pictures of rather high quality of each student and ourselves. We had to make the girls and a few of the boys put their hair behind their ears so we could see them. Some chose to make silly faces (all the better) and others chose to "pose" like their favorite stars on album covers . . . uh, CD covers. We then printed them out at one picture per page on regular paper, adjusting brightness beforehand to get the clearest possible picture. The accompanying figure illustrates the sequence.

Then, each student was given a list of the parts of the head in English with a blank after the English word. Students were then instructed to cut out of their own picture the parts of the head on the list.

The students were instructed to swap each part of their face save one with another student in class. They also were to record with whom they swapped each part on their list. When they had finished their exchange, they were to reassemble a new face with the parts they now had. We also used the business card function of our Print Shop to print out multiple copies of clip art bugged out eyes, vampire teeth, tongues, big noses, glasses, etc. They could use one or two of these if their end picture was lacking an element on the list.

However, the fun did not stop there. After we completed this, we went through a series of oral activities. In our French classes, we have to work on possession in its many forms. In both French and German, we have to practice the irregular forms of the verb "to have." In particular, to German, this provides excellent opportunities to practice the accusative case really reinforcing the noun genders. All this practice was in addition to sentence structure and the vocabulary usage. These new images provided a multitude of opportunities to do all that.

Initially, for example, we asked the students, *Qui a le nez de Charlotte?* Or "Who has Charlotte's nose?" They answered, *Moi, jai le nez de Charlotte.* Or "Me, I have Charlotte's nose." This reviewed irregular verb forms of *avoir,* use of *qui,* and possession with *de.* They then practiced in pairs or small groups. Then we allowed them each to ask the class, *Qui a mon nez?* or "Who has my nose?" With a response of: *Moi, jai ton nez,* or "Me, I have your nose." This reinforces possessive adjectives.

In addition to this, we practiced in our pairs describing our new facial features. *Mon nez est grand et mon oeil droit est vert et grand. Mon oeil gauche est brun et porte des lunettes.* Or "My nose is big and my right eye is green and big." Then they shared some of their observations with the class.

1 Take close-up photos.

2 Cut out parts of head included on the vocabulary list.

3 Swap head parts and assemble new faces.

Three Steps with the Digital Photos

Some variations I am planning to use next semester are allowing the kids loose in small groups with the cameras and letting them compile a series of images illustrating typical dress in each of the seasons. Like "patchwork people," each group of students will have a season and their job will be to photograph people and/or objects. The resulting images will be printed and cropped to include only the essential, then assembled to create a person representative of the season in question. The group will then create a composition or perhaps a dialogue between two people should they choose to make more, describing themselves in addition to the relationship between the weather and what they are wearing.

Creating your own gallery for posting online has several learning advantages. First, the process requires critical thinking in order to choose which of your photos you want to share with the world. Second, constructing the gallery requires learning to use Web editing software. Third, the goal of creating photos for a thematic or genre-specific gallery requires learning or using photographic concepts and skills. Finally, if the gallery is to have a specific topic as its subject, the creator will have to learn something about that topic in order to create a successful gallery.

Preproduction and Planning Steps

Educationally, personally, and artistically, creating an expressive and visually stimulating gallery that viewers anywhere will benefit from seeing is a challenging and fulfilling experience. The following steps provide a sequence of planning ideas and concepts to consider before actually creating the gallery.

Planning Step 1: Search for and Evaluate Online Galleries

The World Wide Web is a tremendous source for viewing the work of thousands of photographers. Many of the photographs are presented as galleries or portfolios designed and posted by the photographers themselves. They consist of all genres, from the strictly personal and artistic to the commercial, from traditional to digital. Yahoo! in particular offers an easy and comprehensive entry into the world of online photo galleries. For example, accessing Yahoo!, then selecting Photography under Arts and Humanities yields many choices of photographic genres and categories. One choice is Photographers. Choosing Personal Exhibits links to a page that allows users to search the personal web sites of photographers by genre or by name. Selecting Complete Listing yields the names of hundreds of photographers with short descriptions of their works. Selecting a name takes the user to that person's site.

The variety of styles and subjects of personal galleries is vast, to say the least. Some are simple or even minimalist whereas others are quite complex. Photos may be categorized by genre or they may be sequential. Some photos may have "thumbnails" to click on to see larger versions. Before creating an online photo gallery, look at a few galleries whose short descriptions you find interesting. Decide which ones you like best and remember why they are successful. Do likewise with ones that are not so successful. There are no specific rules or guidelines for online galleries other than logical and legible design for ease of access.

The same searching process will also yield links to galleries and biographies of master photographers of other eras including Margaret Bourke-White, Walker Evans, Ansel Adams, Imogene Cunningham, and others. A serious perusal of these images is an educational experience in and of itself. Major newspapers such as the *New York Times* and *Washington Post* also display online galleries on their web sites of the work created by their photojournalists. Warning! Due the nature of the vast worldwide collection of photos on the Web, you may want to spend many hours perusing.

Planning Step 2: Choose a Theme or Motif

Plan a theme or motif. The art of photography has a long and rich history consisting of numerous styles, theories, and genres. Approaches to making still pictures can range from the simple "point-and-shoot" to the technical and complex to the unconventional and artistic. When creating images that are to be included in an online gallery, consider the major categories of photography in which your work may fit. The following categories overlap, but they will provide a frame of reference for the choices you must make.

Photojournalistic.   Photojournalists seek to reveal all sorts of events and occasions from wars to natural disasters. But they do much more. Perceptive photojournalists see the stuff of everyday life and often examine the unexamined. They are not content to take pictures *of,* but instead take pictures *about*. In this way, they use the power of images to inform and touch audiences in ways that cannot be done as effectively, or at all, through print alone. Examine the work of Margaret Bourke-White (Figure 4.1) or Eugene Smith, for example, and notice how the power of the images vastly exceeds conventional picture taking. Thus, photojournalists such as Bourke-White and Smith do much more than simply document or record—they reveal. The viewer of a great photograph shares or experiences the captured or frozen moment with the photographer. Even though the greatest photojournalists make pictures that are well composed and aesthetically pleasing to view, their pictures are much more—they anticipate, empathize, or even protest. They do not settle for the easy shot or the cliché. Rather they reveal, persuade, and touch. In that

FIGURE 4.1   Workers on Top of a Large Sluiceway, by Margaret Bourke-White

sense, the best photojournalists are also artists. Therefore, one possibility for creating a thematic online gallery is to follow the traditions of photojournalism. Use still images to share original and fresh perspectives. Invite viewers to share and react to those perceptions. Remember that the chosen subjects need not be spectacular events, but simply fresh views of the "taken for granted" of everyday life.

Photography as Art.   Photography is an important artistic medium. Some artists paint, some sculpt, some write poetry, and some take photographs. Photographers motivated by artistic instincts reveal the world in personal and sometimes unconventional ways. Figure 4.2 is a photograph by the artist photographer Man Ray.

Art galleries regularly display photography. In the late twentieth century, painters seeking to capture the essence of still photography were loosely joined in a movement called "photorealism." Art photographers seek inspiration from nature, from people, from urban environments—from most any subject. Digital photography with its enhanced special effects possibilities expands the potential of the still photographic image as an artistic medium. Refer to the Yahoo! search; then

FIGURE 4.2   Study for *Aurelien,* by Man Ray

seek out and view some examples of art photography. Then consider an artistic theme for your gallery.

Planning Step 3: Curate the Exhibit

Before creating and/or selecting the photographs that will be displayed in the digital gallery, decide on a style or visual design. As with a traditional gallery display, the photographs need to be juried or selected. The images selected may be representative of a theme such as a series of photographs of architectural details and decorations on Victorian era buildings on your hometown's main street. Or you may want to choose a series of photographs exploring a local event such as a music festival or a charity run. Another possibility is a portfolio collection of the works of an artist photographer. Other topics may include patriotic displays on homes and businesses on national holidays or during a time of crisis. Themes can even be categorized according to the nature of the photographs, such as black-and-white images or photos made with a pinhole camera. Of course, the number of possible themes is unlimited. Experiencing or viewing carefully selected gallery works should be a stimulating learning experience for visitors to your gallery. For example, as a result of viewing these images, a visitor to the online gallery will learn something, reflect on an issue, be pleased or entertained, be touched, be exposed to the work of a particular photographer, or have some meaningful reaction to the images. Later steps in this section will describe online presentation options including software and graphics editing possibilities. Keep in mind that outstanding photographs reveal, not merely document or record.

Planning Step 4: Make and/or Acquire the Images

The next step is either to create or to find the images that reflect the chosen ideas and genres. There are two major methods for creating the photos for a digital gallery.

Scanning.   One way to gather and prepare printed images is to digitize them using a scanner. A scanner is a crucial item in multimedia production. Scanners come in an immense assortment of products, designs, features, prices, and manufacturers, yet they all are used for essentially the same task. They are inexpensive, widely available, easy to use, and they provide a way to incorporate the vast and unlimited advantages of two-dimensional images from artwork to photographs. Photographic prints can be created especially for scanning for inclusion in an online gallery. Further, and possibly the greatest advantage of scanning, is the potential of using very old photos.

To use in an online gallery, the scanned photos will have to be saved or converted to the JPEG file format. JPEG (Joint Photographics Group) is a graphic file type for displaying photographs. This can be done either with the scanner's software or with graphics editing software such as *Adobe Photoshop.* Scanning software allows cropping, resolution choices, resizing, and other image adjustment features such as color, contrast, brightness, and so forth. So, even at the scanning step, the photographer has creative flexibility. As with any multimedia production method, trying, experimenting, and retrying is necessary to achieve the best results within the technical limitations and possibilities of the resources being used. If you have your film developed commercially, the scanning step can be bypassed by requesting a CD-ROM or floppy disk containing the digitized versions of the photographs.

Digital Photography.   The second way to make an online gallery is with digital photos taken specifically for that reason. This is an especially creative and expressive option. As is true with most multimedia production tools, digital still cameras are available in a huge and growing array of configurations. Even many digital video camcorders have an option for shooting still photographs. Also, digital video editing software allows users to select and export single frames as digital still images.

Digital cameras can be purchased for less than one hundred dollars or over a thousand dollars. Features such as zoom lenses, automatic exposure, and built-in flash are common. There are several ways that the digital images are stored, depending on the camera. Some cameras have built-in storage space and others may include floppy disk storage, mini-CDs, memory sticks, or various combinations of those. The number of images that can be stored depends on many variables, such as the resolution of images and the available storage space. Most digital cameras allow the user to select a picture resolution. For example, select a high-resolution setting if the photo will be printed as a stand-alone photo, or a lower resolution for a web page or to save more images on the camera's storage device.

The following production steps describe a method for assembling the gallery. As with all projects described in this book, this activity may be adapted to a variety of software.

Production Steps

The purpose of this project is to create a one-person digital online gallery of still photographs. After completing the previously described planning steps, the next step is to lay out or edit the gallery.

Production Step 1: Acquire Basic Materials
Producing a digital photo gallery does not require exotic and expensive resources. The following items are needed for pretty much any style of photo gallery:

1. Still photos. These are photos as described previously.
2. An image scanner if using prints.
3. Photo editing software such as *Adobe Photoshop, Microsoft Paint Shop Pro,* or any software that has photo and graphics editing features. If the photos are acceptable as shot on location, they may not need to be edited. Keep that idea in mind as you shoot the photos.
4. For posting the gallery online, editing software such as *Macromedia Dreamweaver, Macromedia Flash, Macromedia Director, Microsoft Front Page, Adobe GoLive,* or an ability to write line code such as Hyper Text Markup Language (HTML) or Javascript. Other options include *Microsoft PowerPoint* and *HyperStudio.* Depending on the needs of the producer, the gallery may be designed for online or for viewing on a CD-ROM.

Production Step 2: Select, Import, Arrange, Layout

Select ten photos (scanned or digital) and import them into the software. Design a layout for the gallery. This could be a menu-driven design, an automatically playing slide show, an interactive slide show, or a combination of these. Refer again to the previous suggestion of viewing online photographic galleries. Design and presentation possibilities are virtually unlimited. The main idea is to select a design motif, theme, or layout and be consistent throughout.

As an example, follow these steps in producing a ten-photograph gallery based on the theme of timbered buildings of East Anglia using *Macromedia Flash*. The prescanned images are shown in Figure 4.3. Note that *Flash* is a very sophisticated and highly versatile multimedia package. As mentioned earlier and as a short review, this software can be used for a range of activities from creating interactive web sites, to highly animated movies, to simple slide shows. Learning how to exploit all of *Flash*'s potential takes a lot of time, yet the results are well worth it. Also note that the *Flash* lessons under the *Help* menu item provide an excellent introduction to this software. For this assignment, only basic functions are needed to create a still photo gallery, which in effect will be a menu-based slide show. Although there are endless options and variations, the following steps will set up a basic slide show, or gallery. Please note that selecting *Help + Lessons* and completing them is highly recommended for beginning *Flash* users.

1. *Open* Flash. Select *Modify + Movie* (or *Document* in *Flash MX*). Note that it is already set for 550 pixels wide by 400 pixels tall. As you will see, these dimensions can be changed. However, for this project, this default size works very well. Also notice that under *Modify + Movie,* a background color needs to be selected.

2. *Insert frames.* On *Layer 1,* insert eleven blank key frames by either pressing the F7 key eleven times or selecting *Insert + Blank Key Frame* eleven times, from the drop-down menu.

3. *Select actions.* Select *Blank Key Frame* one on *Layer 1* and double-click on it. A *Frame Actions* box appears. Select *Basic Actions + Stop.* Close the *Frame Actions* box. This stops the first frame of the show so buttons may be inserted for various actions.

4. *Place text.* Select *Key Frame* one on *Layer 1.* This is the opening slide. It may contain a title and some introductory text or any other design or image elements. Select the *Text* tool from the *Tools* menu and insert a title. From the menu bar, select *Window + Panels + Character* in order to choose text size, style, color, and other characteristics of the title text. Use the same typeface throughout the show.

5. *Insert buttons.* Select *Window + Common Libraries + Buttons.* When the *Buttons* menu appears, scroll down, select *Push Bar,* and drag it on the title frame. Select it with the solid *Black Arrow* tool, and resize it by dragging the little boxes on the corners to make it much smaller.

6. *Assign actions to buttons.* Assign an *Action* to the *Push Bar* button. Select the button with the *Black Arrow* tool. While it is selected, choose *Windows + Actions.* When

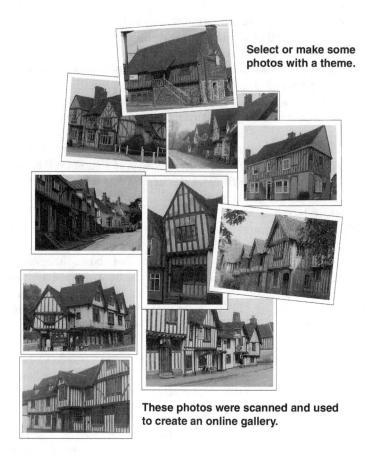

Select or make some
photos with a theme.

These photos were scanned and used
to create an online gallery.

FIGURE 4.3   A Digital Photo Gallery. These are photographs
of timbered buildings in East Anglian villages.

the *Object Actions* box appears, choose *Basic Actions* and double-click on *Go To*. In *Frame 1*, type the number 2, and deselect the box that indicates *Go To* and *Play*. This instructs the button, when clicked, to go to frame 2 and stop. To test the button, select the menu item *Control + Enable Simple Buttons*. Repeat this process for every frame. On the last frame, insert a button action that returns to frame 1. Tip: In order to have a show that runs smoothly, simply select the button with the *Black Arrow* tool and select *Copy* from the drop-down *Edit* menu. Move to the next frame and select *Edit + Paste in Place*. By doing this, the button will remain in exactly the same place from frame to frame. If the action *Next Frame* is chosen from the *Object Actions* menu, actions will not have to be reset for frames 1 through 10. The frame 11 button will need to have an object action assigned to the button that will return to the first frame.

   7. *Test interactivity.* Test the show by selecting *Control + Test*. When the *Buttons* and *Frame Actions* work, make sure the program is saved as a *Flash Movie*.

8. *Place photos.* Import photographs by selecting *File + Import,* and place them in desired sizes and locations on each frame.

A rule of thumb is that photographs require a relatively large amount of memory to display. When imported into *Flash,* photos will increase the file size of the final *Flash Movie,* and thus downloading time to view the gallery will be increased. *Flash* does have ways of optimizing and converting photos, though often at the loss of quality. Thus, when creating a photo gallery, be economical in the use of photos. Be aware of the final file size of the gallery, and seek ways to keep it as small as possible. Use the *Bandwidth Profiler* under *Control + Test Movie* to keep your final product at a reasonable size. "Reasonable" could be interpreted to mean working toward a final *Flash Movie* for posting on the World Wide Web that is around 500 kilobytes (K), give or take a couple of hundred K. Making those judgments comes with practice, experience, and learning.

This process sets up a basic display or gallery for digital or digitized photographs. Figure 4.4 (page 64) shows a completed slide show.

The options are endless. For example, all of the buttons could be placed on a menu page. Then each frame would have a *Return to Menu* button. This basic setup and its endless variations can be used for presenting all sorts of information from artwork to photographs. Shows can also be set up to run automatically by slowing down the frame rate or spacing out the slides.

When finished, export the slide show by selecting *File + Export Movie.* Although there are many possibilities for saving as various file types, select *Flash Player* and give it a name. This creates a Shockwave file that is ready for posting on the World Wide Web.

SUMMARY: THE EVOLVING GALLERY

Creating a gallery such as the one previously described is simple, yet very effective. When the first one works and the producer gains more experience with the software, the gallery can grow or evolve into more sophisticated versions. Most web sites are works in progress, and an online photo gallery is an excellent example of that concept.

THOUGHT PROVOKERS

1. Seek out books on specific photographers. Carefully examine their work and read their statements. Look for a variety in genres from photojournalism to art. The References section contains some titles.

2. Go to a photo exhibit in your hometown or region. Examine the work carefully and write a critique of the exhibit. If the exhibit is a one-person show, look for a consistency in style, theme, genre, composition, and technique.

FIGURE 4.4 A Completed Gallery. The user may view the photos sequentially by clicking on the arrow in the lower right corner or selecting photos to view from the thumbnail images in the menu. The button in the lower left corner returns the user to the menu.

REFERENCES

Agee, James, & Evans, Walker. (1939). *Let Us Now Praise Famous Men.* New York: Ballantine Books.

Loengard, John. (1998). *Life Photographers: What They Saw.* Boston: Little, Brown.

Mellow, James R. (1999). *Walker Evans.* New York: Basic Books.

Nash, Eric Peter. (1995). *Ansel Adams: The Spirit of High Places.* New York: Smithmark.

Smith, W. Eugene. (1998). *W. Eugene Smith: Photographs 1934–1975.* New York: Harry Abrams.

Steichen, Edward. (1955). *The Family of Man: The Photographic Exhibition Created by Edward Steichen for the Museum of Modern Art.* New York: Published for the Museum of Modern Art by Simon and Schuster.

Time Inc. Specials. (2001). *In the Land of the Free: September 11—And After.* Alexandria, VA: Time Inc. Home Entertainment.

Ulmann, Doris. (1996). *Doris Ulmann: Photographs from the J. Paul Getty Museum.* Malibu, CA: The J. Paul Getty Museum.

CHAPTER FIVE

THE MECHANICAL EYE BECOMES THE DIGITAL EYE
Revealing the World with Video

TOPIC OUTLINE

THE CLASSIC STEPS: PREPRODUCTION, PRODUCTION, POSTPRODUCTION
Here are the elements and concepts included in each of the major production steps.

MAKING DIGITAL MOVIES: SKILLS AND CONCEPTS
This section describes and explains the basic skills needed for digital video.

DIGITAL VIDEO EXERCISES
This set of step-by-step exercises is designed to develop digital video production skills.

A CULMINATING VIDEO PROJECT: DOING THE HUMANITIES WITH DIGITAL VIDEO
This is a detailed description of a digital video production based on the traditions of the humanities.

BOX 5.1: USING VIDEO TO CREATE PORTRAITS: TEAM BUILDING WITH SPECIAL NEEDS KIDS
Dr. Kathryn Dipietro describes a creative use of video in special education.

SUMMARY: MOVIEMAKING REFLECTIONS AND TIPS
This section reviews and reflects on the previous skills and exercises.

THOUGHT PROVOKER
This suggests that students view and critique the works of independent video artists.

OBJECTIVES

After reading the topics in this chapter and participating in its exercises, the reader will be able to:

- Describe the three major steps often used in the creation of video projects, and use those concepts in planning and producing individual projects.
- Demonstrate the basic skills of planning, camera operation, and editing, and apply those skills to individual video projects.

- Use video production skills to complete a set of production exercises.
- Plan and produce a short three- to five-minute digital documentary about an interesting aspect of one's own culture, region, or life using the concepts of classical documentary production and humanities study.

Television is so much a part of twenty-first century life that it is almost transparent. This technological phenomenon is taken for granted, and few people can even remember what the world was like before television existed. The influence of television at its best reveals the world in many ways—from documentaries to educational and informational programming to instantaneous news. One wonders what the seminal filmmaker Dziga Vertov who was quoted in the Preface would say about this ubiquitous eye.

Television programming is most often thought of as a product delivered to consumers by an increasing array of networks, cable channels, digital videodiscs, and videocassettes. Despite the continuing debate over the nature and influence of television programming, some of the tools of this technology provide readily available and inexpensive means for virtually anyone to express, to create, and to teach. To borrow the previously quoted words of Vertov's, this modern eye "leads towards the creation of a fresh perception of the world." Of course, this is not new. Consumers with common camcorders have been making home movies for years, and many schools have television production resources that are used for applications such as recording reports to producing in-school news broadcasts.

This chapter describes some specific ways in which consumer and school-level video production tools can be used creatively and effectively. In doing so, this chapter introduces the knowledge and skills needed to use these tools thoughtfully. The topics covered include principles of effective camera methods, principles of editing and postproduction, a frequently used planning method, and descriptions of popular video production genres. In keeping with the approach of this book, the descriptions are conceptual and practical in nature. The chapter concludes with descriptions of specific exercises that can be adapted to locally available resources. The fundamental assumption is that successful media production is founded on creativity and ideas, not hardware. Although having an abundance of tools and the skills to use them provides creative options, successful works based on expressive and resourceful ideas can and often are made with simple tools and limited resources.

THE CLASSIC STEPS: PREPRODUCTION, PRODUCTION, POSTPRODUCTION

Making a video or digital movie of any genre consists of three major steps: planning, or preproduction; creating, shooting, or taping, or production; and finally, editing pictures, sounds, and effects, or postproduction. Approaches to all three of these vary greatly depending on such variables as the nature of the product and the personal working styles of individual producers.

Chapter 3 described a planning model based on preproduction, production, and postproduction. Before describing some basic skills and exercises, review the three steps.

Preproduction Planning

The first step is the preproduction or planning step and includes elements such as outlining a topic, writing a script, or creating a storyboard before the video recording begins. For a production with a specific instructional objective, preplanning also includes such design elements as learner analysis and assessment.

Production

This step includes creating or acquiring the elements of the work. That is, some videos are shot on remote locations, or in the field, while others may be shot in studios or on specially designed sets. Usually, far more video is shot than will be needed to create a final work, which will come together at the postproduction phase.

Postproduction

This step consists of editing shots and scenes, designing and editing sound, and inserting effects. Postproduction can be a complex step or, depending on the purpose of the final product, it may be simple and direct. Some videos may require special effects that need extensive manipulation, or others may require only simple transitional effects.

The following sections will describe key concepts in the production and postproduction steps beginning with the basics of effective camera operation followed by composition basics, editing concepts, storyboarding, video genres, and video production activities.

MAKING DIGITAL MOVIES: SKILLS AND CONCEPTS

Traditionally, a "movie" camera is a camera with some kind of a motor, electric or windup, that takes still pictures at a high rate, usually twenty-four per second. The "software" for the movie camera was, and is, photographic film stock that can be 8mm, 16mm, or 35mm. The film stock has sprocket holes on one or both sides, depending on its use. Claws in the camera grab the sprocket holes, pull down a frame of film, and hold it still over an open gate so the shutter can open a split second, exposing one frame, or picture. Typically, this occurs twenty-four times per second. (Mel Brooks once responded that "putting in the little holes" is the hardest task in making a movie.) When the film is processed, it can then be played in a projector or—through a complex process of work printing, editing, conforming, and release printing—become part of a movie for distribution. In the theater, the eyes and brains of the audience then work together to "see" an illusion of motion created by the fast and persistent projection of the still pictures rendered as shadows on a screen. Figure 5.1 shows the traditional or classic steps in the complex process of making movies.

The illusion of motion created by a sequence of still images is called the persistence of vision. When a bright image from a strip of film strikes the retina on the inside of the eyeball and then disappears instantly, the residue from the bright image fades away. As that fade is occurring and another bright image is presented, the resulting overlap of the two images creates an illusion of motion. For a movie image, this occurs twenty-four times per second and for a video image thirty times a second.

For many years, most movies shown in schools were 16mm prints that were very delicate—susceptible to dust, scratches, and breakage—in addition to being very expensive. The large projected image in a darkened room could be impres-

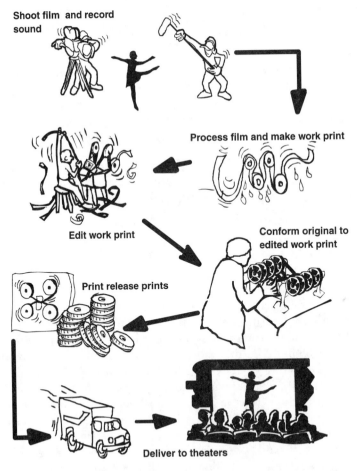

FIGURE 5.1 Making a Movie the Old-Fashioned Way

sive. Producing 16mm films, though, was very rare for most teachers and students due to expense and complexity.

Another popular film format was the Super 8mm movie (not 8mm video) that has all but disappeared, although some independent filmmakers who like its "artsy" look still use it. For example, this renewed interest in Super 8mm filmmaking is supported by a number of World Wide Web sites promoting its use. The popularity of the inexpensive and easy-to-use VHS analog camcorder replaced the 8mm camera as the camera of choice for home and school movies. Now a new generation of digital camcorders is replacing VHS.

Current digital technologies have revolutionized the process of making motion pictures. Digital camcorders are inexpensive, easy-to-use, and the quality of their video recording is excellent. Further, the advantages of digital camcorders combined with the tools of digital editing allow virtually anyone willing to acquire the tools and learn how to use them to create high-quality, expressive videos. Figure 5.2 is a graphic summary of the digital production process.

Skill 1: An Overview of a "Generic" Camcorder

There are numerous brands and models of camcorders. Some of these use analog tape, such as VHS or 8mm, but more and more use digital videocassettes. Specifications and features vary widely but they all share one key characteristic for successful use: an operator who understands and appreciates the creative and expressive potential of the moving picture.

Making successful movies and videos requires concepts and principles supported by practical skills and knowledge. This is true whether using an inexpensive discount store camcorder or a state-of-the-art digital camera. In fact, a sensitive producer with a story to tell or an idea to express, supported by an appreciation and understanding of fundamental expressive methods can use a basic and inexpensive video camera to achieve excellent results that may even win awards at festivals.

Skill 2: Formats and Camera Operation

In film director Frank Capra's (*It's a Wonderful Life, Meet John Doe,* and *Mr. Smith Goes to Washington*) autobiography, *The Name Above the Title,* he said, "There are no rules in filmmaking, only sins. And the cardinal sin is Dullness." This fundamental principle applies to most video productions, whether big budget or small budget. The avoidance of "dullness" begins with the recording and creation of the moving images.

Formats
Analog video is made up of an arrangement of iron oxide particles covering a long strip of tape. The most common analog formats are VHS, 8mm, BetaSP, and 1-inch video. An electromagnetic record head in a camera or tape electronically arranges the particles, and a playback head in a tape deck or camera "reads" the arranged

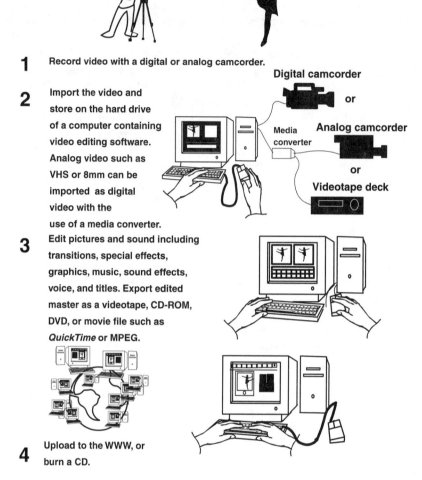

1 Record video with a digital or analog camcorder.

2 Import the video and store on the hard drive of a computer containing video editing software. Analog video such as VHS or 8mm can be imported as digital video with the use of a media converter.

3 Edit pictures and sound including transitions, special effects, graphics, music, sound effects, voice, and titles. Export edited master as a videotape, CD-ROM, DVD, or movie file such as *QuickTime* or MPEG.

4 Upload to the WWW, or burn a CD.

FIGURE 5.2   Making a Movie the Digital Way

particles and reproduces the recorded image. The major disadvantage of analog video is that its duplication and editing require multiple recording generations, with each one of lesser quality than the last. This is especially a problem with VHS, analog 8mm, and to a lesser extent with 1-inch video. Higher-end professional video formats such as 1-inch or BetaSP can be rerecorded several times without appreciable loss of quality.

Editing analog video requires multiple tape decks (sound and video), monitors, and a controller. This can make editing complex and time-consuming. Very sophisticated higher-end analog systems can provide an editor with many video effects.

Compared to analog video, digital video production has many practical and artistic advantages and is thus the preferred choice of contemporary media producers.

Digital videocassette tape formats for use in digital camcorders are mini-DV, or simply DV and Digital 8. On the professional level, digital formats include a digital 1-inch tape format and Betacam digital. Some digital still cameras record on small CDs. A major advantage of digital video cameras is that most of them can also be used to take still photographs, thus alleviating the need to have two digital cameras—one still and one video. Also, many still digital cameras can record short full motion and sound videos. Finally, another prime advantage of digital video is apparent in the editing or postproduction phase. Almost any modern desktop or laptop computer equipped with editing software, including software for special effects, is sufficient for editing digital video. The same resources can also be used for editing analog video, if the computer is equipped with either an internal video digitizing card or an external digitizer. These devices allow the editor to digitize analog video formats for digital editing.

Skill 3: Operating a Digital Camcorder: Some Tips

A vast and growing selection of school and home digital camcorders is available from numerous makers and vendors. Certainly, this makes choosing one for purchase a daunting task. Following the general trend of electronic products, the prices of digital camcorders go down as they become more popular. For school or home use, for example, very high-quality digital camcorders may be purchased for less than $500; higher-end professional cameras may cost more than $2,000. Figure 5.3 shows the parts of a generic digital camcorder. How a camcorder is used is more important than how much it costs. Proper camera operation with an understanding of high production qualities is the most important factor in shooting successful video. That is, an operator who has a basic camera yet understands how to work creatively within the limitations of that camera will be successful.

Figure 5.4 (pages 74–75) shows the step-by-step instructions for operating a camcorder, which may serve as a starting point from which to learn this skill. Features and characteristics vary from brand to brand or from basic cameras to very expensive ones. Nevertheless, there are some basic tips to keep in mind when preparing to operate a camcorder successfully, or even creatively. These steps deal with physically operating the camera. These instructions are not intended to be comprehensive or detailed, but they may be adapted to most camcorders. Of course, this advice is not intended as a substitute for reading the operation manuals that accompany new digital cameras.

1. Note that most camcorders have a camera mode and a VCR mode. Locate this feature and select camera mode. Locate the power switch. Look for the start and stop recording buttons. There may be more than one recording button or switch. For example, one may be on the front near the lens, possibly on or near a handle, and another one may be on the back the camera. Also, check for the Photo button that allows the user to shoot still photos.

Two basic shapes of
digital camcorders

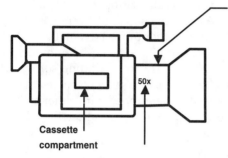

A variable focal length
lens, or a zoom lens, is a
great asset when
composing a shot because
it allows framing
compositions from
extreme close-ups to wide
shots and every focal
length in between.

50x

Cassette
compartment

Every zoom lens has a zoom ratio that indicates
its range or distance between telephoto and wide
angle. For example, a 10x zoom indicates its wide
angle is 10 times longer than its telephoto.
Obviously, the wider the ratio, the more frame
choices; thus, a 100x zoom provides a great
distance between wide angle and telephoto.

FIGURE 5.3   **A Generic Digital Camcorder.** There are numerous
brands and models of camcorders. Some of these use analog tape
such as VHS or 8mm, and some use digital videocassettes.
Specifications and features vary from brand to brand and model to
model. This illustration points out features that can be used
creatively and expressively.

2.   Cassette tapes for digital camcorders may be either the mini-DV format, or
the Digital 8 format. Following the camera's manual procedures, carefully insert
the cassette.

3.   Typically, a digital camcorder has two viewfinders. Look for an LCD panel that
opens from the body of the camera, and look for an eyepiece viewfinder. Shooting
style and circumstances will determine which one to use. Some cameras have a choice
of format, or aspect ratio. These are the conventional video format or the "film" ratio.
The film ratio is for shooting film style and is characterized by black areas at the top
and bottom of the format, thus creating a movie style ratio. Whichever you choose,
remember to be consistent throughout the shooting of a production.

4.   Most cameras have a choice of recording modes from completely automatic
—point and record—to manual adjustments for special exposures. For the novice,

the automatic exposure mode works very well in most situations and with many kinds of available light. Review the manual's description of the recording modes available and locate the setting selector and menu.

5. Check out the focusing and zooming methods. Focusing is obviously crucial for effective, sharp images. Most digital camcorders have manual and automatic focusing. For general steady shooting, the automatic mode works well. However, when in this mode, the camera must be held very still for extended times in order for the automatic focus function to operate properly. That is, moving the camera around rapidly while in automatic mode does not give the camera time to fix a focus. The result is a video recording that goes in and out of focus, thus making the shot unusable. Manual focus requires more attention while recording, but the advantage is that the operator can control where the center of sharp focus is in a shot.

Practice operating the zoom lens, also referred to as a variable focal length lens, a common feature on camcorders. A zoom lens allows the camera operator to choose camera angles from wide to telephoto. The lens can be operated automatically or manually. Generally avoid overusing this feature while recording. Use it primarily for composition. Look for the zoom controls that are usually located on or near the handgrip to allow easy and smooth operation.

6. Examine the built-in microphone, and when recording be aware of the camera's placement in relation to sounds being recorded.

7. Digital camcorders have a VCR mode for preview and playback in the camera or through a television set or monitor. See where this is located and be prepared to switch modes after recording.

8. Note the placement of the camera's battery and examine how it is charged. A fully charged battery can provide flexibility in location shooting. Further, having several batteries or a larger capacity battery is a good idea for a lot of location work. An AC adapter can be used in locations close to wall sockets.

9. Inspect the menu display and functions. Look for various settings and recording modes and options that can be chosen from the menu.

10. Find the ports and cables that are necessary for playback on a monitor and for digitizing and/or dubbing video. A set of cables is included with most digital camcorders.

11. Though there are many other features on digital camcorders, such as editing and special effects, these are best described in accompanying manuals. After examining a digital camcorder with a fully charged battery, turn it on and select the camera mode, automatic exposure, and automatic focus. Use the zoom lens to frame a shot. Holding the camera very steady, push the record button. As a rule of thumb for ease of later editing, shoot several seconds before and after the portion of a shot you want. This will provide editing flexibility and versatility especially for inserting transitions such as dissolves and cross fades.

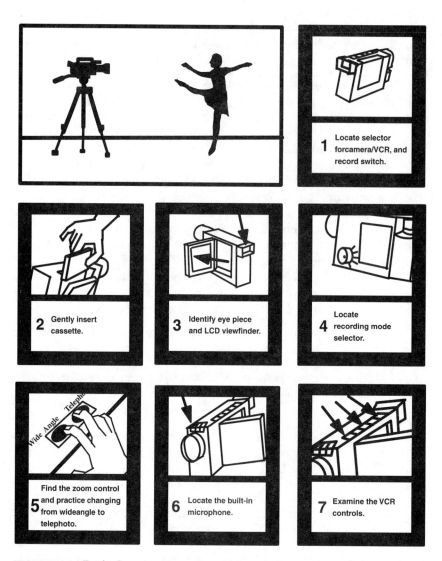

FIGURE 5.4   Basic Camera Operation. Although there are many brands and configurations of digital camcorders, these simple steps point out some things they have in common.

12. Experiment recording a "talking head." Frame a face or head of a human subject, placing the camera so that the built-in mike is as close to the subject's mouth as possible, then zoom out to desired composition. When recording the talking head, have the person look at you, not the camera. Place the subject in front of a simple background with even lighting such as open shade or a brick wall. This will allow

8 Learn how to remove and replace the battery.

9 Locate menu for on-screen programming options.

10 Jacks and plugs are needed for playback and digital video downloading.

11 Practice a few handheld shots.

12 Record a talking head. Hold the camera steady. Try for good sound.

13 Record a variety of shots. Play them back in the VCR playback mode.

14 Critique your work. Look for improvement in camera technique.

These are basic or generic steps to help a novice get started with a digital camcorder before attempting more polished work. The operator's manual that accompanies a digital camcorder is the most important source for learning about that particular camera model.

the auto exposure to light the subject evenly. Bright lights behind the subject will cause the auto exposure to adjust to that light, thus darkening the subject's face. Before having the subject speak, record ten to fifteen seconds of silence, then cue the person to speak. Again, this is necessary for flexibility in editing. Above all, a steady camera is essential and necessary for the auto exposure function to work properly.

13. Record various shots. Vary the compositions. Again, try recording a subject's voice or speech. After accumulating several minutes of video, select the VCR mode, rewind, and play the recording while watching in the LCD screen or connect the sound and video cables to a monitor and play it back there.

14. Critique the video recording. Was it steady? Was it focused properly? Was the sound audible or understandable? How was the lighting? Was the subject's face evenly lit and exposed? Could the composition be improved? Note those and other impressions and suggested improvements.

Accessories that may be useful include a lighting kit for more expression and a tripod. Though most digital camcorders are capable of recording in many available light situations, a basic photographic lighting kit—three floodlights and supports—will provide more expressive possibilities. Also, most camcorders have a light mount for a small photo lamp. These are handy in some situations but may provide harsh, direct light. Lighting a scene requires a lot of practice and analysis.

Shooting video requires patience and above all practice and self-analysis. Do not hesitate to shoot and reshoot. After all, one of the major advantages of the video medium is the possibility of instant feedback and analysis. Though a modern digital camcorder may at first appear to be complicated to operate, that is not the case. However, to use one properly and successfully does require some practice and some time spent reading directions. The effort pays off though when using a camcorder becomes almost instinctive and second nature. Under those conditions, the producer or camera operator can then concentrate on the creative and expressive aspects of digital video production.

The following sections will describe some supporting techniques related to these tips and some exercises that will provide practice.

Skill 4: Three Ways to Keep the Camera Steady

Unless you have creative or stylistic reasons to do otherwise, make sure the camera is steady while recording. In most cases, a camera that rocks and sways distracts from the message of the video or at the very least makes it look amateurish. Again, this is a guideline, or starting point. As creative decisions are made, an obviously unsteady handheld appearance may fit the mood or expressive quality of particular works. Some effective uses of the handheld look are in the popular television show *N.Y.P.D. Blue,* the feature film *The Blair Witch Project,* and numerous commercials and music videos. Here are some effective and simple ways to avoid or minimize unwanted movement and ensure sharp automatic focus while recording. Refer to Figure 5.5 while reading these steps.

Handheld. In many situations and locations, there may be no place for a tripod or any other means of support. Camera operators on mobile news teams frequently have to hand hold their cameras. One difficulty with handheld recording is simul-

1 *Handheld.* **With some practice, one can learn to hold a camera very steady.**

2 *Any firm surface.* **In some video recording situations, a good means of camera support may be a table, a brick wall, a chair, a fence, or any solid surface.**

3 *The tripod.* **The most efficient, versatile, and popular way to avoid unwanted movements while recording is to use one of a great variety of tripods.**

FIGURE 5.5   Camera Support Methods

taneously holding the camera, framing the shot, and operating other features such as a zoom lens; however, with some practice, one can learn to keep a camera steady. Most modern camcorders have an image stabilizer feature that when selected can assist in reducing unwanted movement. The point here, of course, is that even without a physical means of supporting the camera, one should try to steady the shot as much as is possible manually. This important media production skill improves with awareness and practice.

Firm Surfaces.   In some video recording situations, a good means of camera support may be a table, a brick wall, a chair, a fence, or just about any solid surface. Naturally, this depends on how one needs to compose a shot. In some cases, using this means of camera support may even result in an improved or more interesting composition, thus encouraging the camera operator to be creative.

The Tripod.   The most efficient, versatile, and popular way to avoid unwanted movements while recording is to use one of a great variety of tripods, from inexpensive to very expensive. The tripod is such an important tool that all camcorder purchases should include one. In addition to stabilizing the camera, a tripod is needed to perform a variety of camera moves smoothly. (A later section of this chapter describes common camera moves.) The cost of a tripod will depend mainly on the quality of its head, the component to which the camera is mounted. Higher-end professional-level tripods often have features such as a fluid head designed to produce very smooth camera moves easily. Less sophisticated tripods have a head that is mechanical but can still be very effective for stabilizing a camera and performing smooth moves.

Skill 5: Composing and Framing

Thoughtful and creative composition is crucial to the narrative or storytelling medium of video production. There are methods, techniques, guidelines, and rules of thumb for successfully framing shots through a viewfinder. These are important and provide a good starting point, but the best way to develop an enlightened and sensitive perspective that will enhance composition is to seek out, evaluate, and respond to the work of the masters.

Painters since the early Renaissance have known that the essence of visual composition is simplicity and unity. Photojournalists are equally concerned with the relationships between composition, communication, and expression. Cinematographers for feature films study composition from the masters of painting and still photography. Look at the simple yet dramatic compositions of the painters Vincent Van Gogh, Paul Cézanne, Georgia O'Keefe, and Edward Hopper (Figure 5.6), among many others. Examine the strong compositions of photographers such as Eugene Smith, Ansel Adams, Walker Evans (Figure 5.7), and Margaret Bourke-White. The study of these great artists along with the following guidelines should help you use the camcorder effectively.

In the jargon of movie and video production, "shots" are generally referred to as close-ups, medium shots, and wide shots, and there are multiple variations in between, such as extreme close-ups, medium wide shots, tight shots, and so on. In postproduction, editors combine shots to create scenes. Most digital and analog camcorders have variable focal length lenses usually described as zoom lenses. These come in a wide variety and allow the camera operator to choose compositions from wide angle to telephoto. Consider the examples in Figure 5.8 (page 80) while following ideas when composing a shot.

Don't Zoom Too Much.   A variable focal length lens, or a zoom lens, is a great asset when composing a shot, because it allows the camera operator to frame a picture from an extreme close-up to a wide shot and every focal length in between. Zooming while recording can add visual interest when used creatively. However, zooming while recording also presents the danger of annoying viewers if overdone for no apparent creative or expressive reason. On the other hand, combining a smooth zoom with other camera movements, such as pans or tilts, takes practice to execute

FIGURE 5.6   Edward Hopper's Strong Compositions

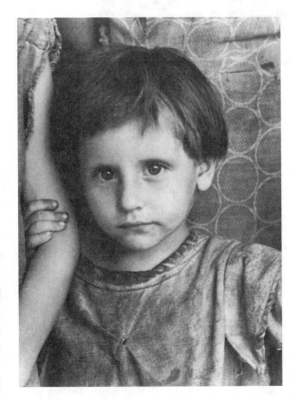

FIGURE 5.7   Walker Evans photos are known for their simple, but dramatic compositions

FIGURE 5.8   **Composition Ideas.** Simple ideas can make a big
improvement in composing pictures—video or still.

skillfully, but can add visual interest to your subject or idea. Keep in mind that too
many unnecessary zooms make editing more difficult, because in most cases an
editor does not want to cut to another shot in the middle of a zoom.

Cropping and Framing.   When framing a shot, choose simple backgrounds that do
not distract from the subject. For example, in a poorly framed shot, trees may
appear to grow out of a head in a close-up of a face, or the subject may get lost
against a busy background. Use the zoom lens to crop out competing background
elements. If possible, either by zooming or by physically moving the camera, get
close to the subject or point of interest. That is, crop the shot so as not to have a lot
of unrelated or unused space in the composition.

   Conventional yet solid composition is necessary to communicate an idea
visually or to provide a narrative structure. Frame composition is part of the

grammar of media production, at least metaphorically. However, shots that are recorded from unconventional and unpredictable angles and positions can make a video production much more visually interesting. Sensitive photographers often shoot from higher than eye level or lower than eye level to give the shots a more dramatic effect. Also effective can be the use of extreme close-ups. Rely on your imagination, placing the camera in unusual locations to enhance the impact of a video production.

Using some object to provide a frame within the frame is an old composition technique that is effective in adding visual unity and structure to a shot. For example, including some tree leaves and branches appearing in the top quarter or so of the shot provides a natural frame for the elements or subjects in the lower portion.

Depending on the type of shot, when framing people, be sensitive to cropping. In a conventional talking head shot, leave adequate headroom in order to achieve a pleasing composition. Imagine that the head has an apple sitting on its top. Frame the shot so that the top of the apple touches the top of the frame. Again, these are only guidelines and starting points.

Another consideration when videotaping people is not to cut off body parts in awkward places. That is, when the main idea of a shot is to show standing, walking, or sitting people from a wide shot, avoid cutting off their feet or the tops of their heads. Also, as mentioned previously, be aware of the background.

Shedding Light. The essence of photography—digital or conventional, video or film—is light. Modern camcorders have automatic exposure meters that read the light and adjust accordingly, thus freeing the operator to concentrate on the other tasks of recording. This automatic exposure works well for the vast majority of situations and depending on the needs of the camera operator, the camera's exposure can also be manually adjusted, thus allowing more flexibility and creative control. Modern camcorders are very sensitive to light and in many situations do not need photo lamps, even in fairly dark situations. However, a basic lighting kit or camera-mounted light allows the video maker to control light sources and angles, thus enhancing creative and compositional possibilities.

When using the auto focus and auto exposure, pointing the camera is crucial to the success of a shot. If the background is in sunlight and the subject in shade, the automatic exposure may expose for the background, thus leaving the subject darkened. Conversely, and depending on what the camera is pointing at, the subject may be correctly exposed but the background may be overexposed. Thus, for that reason, look for locations that do not force the camera to choose between two extremes in lighting. In daylight, open shade provides a nicely exposed, evenly lit shot. Also, early morning or late afternoon sunlight provides good exterior lighting.

Interior lighting presents special problems. Although many camcorders have the sensitivity to make good recordings using existing or available lighting, having a basic photo lamp kit for interior shots is a good idea. When setting photo lamps, avoid direct or harsh light. Bouncing light off of a light-colored surface such as a ceiling or wall provides a softer, more pleasing effect, and the camera's automatic exposure feature will compensate.

Skill 6: Camera Movement

Thomas Edison's early silent movies, made in the Black Maria (his studio building that revolved in order to point its skylight at the sun), were filmed from one fixed position. Edison was imitating live theater; hence, his movies were nothing more than filmed plays. As the art and technique of moviemaking advanced, visionary filmmakers dissatisfied with a single stationary camera learned to exploit the unique properties of their new medium. One way they did so was by moving the camera between the indoors and the outdoors to create a variety of compositions that greatly enhanced expressiveness and audience appeal. An example is Edwin Porter's ten-minute classic, *The Great Train Robbery*, released in 1903. Porter, a former cameraman for Edison, took his camera outside and inside and mounted it on railcars and other locations that were unusual for the time.

The same principle applies over one hundred years later with the very latest camcorders. Smooth and purposeful camera moves are expressive, visually interesting, and easy to do with a good tripod or steady hand. Two basic and commonly used moves are the pan and the tilt. A pan is a horizontal left to right or right to left movement, usually with the camera mounted on a tripod. This move can be used to reveal scenery or to follow an action. A tilt is a vertical movement of the camera from top to bottom or vice versa. Figure 5.9 illustrates both of these simple moves.

With some practice and a very steady hand or tripod, the pan and the tilt can be combined to make expressive shots. Combining a pan or a tilt with a zoom can be a very effective shot as well.

Skill 7: Basics of Recording Sound with a Camcorder

Sound is a crucial element of any video production. If the visuals are excellent but the sound is weak or poorly recorded and edited, the overall production suffers. Sound can be recorded on location or in the field at the production phase; sound effects and additional voices may also be added at the postproduction phase. Sound design complements all the other elements of a video. In that sense, sound is as important as the visual elements in a media production. Sound recording, design, and editing can be a complex process requiring special skills and experience, but successful sound can also be achieved by considering a few basic techniques.

The built-in microphones that come with most camcorders are adequate for general-purpose recording. Better-quality sound can be achieved, especially for recording voices, by connecting a lavalier mike to the camera. The lavalier microphone clips to the subject's clothing about a foot below the mouth and is used by news anchors in television studios. Another kind of external mike is the handheld microphone that television correspondents often use.

The ultimate sound recording microphone is the wireless mike worn by the subject, or talent. Wireless mikes allow maximum flexibility in following a moving subject, but they are very expensive and require a lot of battery power.

When a lavalier mike, a handheld mike, or a wireless mike is not available, the built-in microphone can record voices successfully if placed correctly. Figure 5.10

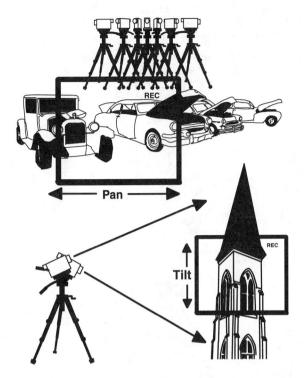

FIGURE 5.9   **A Pan and a Tilt.** A pan is a horizontal left to right or right to left movement, usually with a camera mounted on a tripod. A tilt is a vertical movement of the camera from top to bottom or vice versa.

(page 84) illustrates two voice-recording methods. When recording voice or dialogue with the built-in mike, the camera needs to be placed as close as possible to the subject in order to record clearly and accurately. For this purpose, the zoom lens can be set on a wide angle, thus allowing the camera and its built-in microphone to be placed reasonably close to the subject. An external microphone provides more control over placement. For example, an external mike connected by cable to the camera allows for an ideal placement—usually about 8 to 10 inches below the person's mouth. In all cases, experimentation with particular equipment and locations should result in the best possible sound and picture recording with the tools available. Good-quality location sound pays off in postproduction and editing.

Skill 8: Digital Editing

Postproduction is the step in which all the shots, scenes, and video recordings are combined with additional creative elements such as sound and special effects in

Recording voice with the built-in microphone works best if placed as close to the subject as possible while setting and focusing the zoom lens at a wide angle. If possible, place the subject in front of a solid wall.

Recording voice with an external microphone connected to the MIC terminal may provide better-quality audio. External microphones may be wireless, handheld, mounted on a boom, placed on a stand or table, or clip on. No matter what type of microphone is used, the most important factor in obtaining excellent audio is placement.

FIGURE 5.10   Microphone Placements

ways that express, teach, explain, or tell a story. In a metaphorical sense, editing is the basis of the "language" or "grammar" of media production. This section presents a basic historical and conceptual explanation of motion picture editing and provides an introduction to digital editing.

A Conceptual Framework for Digital Editing
The essence of editing is making decisions. Video and movie editors juxtapose and sequence shots and scenes in ways that make assertions that lead viewers to make inferences. For example, a shot seen alone or in isolation may have little or no meaning. However, by placing a shot or image before it, an editor leads the viewer

to infer the meaning of the image or shot that follows. This concept was described by Sergei Eisenstein in *The Film Sense:*

> This property consisted of the fact that two film pieces of any kind, placed together, inevitably combine into a new concept, a new quality, arising out of that juxtaposition.

A famous experiment by film theorist V. I. Pudovkin contributed to the theoretical framework of editing as described by Eisenstein. To conduct this experiment, Pudovkin filmed a close-up of an expressionless actor. Then he filmed close-ups of a bowl of soup, a small girl playing with a teddy bear, and a dead woman in a coffin. His next step was to combine the shot of the expressionless actor with each of the other shots. That is, he edited three separate sequences consisting of the actor followed by the bowl of soup, the actor followed by the small girl playing with the teddy bear, and the actor followed by the dead woman in a coffin. When these three film sequences were presented to viewers, he discovered that depending on the combination, audience members interpreted the expressionless actor as thoughtful, sorrowful, and smiling. Of course, the actor's expression was exactly the same in all three combinations. Pudovkin's juxtaposing of the face with the three different shots led the audience to interpret the actor's moods differently, even though his face was deliberately expressionless in all three combinations. Thus, the editor, not the actor's talent, accounted for the difference in interpretations.

Like early moviemakers, contemporary feature moviemakers make editing choices by actually cutting the film and splicing the scenes together with tape. The film they cut (thus, the term *cutting room floor*) is a copy or print of the original footage that was shot on location or a sound stage. This duplication of the original is called a work print. As the work print is edited or cut and spliced, directions to the film lab for various effects are written directly on the edited work print with a grease pencil. The edited work print with an edited synchronized soundtrack containing voice, sound effects, music, and presence is then sent to a motion picture lab, which matches or conforms the camera original to the editor's edited work print. From this extremely expensive and tedious process, the lab makes release prints that become the movies projected in theaters.

The preceding is a simplified description of the extremely complex process of editing real movies for theatrical distribution. For obvious reasons, this process is very expensive, exclusive, and time-consuming, and it requires many skilled practitioners. However, modern digital tools have revolutionized the editing process. Now all that is needed for virtually anyone who is interested in editing creative and expressive movies is a good computer with some specialized editing software and the means for digitizing video.

Digital Editing: Hardware and Software

Any computer to be used for digital video editing needs to have a substantial amount of random access memory (RAM) and a large hard drive. A computer with

256 megabytes (MB) of RAM provides reasonably good performance for editing. Even 128 MB will work fairly well. A large hard drive is essential for importing and storing either video clips directly from a digital video camera or digitized video from an analog format such as VHS. For example, a 40-gigabyte hard drive provides enough storage space to save the amount of unedited video that most school or personal projects would require. Of course, more is better. In fact, large hard drives of up to 100 gigabytes or more are not unusual on modern computers. Also, due to the intensely visual and precise process of editing, a high-resolution monitor is also highly desirable.

Editing software appropriate for use in schools is produced by a variety of vendors. Much of it is simple to learn and use, yet contains plenty of creative and expressive features, and some of it is fairly complex with a steep learning curve but containing many sophisticated effects. An excellent example of a simpler choice is Apple's *iMovie*, which can be learned quickly, is easy to use, and offers many choices for titling, transitions, sound editing, and exporting as various files and formats. Two popular choices for editing software that are more complex but allow for more creative editing choices are *Adobe Premiere* and *Final Cut Pro*. As described in Chapter 3, *Studio Deluxe* and *Video Wave* are excellent choices for digital editing on PCs. Both are easy to learn and use.

In order to import analog video for editing, such as VHS, the system needs a digitizing capability. One way to do so is by acquiring a converter for that purpose. The advantage of having a media converter is that ordinary VHS camcorders can be used for shooting video for various projects. Further, older VHS tapes can be a rich source of material that can be included in video production projects.

Digital Video Editing Basics

As with the varied features of digital camcorders, digital editing tools available for school and home also have many features. Some basic fundamental steps are common to most digital editing systems. Try this simple editing exercise:

1. Following the videotaping steps described previously, record about five minutes of digital video. Choose a subject that is visually interesting. Vary the shots and compositions. A digital camcorder or an analog camcorder will work. Several short shots will be better than fewer longer ones.

2. To prepare for digital editing, import and store the digitized video on the computer's hard drive. In most cases, the digital camcorder can be connected directly to a computer's digitizing card, via a *Firewire* connection, for example. For analog video from an analog camcorder or VCR, your computer needs either a media converter or a digitizing card that can digitize analog video.

3. Using the VCR-type controls in editing software, such as *iMovie, Final Cut Pro,* or *Adobe Premiere*, preview the shots and scenes that are needed for the final edited master. Due to the enormous amount of space that digital video requires to be stored on the hard disk, import only the essential scenes. In fact, previewing the shots on an unedited videocassette before deciding what to import is a good idea.

One way to keep track of the unedited video is to create a descriptive list, or log, in order of the shots on the tape. This process helps to quickly identify and select shots and sequences to import.

4. Learn the editing software. One key principle to remember is that editing is about making choices. In most cases, simpler is better. Though many transitional and special effects are possible with digital editing software, only a basic knowledge is needed to begin editing. There are many possible ways to learn particular digital editing software packages. Of course, user's manuals come with the software, and online tutorials are available for many types of software. Special workshops are often offered for little or no fee for various ages. Some sources for these may be community college courses, workshops associated with film and video festivals, or special video production camps. Also, look for community outreach programs offered by various local educational institutions. For students and employees of educational institutions such as school districts and universities, professional instructional technologists and media specialists provide support.

5. Begin editing by selecting and dragging or placing video clips (shots) in desired sequences. The shots themselves more than likely will need to be edited or trimmed. Deciding what to cut takes a lot of experimenting. Place the edited clips in various combinations and sequences, and play them back frequently. Move the clips around to try different combinations and transitions. No two editors will interpret a project in the same way. To demonstrate this, try the train editing exercise later in this chapter.

6. Sound editing is a crucial component of the finished production. Poor sound quality will ruin an otherwise excellent movie. In many cases, sound editing will be minimal, because the location sound will suffice, depending on the nature of the production. Digital editing software provides a lot of flexibility for combining sound effects and music with edited images, and is done much the same way as editing the images. The section on sound in this chapter provides more detail about making sounds, recording, and importing.

7. Edit the five minutes of video down to not more than one minute. Preview and critique it. Try re-editing the digitized video into different versions of the same video.

The preceding steps are simply a starting point. The following sections will describe some creative elements and concepts of editing.

Telling the Story: Transitions

In moviemaking terms, a transition is the means a shot or scene uses to change to the next shot or scene. An editor uses transitions to help develop a topic or tell a story. In the following description, a shot is one take or one camera angle and functions much as a sentence does in writing. A shot can be as short as a fraction of a second, or it can have a long duration, in some cases taking up most of an entire production. A scene usually consists of several related shots and functions as a paragraph in writing. Thus, transitions are crucial elements to the structure or language of a video or film in changing from shot to shot and from scene to scene. Three fundamental transitions most viewers understand are the cut, the fade in or out, and the dissolve.

Cuts.   The term *cut* comes from the motion picture editing tradition of physically cutting the film and then splicing the strips of film together in the desired sequence. Cuts therefore proceed from one shot to the next instantaneously. Cuts can be used to establish a rhythm of shots accompanied by music, or they can be used to cut to various shots within a scene. As an illustration, cutting to close-ups of faces reacting to dialogue or action can be effective in adding expression to a scene. The cut is also very useful when editing in the camera. Cuts can be made with the digital editing software, or with careful planning and camera work, a video can be edited in the camera by simply pausing, changing a setup, or framing a new shot then restarting. The effect of pausing, then starting is a cut.

Fades.   Another traditional transition is the fade in and fade out. The basic function of a fade is to avoid the abruptness of the cut. A case in point is a common thirty-second television commercial that fades in from black, runs through its shots, and fades out. The use of the fade in this instance is to provide a smooth beginning and ending. As a storytelling device, the fade indicates the beginning and ending of a scene or the passage of time. Many camcorders allow the user to fade scenes in and out, therefore allowing the operator to include some in-camera transitions similar to an in-camera cut as described previously.

Dissolves.   This transition is created by overlapping one shot over another. In that sense, a dissolve is created by one shot fading out as the next one fades in. Dissolves can be so short that they actually function as very smooth cuts, or they can be so long that viewers may not even be aware of them. If you are planning to use a lot of dissolves in editing a production, remember to shoot enough to cover the lengths of the dissolves. That is, make sure that there is enough time at the beginning and end of shots so that you will be able to create overlapping shots and scenes.

Video editors use dissolves to make very smooth transitions from shot to shot. For example, long dissolves may fit the mood or feeling that the editor is trying to establish, or dissolves may reinforce a musical score. Dissolves may be used to create simple special effects. Shooting from a tripod, the camera can record a protracted shot of an abandoned city street. The camera is then stopped or paused, people or other props are inserted into the shot, and the camera records the shot again from exactly the same position and angle. In the editing phase, the editor can dissolve or cross fade the shots in order to make the people and props appear and/or disappear as the background stays exactly the same. This simple effect can be used very imaginatively with the creative possibilities of digital editing software.

Others.   The cut, the fade, and the dissolve are fundamental transition devices for effective editing, but digital editing, software offers hundreds of additional transitional effects such as rolls, wipes, peels, page turns, and sweeps. Due to the abundance of special transitional effects packaged with digital editing software, the temptation is to overuse them. These effects are fun to use and they do provide creative room for the editor to wander around, but they should not be overused. In keeping with the principles of simplicity and elegance, skillful and sensitive editors rely on basic transition choices most of the time. On occasion, special transition effects can be used to achieve expressive effects that add impact and reinforce the concept of the work. Generally transition effects should be used in ways that enhance and support the message or expressiveness of the production in which they are used.

To achieve flexibility, for editing it is best to use a combination of software. Unlimited postproduction possibilities can be found by using *Adobe Premiere* for picture and sound editing. *Adobe AfterEffects* for motion picture special effects, *Adobe Photoshop* for graphics editing, and *Adobe Illustrator* for creating original images provide unlimited postproduction possibilities. These and similar software provide the production capability for creating a range of movie formats from stand-alone digital movies for film festivals and television broadcast to movies made specifically for access and distribution on the World Wide Web.

Introduction to Sound Editing

The section on camera operation explained some methods for recording sound with the camera's built-in microphone. For some projects, good-quality sound, for example, of a person speaking, may be all that is necessary. However, sound added during postproduction can enhance and reinforce the message or story of the production.

Sound recording and editing can be a highly specialized and complex process. That is why some independent media producers work very closely with music composers, sound designers, and recording engineers. On the other hand, digital production tools can be relatively easy for almost anyone to learn and use for recording and editing sound. Here are some sources for sounds to use in digital video productions.

Camera-Mounted Microphone.   This microphone is mounted on the camera and works well for general recording. The camera can also work as a tape recorder by leaving the lens cap on while recording sound only. This technique works well for recording a narrator. The advantage of this method is that the microphone can be placed closer to the narrator in order to record good-quality digital sound. This technique is also an excellent way to create sound effects—footsteps, car motors, splashing water, and others. In postproduction, this sound will be imported into an editing system.

Recording from Audio CDs.   Sound effects and music can be recorded from the common audio CD. Modern desktop computers contain the software to do so, plus many selections of inexpensive software packages can be used such as *QuickTime Pro, Real Producer,* and *Goldwave.* Just remember that recording material off of commercially produced CDs for the purpose of using that material in a media production is subject to copyright laws and fair use guidelines described in Chapter 3. Another popular source for sound off of CDs are sound effects libraries. These too are ordinary audio CDs from which you can record hundreds of sound effects. In most cases, the purchaser can legally use the material on these CDs. When the sound has been recorded and imported, it can be edited in many ways to include in a digital media production. Also, imported sound can be converted into a number of audio file formats for various applications from web pages to stand-alone digital videos. Chapter 3 on software describes these file formats and their uses.

Importing Effects from CD-ROMs.   Sound libraries recorded on CD-ROMs are an excellent source for a wide variety of easy-to-use effects. Usually the sound files, from music to effects, are in the WAV or Midi format. These effects are easily imported and converted to whatever file the editor needs.

The World Wide Web.   A vast collection of music and sound on the WWW can be downloaded for use in digital media productions. Again, the use of this material is subject to copyright laws. Sound can be purchased and then downloaded from online libraries; some sites allow free use of selected sounds and music.

Original Scores.   One of the most fulfilling aspects of digital media production is being able to incorporate as much original work as possible. Working with a composer to create, record, mix, and incorporate music written especially for a particular digital production is a collaborative creative experience. This process can be very complex, involving the hiring of musicians and the renting of postproduction facilities. On the other hand, the process can be simple by collaborating with a musician or composer who has recording and mixing facilities.

Sound design is a highly complex and specialized process, yet the tools of modern digital media production make the use of sound accessible, flexible, and expressive. As mentioned earlier, sound quality can make or break a digital video production. The slickest photography and picture editing cannot compensate for poorly realized and executed sound.

DIGITAL VIDEO EXERCISES

Operating a camera effectively, editing the video in a way that communicates, and understanding genres lead to successful and expressive results. Combining the numerous elements of a digital video production requires planning because one cannot expect to achieve excellent results by accident. The following section describes projects and activities that incorporate the ideas and skills presented in the previous sections. These activities provide practice in camera operation as well as the common and traditional media planning method of storyboarding. The projects are described conceptually and step-by-step and can be adapted to locally available resources. Above all, these projects are all field-tested, having been used in educational settings from kindergarten through twelfth grade to graduate school to teach the concepts and skills of media production. Further, these activities can be modified and enhanced in unlimited creative, personal, and expressive ways. Each exercise is broken down into the categories of planning, production, and postproduction.

Exercise 1: Making a Storyboard

An effective way to visualize a digital video production before producing it is to create a storyboard. The storyboard originated in the Walt Disney Studios of the early 1930s, according to motion picture historian, scholar, and critic Richard Schickel. Webb Smith of the story department devised the practice of pinning rough sketches of cartoon gag ideas to the wall, and later to corkboard, in proposed sequences. This helped communicate the structure and rhythm of the cartoons as they were being planned.

Preproduction
Concept. A storyboard, whether rough or elaborate, assists a production team in planning everything from possible camera angles and locations to sound effects and props.

A storyboard can be constructed in many ways, from very informal to polished. Figure 5.11 (page 92) illustrates three commonly used formats. They can be drawn on sheets with multiple frames, or they can be drawn on separate cards. Drawings can be made with everything from pens, pencils, and felt-tipped pens to computer graphics. Also, the use of a storyboard often depends on the structure or genre. For example, a storyboard may not work well for productions that may be unpredictable in character such as experimental works or some documentaries. On the other hand, the storyboard is a crucial element in designing works that may have a specific purpose or objective such as an instructional or informational work or a work that develops a topic or plot. Figure 5.12 (page 93) is a detailed storyboard made with computer graphics. Some producers rely on storyboards, and others may prefer not to use them, in effect letting the move come to them.

Materials. Only simple materials are needed to create a storyboard of a story or script. Choose from the following items:

- Conventional bond typing or printing paper to draw the boxes or frames on.
- Five- by eight-inch unruled index cards.
- Number-two pencils or black fine tip, felt-tipped pens for simple sketches.
- Copies of the storyboard masters in Figure 5.13 (page 94) and Figure 5.14 (page 95) for ready-made formats.
- Thin cardboard sheet with rectangular frames cut out in order to make a storyboard stencil.
- A simple computer paint program such as *Microsoft Paint* to create a computer graphics storyboard. Other choices include *ClarisWorks Drawing, ClarisWorks Painting, PowerPoint,* and *HyperStudio.*

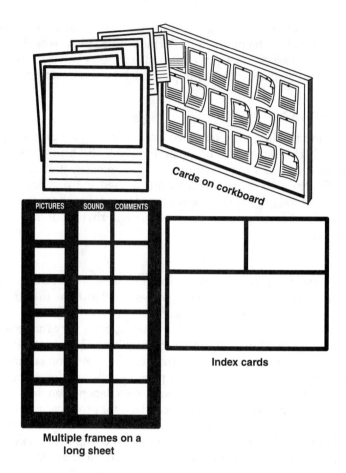

Cards on corkboard

PICTURES   SOUND   COMMENTS

Index cards

**Multiple frames on a
long sheet**

FIGURE 5.11   **Storyboard Formats**

- Additional items for creating storyboard images may include a scanner and digital camera.
- A story. This need be only 300 words at the most (about one typewritten page, double-spaced with 12 point type). Story sources include the following:
  - Story by a class member or teacher
  - Family story
  - Story a friend tells
  - Local or regional legend or folktale with a cultural flavor
  - Public domain fairy tale
  - True story based on a class member's memorable experience
  - Retelling of a memorable local event
  - Local historical event
  - Story from a creative writing assignment
  - Story "Top This" by Errol Hess in Figure 5.15 (page 96)

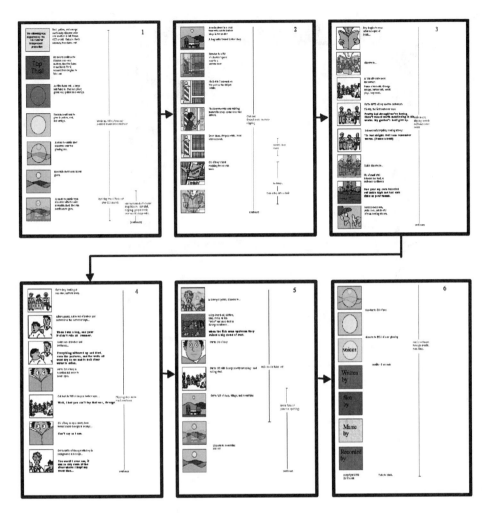

FIGURE 5.12 A Detailed Storyboard. This more refined storyboard was made with computer graphics and includes such elements as dialogue, transitions, and music.

Production

After selecting a story, transcribe it and type it as a script. If this is a group activity, make copies for each member of the group. The reason for doing this as a group activity is to compare the many interpretations of the same story.

Include framed drawings for each shot suggesting camera angle, composition, and transition to the next shot. Parallel to the storyboard frames include narration, dialogue, and descriptions of score, locations, props, and any information that helps

FIGURE 5.13   A Single-Frame Storyboard

the reader visualize the proposed production. Construct your storyboard so that your reader looking at it can form a mental interpretation of what the proposed project will look and sound like when finished.

Your first storyboard can be made by hand and be spontaneous and informal, like the sample in Figure 5.16 (page 97). When this one is complete, you may want to make a more refined version with computer graphics such as the one in Figure 5.12 (page 93). For supporting images, use computer graphics to draw directly on the storyboard, examine clip art collections, use a digital camera, or scan drawings and photographs or combinations of those. Another option is to create the images and related items on index cards that can be rearranged. Typically, five- by eight-inch unruled cards work well for this. When pinned on a corkboard, the cards can be arranged and rearranged and presented to a production team in a storyboard conference.

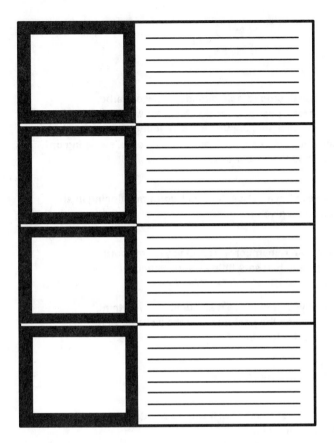

FIGURE 5.14   A Four-Frame Storyboard

Postproduction
When you have finished your proposal for the story you selected or for "Top This," compare your storyboard for the story with the storyboards of others. While examining how others have interpreted the story, consider the following:

1. Count the frames or shots per storyboard, and look for indications of transitions.
2. What were some of the sounds used to support the story?
3. Look for suggestions as to whether the storyboard producer saw this as a live-action or animated movie.
4. Identify elements, details, and items that are particularly creative, surprising, or unusual.

TOP THIS
by Errol Hess

Setting:

A typical barbershop, with striped pole outside, a row of barber
chairs, wall-length mirrors, coatrack, facing chairs for waiting customers,
table or rack with magazines and comic books. A young boy loafing there
reading comic books half watches his Great-Uncle George, sweeping up
hair while customers and the barber talk.

FIRST OLD MAN:
Pretty bad drought we're having. Hasn't rained worth mentioning in six
weeks. My garden's about give up.

SECOND OLD MAN:
It's bad all right. But I can remember worse. One year my corn
tassled out ankle high and had ears little as your thumb.

THIRD OLD MAN:
When I was a boy, one year it didn't rain all summer. Everything
withered up and dried, even the pastures, and the wells all went
dry so we had to boil water to drink.

BARBER:
Well, I bet you can't top that one, George.

UNCLE GEORGE (slowly):
Can't say as I can. The worst I ever saw, it was so dry down at
the river where I kept my trout line,
when the fish swam upstream, they raised a big cloud of dust!

FIGURE 5.15   A Script for "Top This." Follow the steps in Exercise 1—
be inventive and creative! Share and compare versions with your
classmates, and compare them with the rough storyboard in Figure 5.16.

5. Note whether the storyboard contains enough detail and description to assist
the reader in accurately constructing a mental image of the proposed project.
If not, suggest what additional elements would make it complete.
6. If you storyboarded "Top This," view a two-minute completed version of it
on the accompanying web site (www.ablongman.com/counts) and compare
that version with the interpretations created as a result of this activity.
7. Finally, discuss the advantages of creating a storyboard as a part of the planning process; also determine media productions or genres for which a storyboard may not work very well.

A storyboard does not have to be fancy to be helpful. Visual thinking, even doodle-like drawings, helps visualizing a production.

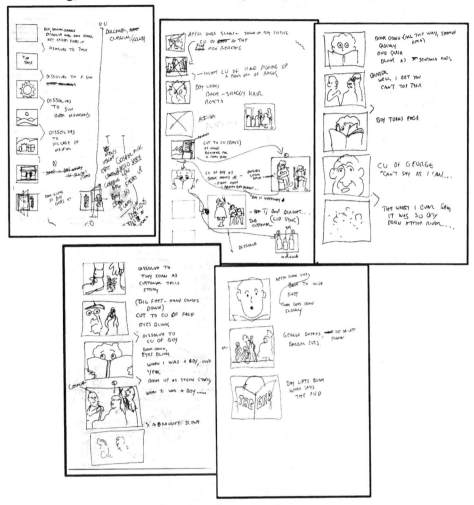

Compare this rough storyboard to your storyboard interpretation of "Top This."

FIGURE 5.16   A Rough Storyboard for "Top This"

Finally, this storyboard exercise can provide insight into the planning process of all media production. Storyboard methods vary from producer to producer and even from genre to genre. However, one can assume that in most cases, successfully realized media productions do not happen by accident.

Exercise 2: A Basic Camera Move—the Pan

Solid camerawork is crucial to any successful production. Fortunately, this is easy to achieve by following a few basic principles and techniques. The following exercise will describe how to practice the fundamental camera move called a pan.

Preproduction

Concept. A pan is a horizontal movement left to right or right to left. Although this is seemingly a simple concept, learning to execute a smooth pan does take practice. A smooth pan allows the producer to reveal a wide vista slowly and expressively. Unwanted movements or hesitations ruin the effect, so this exercise involves using a tripod and a camcorder, digital or analog. Follow these steps and refer to Figure 5.17.

1 This exercise requires the use of a tripod, a camcorder, and an actor.

2 Mount the camera at eye level on a tripod.

3 Choose an uncluttered background in even light, such as open shade.

4 Maintain the actor's position in the viewfinder while panning as smoothly as possible.

5 Shoot several practice takes.

Frame the actor in the center of the viewfinder or LCD screen.

Direct the actor to walk at a normal pace from left to right while panning and recording.

FIGURE 5.17   Pan Practice

Materials.   This exercise requires the following:

- A video camcorder and blank tape. Any format will work—digital or VHS.
- A tripod. Although a smooth pan may be executed with a steady handheld camera, a sturdy tripod is essential for this exercise.
- An actor.
- An evenly lit space in front of a simple background such as a brick wall.

Production
The following steps describe a simple yet effective way to practice making smooth pans.

1. Mount the camera at eye level on a tripod. Set the head of the tripod so that it will freely rotate 360 degrees.
2. Find a recording location that provides an uncluttered background, such as a brick wall and even light, for example, open shade or overcast skies.
3. Recruit an actor.
4. Position the actor and direct him or her to walk at a normal pace from right to left on cue. That is, place the actor, start recording, and after about five to ten seconds cue the actor to walk from left to right while you pan.
5. Place the actor in the center of the frame and try to hold that position all the way through the pan. Shoot several takes, varying starting and stopping points, high camera angles, low camera angles, distance from camera to actor, focal lengths, walking speeds, and other variations.

Postproduction
After collecting a series of pans, play them back and critique them for smoothness. Because this is simply an exercise, there is no postproduction in the conventional sense. However, you could use some of the pans to practice editing. Some of the better ones, for example, could be edited into demonstrations of panning.

Exercise 3: Tilt!

Preproduction
Concept.   Another basic camera move is the tilt. This is in effect a vertical pan; therefore, the basic techniques are similar. An interesting way to learn about a tilt is to complete the following exercise, which also introduces the concepts of matching action. Matching action refers to the editing method of creating a natural and logical flow to a movement. For example, filming an actor opening a door is matched by a shot of the same actor on the other side of the door exiting the room. Follow these steps and refer to Figure 5.18 (pages 100–101) to complete this exercise.

Materials.   This exercise requires the following:

- A video camcorder and blank tape. Any format will work—digital or VHS.
- A tripod. Although a smooth tilt may be executed with a steady handheld camera, a sturdy tripod is essential for this exercise.

1 Mount the camera at eye level on a tripod. Set the head of the tripod so it will easily and smoothly move up and down.

2 Direct an actor to stand a couple of feet from the camera lens facing away from the camera.

3 Direct the actor to walk away from the camera while recording.

4 Tilt down while zooming to a close-up of the actor's walking feet. Stop the recording as the actor walks out of the frame.

FIGURE 5.18   Tilt Down and Zoom Up

- An actor with a change of clothing and/or a selection of props.
- An editing system—digital or analog.

Production

The following steps describe a simple yet effective way to practice making smooth tilts.

1. Mount the camera on a tripod at eye level. Set the head of the tripod so that it will move up and down easily and smoothly.
2. Recruit an actor. Direct the actor to stand a couple of feet from the camera lens facing away from the camera.
3. Direct the actor to pause a few beats after the action command and then walk away from the camera at a normal pace.

5 Make a major appearance change— have actor change clothes, put on a costume, and so on.

6 From the previously paused shot, have the newly changed actor continue the walk away from the camera. Tilt up as the camera zooms to a wide angle as the actor walks away.

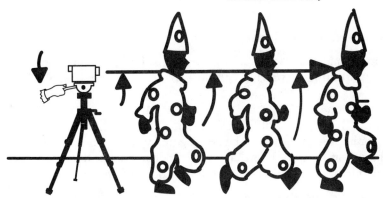

Using a digital video editing system, make a matching action edit or cut between the close-ups of feet. Try to make this as smooth as possible to enhance the effect and surprise.

4. As the actor walks away from the camera lens, tilt down while zooming into a close-up of the actor's walking feet. Pause the recording on the close-up as the actor walks out of the frame. Several takes may be necessary.
5. Have the actor change clothes, put on a costume, or make any extreme and contrasting visual change.
6. From the previously paused shot, have the newly changed actor continue the walk away from the camera. Tilt up as the camera zooms to a wide angle as the actor walks away.

Postproduction
This exercise combines several creative and expressive ideas. These include camera tilts up and down, in and out zooms for specific expressive purposes, creative decisions, and shooting for continuity and matching action. Further, if you plan to

execute this task carefully, you can edit in the camera by pausing at precisely the right point after the tilt down and continuing the recording as the actor walks away in a changed appearance. Of course, with access to video editing resources, editing and matching the action from the tilt down to the tilt up is much easier and more effective, with more precise control. As with the pan exercise, you may create an edited collection of the shots in this exercise.

Exercise 4: A Video Quest

This traditional exercise has many variations. Its purpose is to provide some creative opportunities to practice composing and recording symbolic shots.

Preproduction

Concept.   The objective of this exercise is to list a number of concepts, thoughts, ideals, or impressions that can be represented visually and then to use a camcorder to compose and record shots that represent or symbolize those concepts. For example, what images or subjects would you record to symbolize authority?

Materials.   Because this project is about ideas more than technique, minimal materials are needed. They include the following:

- A camcorder for composing and recording the symbolizing shots.
- A tripod is preferable, although this exercise can also provide an opportunity to practice shooting steady handheld shots.
- Materials to make and copy the list of concepts to be symbolized.
- A group of participants to generate and record the concepts.

Production

At this step, take the cameras into the world in search of the designated symbols.

1. Make a list of concepts to symbolize. For example, find and tape symbols of authority, education, oppression, patriotism, nature, and many others. Make a list of at least ten ideas. This can be a group activity. Also, the list of concepts can be based on a theme. Copy the list for each individual or small group. Figure 5.19 suggests some terms.
2. Using the camcorder, compose and record shots that provide a visual metaphor or representation for each concept on the list. Look for representational shots outside and inside, day or night, with supporting sound when possible.
3. Do not settle for visual clichés. Try wide angle shots to extreme close-ups. Use tilts and zooms to reveal and surprise. Make sure all shots are steady and last at least ten seconds. In effect, edit in the camera. Record for ten seconds, pause or stop, set up the next shot, record for ten seconds, pause or stop, set up the next shot, and so on. Use the tripod for some shots, and try some steady handheld shots.

Peace		Comfort
Urban		Confident
Rural		Insecure
Old		Working
New		Relaxing
Fear		Teaching
Courage		Learning
Love		Neat
Hate		Messy
Diversity		Happiness
Family		Sadness
Friendship		Waste
Conflict		Greed
Cooperation		Pain
Win		Make a list of
Lose		your own:
Satisfaction		_____
Frustration		_____
Down		_____
Up		_____

FIGURE 5.19   Examples of Visual Symbols for a Video Quest

Postproduction

Although editing of the shots in postproduction is not necessary to achieve the objective of this exercise, you may want to create a polished edited version. The major postproduction activity is sharing and reacting to the diversity and individuality of the many interpretations.

This activity is especially fun and revealing when done as a group activity. When twenty people complete this activity using the same list of ten or so concepts, you will see a fascinating variety of interpretations, compositions, and camera work. Most important, all of the people in the group can learn from each other while sharing their results, perhaps in a classroom video festival. In fact, although in the context of this book this project is about effective camcorder operation, this activity also can be used in virtually any discipline to encourage thoughtful observation of various issues and subjects and to inspire discussion.

Exercise 5: A Mystery Video

Preproduction

Concept.   Another way to practice steady shots, interesting compositions, and varying focal lengths is to use a camcorder to break familiar objects into multiple frames. Examine the example in Figure 5.20 (pages 106–107). This too is an excellent class or group activity.

Materials.   Only basic video production items are needed for this exercise. These include the following:

- A camcorder and blank tape.
- A tripod will be useful, as this activity will provide practice in using a tripod. Steady handheld shots will also work.
- An object or thing to tape. The possibilities are limitless: a lamp, a chair, a lawnmower, a bicycle, a computer, a pitcher, a car, a grill, a fireplug, or anything else that appeals to you.

Production

This is the step at which this activity becomes creative.

1. Choose the item you are going to examine visually with the camcorder.
2. Record the object from a number of unusual angles, focal lengths, and compositions that are visually interesting, yet do not reveal what the object is. Be creative and unpredictable with the compositions. Try starting with some extreme close-ups, shooting five or ten seconds per shot. Widen the shot a little, and shoot a couple of more from different angles or perspectives, in effect, editing in the camera.
3. Continue step 2 while still trying not to reveal the object's identity for as long as possible. Of course, the wider the focal length or zoom setting, the more difficult it will be to disguise the object. Again, continue to edit in the camera by recording a shot and pausing, zooming out a little, recording another shot, and pausing. Continue this for at least ten shots, from close-ups to telephotos. Do not zoom while recording.

Postproduction

When finished, group members can share their mystery object videos while the others try to guess what is being pictured. This activity synthesizes such techniques as composition and framing, holding the camera steady, and setting focal lengths, all of which are needed for sophisticated video work.

Again, as with the previous exercise, editing of the shots in postproduction is not necessary to achieve the objective. However, you may want to create a polished edited version.

Exercise 6: Multiple-Choice Editing

Preproduction

Concept.   Editing video is an intriguing and intuitive endeavor because of the many possible interpretations of a set of shots. In most cases, many hours of video recording must be edited into a relatively short program that tells a story, develops a topic, teaches, or informs. Thus, the process is necessarily complex and interpretations of the shots are unique to each editor.

Materials.   The primary resources required for this exercise are a computer with some editing software. More specifically, these are the following:

- *Multimedia computer.* The computer for this exercise needs to have enough storage space on its hard drive for digitized video shots. Virtually all recently produced computers have multimedia capabilities.
- *Editing software.* This software can be relatively simple such as *QuickTime Pro* The advantage of *QuickTime Pro* is that it provides easy-to-use picture and sound editing features and can import, export, compress, and/or save a number of image and file types. For more features and effects, software such as *Final Cut Pro* and *Adobe Premiere* are necessary. These have fairly steep learning curves and work best on computers with substantial random access memory and large hard drives for storing digitized video. Although both are professional-level packages, they can be used to edit everything from little movies for web pages to professional works mastered on digital videotape formats for broadcast.
- *Video clips.* In this exercise, each member of the group is going to edit the same clips. That is, you will need to shoot fifteen to twenty shots of a selected topic and arrange for each editor to have those shots on his or her computer.

Production

The production step in this exercise is actually the postproduction step in conventional media production. Because the objective of the exercise is to produce an edited version of a set of unedited shots, the following are the production steps:

1. Have a member of the group, or the teacher, select a topic or subject and shoot fifteen to twenty digital video shots of it. For example, shots of a little train running around a model railroad layout are used for these steps in Figure 5.21 (pages 108–109).
2. Download, import, transfer, or copy the shots to the hard drive of each participant's computer. These shots can be downloaded from the camera to each hard drive, or they may be copied onto a CD-ROM that each editor can use. Or, you can make a CD-ROM of the clips for each editor.
3. Examine the separate shots on the CD. They are from a variety of angles and focal lengths and total about five minutes of recording time.
4. Using the editing software, sequence the images in a logical, continuous, or creative manner. The edited version should be about one minute in length.

1 Choose a visually interesting object—a lamp, a chair, a lawnmower, a bicycle, a car, a grill, a fireplug, or a ceramic dog.

2 Use a camcorder to compose shots of the object from many different angles.

FIGURE 5.20   Mystery Video

5. Try several edited versions: one that is smooth and logical and one that is more creative, for example. Although it is not necessary to demonstrate the idea of this exercise, you may want to locate some sound files and add those to enhance and support the idea.

6. Editing software allows several choices for exported edited videos. For this exercise, export the edited video as a *QuickTime Movie*. The movie does not need to be full-screen size. Small movies are easier to move around, e-mail, or post to a web site.

7. As a group, watch each of the group members' movies. Movies may be grouped onto a disk, a CD-ROM, or posted to a web site.

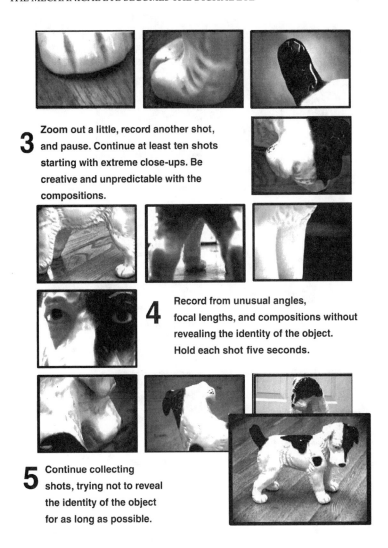

3 Zoom out a little, record another shot, and pause. Continue at least ten shots starting with extreme close-ups. Be creative and unpredictable with the compositions.

4 Record from unusual angles, focal lengths, and compositions without revealing the identity of the object. Hold each shot five seconds.

5 Continue collecting shots, trying not to reveal the identity of the object for as long as possible.

Postproduction

This short editing exercise reinforces the fact that every editor has a unique perspective and vision. Some may use very few shots, for example, and others may use many shots. Others may edit at a very fast pace using the same shots more than once. Depending on the capabilities of the editing software, some versions may have many special effects and transitions, whereas other versions may be simple yet elegant. Sound adds another dimension that may change the whole mood and style of the work.

No matter what style or creative choices are made, participating in these exercises will instill an appreciation for the skills, ideas, and expressiveness of editing.

These are still frames from twelve shots of a model train traveling around a layout. Each shot is ten to thirty seconds long. They were recorded with a digital video camcorder.

Passing coaches

Passing some buildings

Overhead wide shot

Moving toward camera

Overhead following

High angle

FIGURE 5.21   Editing: Multiple Interpretations. Editing video is an intriguing and intuitive endeavor because of the many possible interpretations of a set of shots.

Finally, as befits the motif of this book, the technology and machines are new, but the concepts and processes of editing are fundamental and as old as the moving picture. Box 5.1 (pages 110–111) exemplifies an especially thoughtful and creative video activity developed by Kathryn Dipietro when she was a special education teacher.

A CULMINATING VIDEO PROJECT: DOING THE HUMANITIES WITH DIGITAL VIDEO

One of the most important uses of contemporary media and technology tools is to create, or even discover, one's identity, heritage, self, community, and culture.

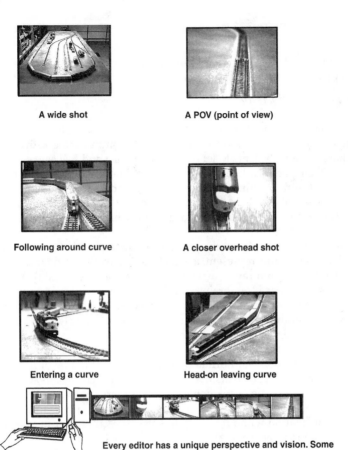

A wide shot

A POV (point of view)

Following around curve

A closer overhead shot

Entering a curve

Head-on leaving curve

Every editor has a unique perspective and vision. Some may use very few shots and others may use many. Depending on the capabilities of the editing software, some versions may have many special effects and transitions whereas other versions may be simple yet elegant. Sound adds another dimension that may change the whole mood or style of the work.

Artists, filmmakers, and scholars have traditionally used the tools of their day to observe, document, and interpret. Major producers of commercial media, such as theatrical motion pictures and television programming, produce works that they hope will have wide audience appeal, although in some cases, movie directors are able to produce highly original works that do display independence and unconventionality. Major software distributors also respond to the reality of the marketplace by producing and distributing works that appeal to very large audiences. As with any medium, some of that work is outstanding and much is mediocre. So who does that leave to document the richness of everyday life and culture with sensitivity, empathy, and respect? Answer: virtually any people who are sensitive enough to want to "see" the world around them, capture what they see, and share

■ ■ ■ ■ ■

BOX 5.1

USING VIDEO TO CREATE PORTRAITS: TEAM BUILDING WITH SPECIAL NEEDS KIDS

Kathryn Dipietro, Lehigh University

As a teacher of kids with emotional problems and learning disabilities, one of my challenges was to help the students find ways to communicate with each other. Often it was hard for my students to let down their guard and feel safe enough to divulge aspects of their personal lives to each other. While teaching special education at an inner city sixth-grade center in Duval County, Florida, I devised the following video activity that seemed to help students overcome their anxieties in sharing personal information. We used a combination of activities that culminated in the production of a movie titled "Portraits."

First the class explored the concept of portraits. We found the various ways that individuals could represent themselves. We explored how music, art, poetry, writing, and film could reveal aspects of the creator's personality. With that knowledge as a springboard, we brainstormed ways that we could represent ourselves using a variety of mediums. Finally we decided that we would combine several methods and produce a movie as a final portrait of our class. While we were discussing the movie, many of the students relayed their hesitancy to be filmed. They were somewhat reluctant to reveal certain aspects of themselves and were even more hesitant to share personal information in a face-to-face dialog or in front of the camera. Also many of the students had reading and speech deficits, which presented a unique problem. Talking or reading in front of others could be intimidating. We kept this in mind as we developed our project and devised a way for students to share personal information without having to speak directly either in front of their classmates or in front of the camera.

Our next task was to decide how we would use each of the mediums within our movie. We began by discussing very generally the concept of our movie. It was to be a documentary of our class and its members. We would do this by using a visual to represent the class as a whole and then focus more specifically on each class member. We storyboarded our movie on the blackboard to create an outline and guide. Each scene was sketched out and this helped break down the project into manageable parts as well as make sure we were "all on the same page." As mentioned, students were somewhat uncomfortable performing in front of each other as well as the camera. I kept this in mind as we developed our project.

To represent ourselves visually using an art concept, we decided to create paper silhouettes of ourselves. Using paper silhouettes with soft lighting would create the effect of the students being in front of the camera; however, they would be safely hidden behind their construction paper silhouette. Also this would allow me to be behind the paper silhouette with them so that I could assist with reading or speaking as needed. To create the paper silhouettes we used a dark coatroom with a utility light rigged up, a piece of black construction paper, and a white piece of chalk. Students worked in teams to trace the outline of each other's silhouette projected on their black construction paper by the light. After creating silhouette portraits, cutting them out, and pasting them on a white posterboard, we considered how to represent ourselves in prose.

As I mentioned, in addition to having some emotional problems, many of the students had learning disabilities that manifested themselves in written and/or oral expression. To move the students beyond this, we worked as a team to develop an outline of the type of information that we'd all like to both divulge about ourselves and learn about each other. We all brainstormed the types of things we'd like to share about ourselves as well as what we'd like to know about each other. We developed an outline that included a list of questions or topics. With assistance as needed, the students outlined their information and it was then put in a prose form. Once we had finished, we were ready to give consideration to music.

Students agreed to bring in selections of music to be played during the introduction to their personal portrait. They were encouraged to use music that would further reflect aspects of their personality and to be able to justify how and why their selections represented them. Now that the stage was set (so to speak), the filming was ready to take place.

We darkened the room, used some well-placed soft lights, aimed the camera at the silhouettes, and played the music. The effect was haunting as the camera focused in on the silhouette with the music playing in the background and then a student's voice rose from behind the silhouette softly revealing bits of personal information.

Once the film was completed, we watched it. As we watched it, I reflected on the process. This project had done more than I had hoped. Not only had students become more communicative and comfortable with each other, students with emotional handicaps and learning disabilities had also pulled together as a team to create a project that would reflect our class.

what they see. Contemporary media and technology tools make that possible and practical in ways as never before.

Preproduction

Concept

The following project describes and reviews some of the ideas and activities described previously in this chapter. In that sense, the project is a synthesis of those ideas and the ideas of a video producer.

The objective of this project will be to produce an at least three- to five-minute minidocumentary about a unique local subject within the producer's community. This will consist of a conceptual, historical, critical component followed by the production component. As with the previous projects and exercises in this book, this project will consist of the classic media production sequence of preproduction, production, and postproduction.

Materials and Resources

- *The camera.* Any consumer-level camcorder will work. These include the analog formats of VHS, 8mm, or Hi8 and digital camcorders that use mini-DV tape. Most camcorders have a built-in microphone that is adequate if placed properly, but an external mike will allow more flexibility, especially if recording voice in a variety of situations.

- *The tripod.* Whenever possible and practical, a tripod should be used to avoid unwanted camera movement while recording. As with all types of media production hardware, these have various prices, but even a relatively inexpensive one can provide adequate support while allowing basic camera movements. Of course, in many situations the use of a tripod is not possible. In these cases, practice steady handheld shots or look for other means of camera support such as brick walls, furniture, or any solid, firm surface.
- *Editing resources.* Being able to sequence shots and scenes to carry your message is the essence of producing a video documentary.

After acquiring the shooting and editing resources and then learning to operate them, some preparation and planning will pay off in the quality of a finished product.

Group Preparation: Discussion and Presentation

The preproduction step concerns the nature of documentary video or film production. Chapter 2 presented a traditional concept of the "classic" documentary form, which was described as usually dealing with an issue from a particular perspective. In particular, independent documentary filmmakers seek to present inadequately represented views and perspectives often from the point of view of underrepresented social groups. These alternative views are usually absent from big-budget mainstream producers who are concerned with audience size and advertising revenues. Thus, that leaves independent filmmakers to explore and share unique viewpoints. They may not have big budgets, but they frequently make up for that shortcoming with passion, creativity, and energy.

Therefore, it should not be surprising that video producers who have been exposed to and understand the uniqueness of documentary production will bring some of that insight into their own work. Some preproduction instruction and activities will help these novice producers develop an appreciation for the process, thus creatively nourishing the work they will do. Some preproduction instruction may include the following activities and ideas or adaptations of them.

Because the emphasis on this project is in the creation of a unique or personal observation of a particular issue or subject, examine the nature of what is referred to as the "humanities." What are the humanities? Why are they important? How can students and teachers use multimedia to address the humanities? Select a documentary that fits the classic documentary genre, review it, and prepare comments that could be used before presenting it to an audience. The title selected does not need to be very long. Even a five- to ten-minute work that exemplifies the documentary tradition will work.

Share the comments with the group, screen the movie, and then lead a discussion concerning the nature of documentary film and the relationship of that genre to the humanities. That discussion may include the moviemaker's perspective on an issue and a rationale for that issue. Other discussion items could include locations and places, biases, cultural factors, and individual audience members' impressions and reactions.

Next, transfer the experience of seeing and discussing that film to a conversation inspired by the words of Jim Wayne Miller:

> Those things we see every day of our lives, and therefore take for granted, are the very things we may never really see at all. But what if we deliberately inspect what is ordinarily not examined and, by considering what we can see, draw conclusions about what we can't see—about our values and assumptions? This human activity we ought to call *doing* the humanities.

In this project, the digital technology in the form of video production will be used to "do the humanities" and "inspect what is ordinarily not examined." All communities have uniqueness, individuality, distinctiveness, character, local flavor, and personality. List and discuss some interesting though taken for granted characteristics of the local community; that is, the community in which this project will take place. Consider local architectural details, historical monuments and landmarks, and regional festivals. Identify interesting personalities such as artists, craftspeople, musicians, business owners, hobbyists, and senior citizens and their stories. Local natural environmental characteristics may make informative works. Issues of social change may provide material such as the fading of the traditional downtowns and the impact of industry and technology on local culture. Other perspectives may include the richness and value of cultural diversity, and profiles of local institutions such as schools, libraries, and museums. Various community political issues can be examined from unique perspectives. Of course, there are many other ideas and many variations of those. Brainstorm ideas and consider unconventional perspectives and presentations. Choose a "point of view" or distinct perspective for each issue. Suggest unusual locations for the camera and compositions. Do not settle for the cliché.

Finally, storyboard some ideas. When shooting actually begins, a storyboard provides a map or starting point and help in selecting locations. Of course, the storyboard that is created for a particular subject will more than likely change over the course of actually recording the various scenes. When developing the storyboard, consider some stylistic and production design qualities that will provide consistency. Avoid the use of a narrator. Instead, let the camera reveal the subject with images and sounds, and when profiling people, allow them to speak for themselves. Of crucial importance is to limit the concept. Do not try to do too much! A direct, well-shot and -edited five-minute piece is better than a rambling thirty-minute piece. When shooting a short three- to five-minute documentary, feature one specific idea. For example, instead of Historical Architectural Landmarks of East Tennessee, choose one landmark, or structure, and use the camera to examine it.

Production

Shoot the documentary applying the skills and concepts presented in this chapter. That is, steady the camera with a tripod if possible and do not overuse the zoom feature. Think about composition elements such as headroom and shot framing. Use the zoom lens primarily for composition, and make smooth camera moves, pans, and tilts, using a tripod or a very steady hand. Look for interesting, even unusual compositions and do not hesitate to zoom or move in close to a subject. Remember that great pictures are worthless if the sound is bad, so select good locations (as quiet as possible with little or no echo) for recording voices and, if using the camcorder's mike, get as close to the subject as possible. One suggestion here is, if possible, to place the speaking person a few feet in front of a solid wall and place the camera close to the face and zoom out to compose the shot. Before recording voice, activate record and let the camera run for five to ten seconds before having the subject speak. This will make editing the shot a little easier. In addition, be sure to obtain permissions from any people who are in the shots. A good idea is to prepare a simple model release.

Effective and creative editing, or postproduction, requires a lot of shots to choose from. Therefore, shoot at least two or three times more tape than will be needed for the final edited master.

Postproduction

As described earlier in this chapter, it is the postproduction phase in which all of the elements are combined and edited into a finished product. Review that section and incorporate the ideas and methods into the presentation of this subject.

Sharing the final production is what multimedia is all about, and there are several possibilities for that. These may include the following:

1. Presentation in school as part of a report or in conjunction with other activities. In this case, making a VHS or DVD copy will be necessary for group presentation.
2. Inclusion on a group-produced web page with other productions with each movie linked to a menu item. To do this, the movie will need to be exported as a movie file such as *QuickTime, RealMedia,* or *AVI.*
3. Submission to online World Wide Web festivals that solicit independent video works. There are web sites devoted to the promotion and display of independent "microcinema." Often they may request a VHS version that will be converted to an online file format. Some will request it as an attached file. A popular site fitting into this category is *ifilm.*
4. Submission to independent film festivals, especially those that solicit student produced works. There are numerous festivals for independent video, usually in community locations such as colleges and theaters. In fact, some schools plan and present school-wide festivals to share the work of students in that school.

Technology does make the world a "global village," but it also can help us focus on self and community. The expressive use of digital tools can force us to see ourselves and our communities in ways we may never have considered. In that way, technology supports and expands the traditional role of the humanities.

SUMMARY: MOVIEMAKING REFLECTIONS AND TIPS

The motion picture is as fascinating and entertaining as it was over one hundred years ago, and most important, the means for making motion pictures is widely available to teachers and students at all levels. Early classroom use of computers was often mundane and unimaginative. The software was little more than expensive flash cards. The computers programmed the students. The quantum leap of technology, however, has changed all of that. Effective application emphasizes the need of people to communicate, teach, and express. That is, computer technology and its accompanying peripherals, related tools, networks, and digital media processes require thought, planning, and creativity, all of which are highly desirable educationally. The use of these tools to create a wide range of digital videos and movies exploring an unlimited selection of subjects is a case in point.

This chapter introduced the fundamentals of creating digital video, or movies. Using these skills and concepts and following the described activities to practice them will improve the quality of work created with digital media production tools. In other words, follow these tips:

1. Learn the features of the camera and how these can be used expressively and creatively.
2. Be careful to keep the camera steady during recording. A tripod is best for this, but any firm surface will work as will practicing steady handheld shots.
3. Look for interesting compositions and move in close to the subject if possible. Be aware of camera angles and light.
4. Consider location and circumstances when recording a subject's voice. Place the camera and its microphone in a position that will achieve the best sound quality.
5. Learn some basic camera moves and how they can be used effectively.
6. Learn the basics of editing pictures and sound including familiarity with editing software and the use of transitions and special effects.
7. Practice the art of storyboarding as a planning method.
8. Understand the various genres and subgenres of media production and how to incorporate related concepts and ideas.
9. Submit your completed work for all to see via the World Wide Web and other venues such as festivals and exhibits.
10. Decide what to say to the Academy.

Most important of all, do not settle for clichés. Instead, experiment and do not hesitate to break the "rules" if breaking the rules enhances creativity and impact.

After all, push the technology. That is what the vast amount of creative potential available in digital media production tools is for. Not to exploit that potential defeats the purpose for which they were designed.

THOUGHT PROVOKER

Critical analysis and discussion of works from various genres help in developing a repertoire of media production knowledge and skills. The serious student of digital media production seeks out and critically views a wide range of works, especially those produced by independent media artists. The work of independents is often highly original and often daring and unconventional. The best sources of this work are film festivals that screen independent work, web sites dedicated to promoting the work of independents, audiovisual collections in college and public libraries, and public broadcasting stations. Unfortunately, mainstream commercial networks rarely air the work of independents. Based on that, seek out, watch, and critique some independent works from various genres and subgenres. As a group activity, class members can obtain—rent, borrow, check out, download, bookmark, record—selected works of independent producers to present to the class for discussion.

REFERENCES

Capra, Frank. (1971). *Frank Capra: The Name Above the Title.* New York: Macmillan.

Eisenstein, Sergei. (1942). *The Film Sense.* New York: Harcourt, Brace.

Miller, Jim Wayne. (1983). *Doing the Humanities.* Unpublished essay, Kentucky Museum and Library, Western Kentucky University.

Schickel, Richard. (1968). *The Disney Version: The Life, Times, Art, and Commerce of Walt Disney.* New York: Simon and Schuster.

Zettl, Herbert. (1990). *Sight Sound Motion: Applied Media Aesthetics.* Belmont, California: Wadsworth.

CHAPTER SIX

LIVING PIXELS
Digital Animation

TOPIC OUTLINE

THEORIES AND METHODS OF ANIMATED MOTION: HOW IT WORKS AND HOW TO MAKE IT WORK

This section introduces and describes how the illusion of movement is created by animators. It also includes descriptions of popular animation methods.

BOX 6.1: NEIGHBORHOOD STORIES: A CASE STUDY IN CLAYMATION

This is a description of how two filmmakers, Ron Schildknecht and Ruben Moreno, worked with school students in creating community-based animated movies.

DRAWING ON THE COMPUTER

Two fundamental and traditional drawing exercises are presented, which can be adapted to drawing and painting software.

ANIMATION EXERCISES AND PROJECTS

This section contains sixteen step-by-step animation projects.

INFORMATION SOURCES AND IDEAS FOR LEARNING ABOUT ANIMATION

This is a selection of print, video, and online sources of information about animation. It also includes information about festivals and organizations.

SUMMARY: HAPPY ANIMATING

This summarizes the goals of this chapter's animation exercises.

THOUGHT PROVOKERS

Here are some ideas designed to encourage reflection on animation as a multimedia design method.

OBJECTIVES

After reading the topics in this chapter and participating in the production activities, the reader will be able to:

- Understand how animators use various tools and processes to create an illusion of motion, movement, and life.
- Use computer graphics and art software to make simple contour and gesture drawings.

- Create animated products as a result of following the described animation exercises and projects.
- Use a variety of sources—print, video, web sites—to locate information about the concepts and techniques of animation.

Animation is a genre that has exploded with the vast improvement and availability of multimedia tools and processes. Possibly no other multimedia production element has benefited more from technological media production advances than has animation. The term *animation* is very broad and can refer to any action, motion, effect, or manipulation of a frame of film, video, or computer software. Animation can also refer, for example, to graphics, shapes, colors, and text flying and dancing in movies or videos as are commonly seen in television graphics. Not surprisingly, this broad definition is at odds with the way that the great character animators used the term. To Walt Disney and his animators and storytellers, animation meant life. Two of Disney's greatest animators, Frank Thomas and Ollie Johnston, expressed this view in their classic book, *The Illusion of Life.* They and others during the golden era of studio animation strove successfully to create seemingly living, breathing, and feeling characters that have moved and touched audiences for many years. Disney's animated features established animation as a powerful storytelling tool, and the Warner Brothers, MGM, and Fleischer brothers' cartoons established animation as an often irreverent and satirical force. As explained in Chapter 2, animated movies date back to the earliest period of motion picture history. Animation in contemporary technology applications includes unlimited possibilities of movements and effects. Anyone who watches television is bombarded by an array of flying logos, three-dimensional text, morphing products, elaborate opening and closing sequences, simulations on news and sports, and manipulated live-action shots. In feature films, special effects artists create computer animation that blurs the distinction between what is real and what is animated. Hundreds of passengers in James Cameron's primarily live-action epic *Titanic,* for example, were created with computers. World Wide Web sites contain all sorts of animations from animated bullets to streaming cartoons. Driving the interest in animation is the availability of relatively inexpensive software to students, teachers, instructional technologists, and artists to create sophisticated effects for web pages and self-contained movies. Computers in schools, businesses, and homes have animation power through such common software as *PowerPoint* and *HyperStudio.* Thus, multimedia designers see animation as a diverse set of methods from simple moving shapes to highly refined character development.

THEORIES AND METHODS OF ANIMATED MOTION: HOW IT WORKS AND HOW TO MAKE IT WORK

An animated film works on the same principle as a live-action film. The difference is in how the individual frames on the film are made. To make a live-action film, a camera simply records a series of still pictures at regular intervals, usually 24 per second for film and 30 per second for video. When projected at the same rate, the illusion of movement is achieved. To make an animated film, each frame of the film has to be drawn or created by hand. Instead of just pointing a camera and pushing a shutter release or record button, an animator must draw or create each position of a movement. Animation production also requires a camera that can take one frame at a time. For very smooth and fluid motion, this requires 24 drawings per second. At this rate, a 30-second piece of animation on film takes 720 drawings. Most animators, however, find that they can achieve acceptable smoothness by making one drawing and filming it in two frames. With two-frame animation, the animator needs only 360 drawings or setups for 30 seconds of film.

Although teachers and their students are not going to make multimillion-dollar animated features in their schools, they can apply some basic animation concepts to a variety of in-school multimedia projects. So, how *do* animators bring life to their work? The appeal of the art of animation is that the result, or the expressiveness, depends on elements distinct from the tools used to create it. For example, an animator who understands that the essence of the art form is the illusion of motion can make successful works whether using index cards and pencils or the latest digital tools. Norman McLaren, the late Canadian animation artist at the National Film Board of Canada, proposed a model of animated motion. Through a series of instructional movies he made in the late 1970s, he described animation as an interaction of motion, tempo, and change with tempo determined by the motions of constant, accelerating, decelerating, zero, and irregular. The premise of this model was that motion and movement—whether in humans, animals, objects, or nature—is a combination of acceleration, deceleration, irregular, and/or constant. For example, movement and motion can be predictable, regular, and constant, or, as some animators may say, lifeless, stiff, and boring. Movements may accelerate and decelerate, thus adding energy and life. Sometimes there is no movement at all, and sometimes motion is irregular. Creative animators combine these motions to tell stories, to teach, to inform, or to express. For example, a ball rolling up and down hills, accelerates going down, decelerates going up, then accelerates going down again. An animator who understands this concept will create work that is lively and expressive, not simply constant and boring. The beauty of this model is that its principle applies to a school student creating a simple animated GIF for inclusion on a web page just as it does to the latest production of a big-budget animated feature.

How Animators Create Life: Methods and Materials

As an art form, the process of animation is unlimited in creative potential. Simply put, most anything can be animated—people, drawings, paper, objects, modeling clay, beads, sand, photographs, toys, food, pixels, puppets, paint, plants, shoes, hats, text, words—anything that can be placed on an animation stand or framed in the viewfinders of cameras. Although the traditional method of animation is based on photographic motion picture film stock, the arrival of digital production tools expands the possibilities of animation even more. Most important though is that animation is no longer an exclusive genre requiring big budgets and expensive hardware. The aesthetic and expressive properties unique to traditional animation materials and methods are often adapted to the special qualities and advantages of digital media production resources. The following section describes the major categories of animation techniques and tells how they are being carried on by contemporary digital production methods.

Line Animation

The simple elegance and directness of the drawn line has been the backbone of animation since the earliest days of this art form. Winsor McCay's film *Gertie the Dinosaur* was created with black lines on 10,000 cards, yet he achieved a stunning illusion of life. Although the black line on white paper was the primary animation method during most of the silent era, the invention of celluloid or cel animation led to the use of line animation mainly for planning and making rough sketches. Figure 6.1 (pages 122–123) illustrates a couple of samples of line animation art. This was true till independent animators seeking personal expressive styles rediscovered the line and its rich potential. Line animation again is an important production choice of multimedia creators because of the computer's virtually unlimited ability to manipulate lines and shapes. The line is a natural extension of creative technological tools such as scanners, graphics tablets, and a great variety of off-the-shelf graphics software packages. The projects section of this chapter describes some specific ways the concept of line animation can be used with computer graphics and animation.

Multiple-Cel Level Animation

For early animators, drawing or tracing every element or line on every card for every frame was very time-consuming. For example, an animated movie that lasts 7 minutes and plays at 24 frames a second requires the animator to create 10,080 frames. Another disadvantage of this method was that each line on each drawing was slightly different than the lines on the drawings before and after. Even very carefully traced drawings fluctuated throughout the movie, distracting viewers.

The solution to this problem, although simple, revolutionized cartoon production and ignited the golden era of studio animation. The animator Earl Hurd is credited with coming up with the idea of making the drawings on clear celluloid sheets, thus allowing the background to show through in every frame. Figure 6.2 (page 124) shows the concept of cel animation.

Separate actions could be drawn on each celluloid level. Preliminary drawings were done on paper and traced or inked onto the cels. The drawings were then painted on the opposite side. When the color process was perfected, this multiple-cel level animation allowed animators to create colorful and rich cartoons, which are still very popular. The disadvantage of this process was that handling the cels was difficult, and filming could be a problem because of dust, fingerprints, and reflections. Throughout the subsequent years, millions of these cels were created, so many in fact, that collecting cels is a popular hobby. Rare cel drawings from important works can be lucrative investments.

In the digital era of computer animation, software designers perpetuate the unique properties of traditional cel animation. Popular movie software such as *Macromedia Flash* mimics the process of cel animation by allowing the animator to use multiple layers to create independent actions and complex interactions among the layers. This is another example of how older media production concepts are adapted in the creation of new technology works. Traditional cel-level animation (created on acetate sheets) is still used in many animated works, often in combination with digital production methods.

Cutouts and Collage

Line animation and cel animation, although very effective for studio and commercial work, can be very complex and extremely time-consuming and expensive to create. Using cutouts instead of hundreds or even thousands of drawings has some distinct advantages. Independent animators especially like the distinct aesthetic quality of cutout animation and the relative ease of creating the artwork. For example, the separate heads in Figure 6.3 (page 125) were created as cutouts so they could be filmed in sync with sound. In particular, drawing and cutting out characters and props works especially well for school students. A character may have separate cutouts for arms, facial features, and mouth shapes. Filming cutout animation, on the other hand, can be a tedious process. Filming or recording on a copy stand with a digital camcorder requires total concentration but is not very difficult to do. Basic editing software can be used to complete a cutout animation movie.

Ideas for cutout animation include traditional storytelling movies with characters and plot, or cutouts can be manipulated in expressive and abstract ways in sync with music or sound. One of the more outstanding examples of collage or cutout animation, released in 1973 by independent animator Frank Mouris, was *Frank Film,* a short movie consisting of about 35,000 images cut from catalogs and magazines and filmed on an animation stand. These images were accompanied by a double voice-over soundtrack of autobiographical comments by Mouris. This film and its overwhelming rapid pace of cutout consumer products can be interpreted as a comment on our consumer-based culture. *Frank Film* was awarded an Oscar in 1973 for best animated short.

A meshing of this traditional method with modern digital tools has great creative potential. Artwork may be created on drawing paper or cut out from catalogs, magazines, books, or any source of printed images, or cutouts can be drawn on a computer. Either can be printed and filmed on a copy stand with a digital camera. Alternatively, the concept of cutout animation can be used to manipulate computer graphic shapes with various multimedia software.

Object, Stop Motion, and Clay

Bringing life and motion to inanimate objects is called object animation or stop motion animation. This is accomplished by placing a camera on a tripod and recording single frames of objects that are moved between frames. Figure 6.4 (page 126) shows a typical setup for stop motion animation.

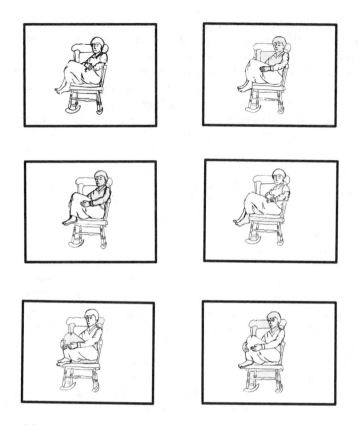

Line art drawn on white bond paper or index cards

FIGURE 6.1   Line Animation

For example, if the animator wants a toy car to move slowly from left to right through the viewfinder, the process is to move the toy a short distance, record a still picture, move the toy again, record a still picture, and so forth. The concept is simple, but it can be used to produce stunning results. Claymation, as clay-based animation has come to be called, was popularized by the 1950s television characters Gumby and Pokey by Art Clonky. Later, Claymation artist Will Vinton and his studio created a series of award-winning works, including the 1986 commercial "Heard It Through the Grapevine" for California Raisin Growers. An outstanding feature film created with stop motion and clay was Tim Burton's *The Nightmare Before Christmas.* In England, Nick Park created the highly popular Academy Award–winning *Wallace and Grommit* shorts and the feature *Chicken Run.*

Line drawings on 9 by 12 Acme punched animation bond paper

Claymation has great versatility and can be used for simple yet expressive movies as well as highly complex works such as Nick Park's *Wallace and Grommit* movies. Box 6.1, Neighborhood Stories: A Case Study in Claymation, on pages 127–133, describes a highly successful approach to using this method with school students.

Pixilated Movies
A popular variation of stop motion animation is the pixilated movie. In this method, people are the objects that are animated, so that they appear to be pixie-like. The process is executed with a camera mounted on a sturdy tripod. The human subjects are framed in the viewfinder and directed to hold a pose while the camcorder records a still picture. The setup shown in Figure 6.5 (page 134) illustrates this concept.

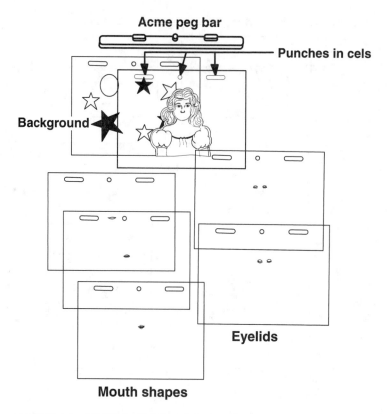

FIGURE 6.2   **Multiple-Cel-Level Animation**

As with any kind of video animation, how the still frame is recorded depends on the camera, for example, whether the camera can record a true single frame of video (one-thirtieth of a second). Some digital camcorders can record a still picture or photograph. When the photo button is pushed, for example, the camera will automatically record a still picture for a few seconds. In the editing stage, single frames may be removed to build a pixilated movie. The process continues with the actor holding a pose while the camera records a still picture. This process is repeated over and over. When the tape is played back, people appear to move around without moving their feet. Many people may emerge from a small car. A person can simply disappear and reappear. In *Neighbors* by Canadian animator Norman McLaren—one of the most astonishing examples of pixilated short film—two actors play neighbors who feud over the location of a property line. The feud gets progressively more violent. All of the action is pixilated or stop motion. The most remarkable visual quality of this movie is that the actors were filmed as they jumped. That is, the actor was instructed to jump while bending his legs at the apex of this jump, thus capturing a still image of the actor appearing to float. This paci-

FIGURE 6.3 Cutout Animation. These multiple cutout heads were designed to be filmed in synchronization with dialogue.

fist pixilated movie, though eye-catching, is about making love, not war, an example of animator as social critic. *Neighbors* and other outstanding films are available from the National Film Board of Canada. Also, McLaren films are often available in audiovisual collections in school, college, or public libraries.

Pixilated movies are relatively easy to produce yet the effects can be very effective and entertaining. They make excellent group projects, and as with the previously mentioned methods, pixilated video recording can be edited for maximum effect. For this reason, the production of pixilated movies has great potential for school-based media production.

Experimental Animation

Experimental filmmaking has a long history. In fact, many techniques of animation that are now taken for granted were at one time experimental. Figure 6.6 (page 135) exemplifies this approach by showing a sequence of linear shapes that would appear to be dancing.

Usually, experimental works are short and often are made with unconventional combinations of tools and ideas. Computer-based animation, for example,

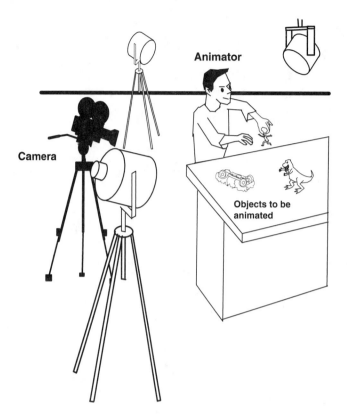

FIGURE 6.4   Stop Motion Animation. Stop motion
animation can be used for very simple works, or it may be
used for complex feature-length works such as *The Nightmare
Before Christmas.*

was once considered to be experimental. Norman McLaren's work was experimental in nature because he was interested in exploring the expressive potential of a
range of tools and materials. He worked with an optical printer, a motion picture
printing device, to create beautiful multiple image and motion effects in *Pas de Deu.*
McLaren also manipulated optical soundtracks to create very unusual yet dynamic
combinations between pictures and sound. Again, seeking out and viewing the work
of McLaren is one key to developing an appreciation of animation as art and social
commentary. Another early experimental animator was Oskar Fischinger, whose
work with intensely colored and animated 3-D objects accompanied by jazz or classical scores pioneered the concept of the animator as "abstract" artist. For that very
reason, Walt Disney sought his assistance in conceptualizing the movie *Fantasia.*
Fischinger's influence on the concepts in that film are strong, although the combination of the commercialism and sentimentality of Disney with the avant-garde work
of Fischinger was somewhat odd. Viewing the work of Fischinger can enhance one's

■ ■ ■ ■ ■

BOX 6.1

NEIGHBORHOOD STORIES: A CASE STUDY IN CLAYMATION

Ron Schildknecht and Ruben Moreno, Louisville, Kentucky

Claymation, an animation technique using clay figures and stop motion photography, is an excellent device for teaching children the basic principles of filmmaking, to include writing, camera work, and editing. Fifth-grade students at a parochial school in Louisville recently had such an opportunity with the assistance of two video artists—Ruben Moreno and myself—which took place over a three-week period.

Using the theme of the uniqueness of our city's neighborhoods, several grants were written and received to fund the project. The major expenses were Mr. Moreno's time and the cost of the materials (my time was donated as a parent of one of the students). A significant amount of the financial support was provided by our state arts council's artist-in-residence program, which is available in most states.

We began the project by discussing the value of communities in the students' lives. This discussion really could have been about any particular subject area, just as long as they had some specific content to focus their ideas on. This also sets established parameters for the students and prevents them from being overwhelmed by what to make their first film about.

The next step was to split the class into groups of four or five. Each group was to work together to come up with a story that involves their neighborhood. Most of the students live near the school, so most have similar experiences to share. This activity, as does the actual filming, requires teamwork and collaboration, and reinforces writing skills.

This process was followed by storyboarding, the very heart of filmmaking. This is how filmmakers become storytellers, creating a play-by-play blueprint of turning their verbal stories into a cinematic sequence. We helped them in this activity by discussing the visual syntax—the language of film—used in telling stories visually. The easiest way of doing this is by creating a simple scene—something with a beginning, middle, and end—then as a group, breaking down the story into individual shots. Comic books serve as a good example of this. We also provide them with the appropriate vocabulary—long shot, extreme close-up, pan shot, and others.

MAKING THE CHARACTERS

After the storyboards are completed, the fun begins. Students finally get to put down their pencils and get their hands on some clay. An assortment of tools and clay are used in creating Claymation figures. Under careful instruction, they create the heads of their characters—typically modeled after themselves—then the bodies. Keeping the two separated allows for greater stability in the figures.

The next step has to do with students learning about scale. Scale in a production has a lot to do with the size of the figures. Using modeling clay (plasticine clay), a very soft and colorful clay, one has the ability to make interesting clay figures in multicolors, which can increase the beauty and value of the character. So the construction of the characters also includes the assembling of the colors of the characters. Clay figures can vary in size. We have found that unless we want to get into making armatures, the best thing to do is to be truthful to the modeling clay material itself and not build a character that is so big that the weight of the torso can crush the legs beneath it. Figures

(continued)

BOX 6.1   CONTINUED

Claymation Tools

between 3 and 4 inches tall suit this method of construction well for a production. Given that a character would be 3 to 4 inches, that sets the scale for the production's doorways, buildings, and windows.

Once that is completed, the students have a chance to create their own characters. They started off by building heads that were roughly about the size of a small robin's egg and from there trimmed them down.

Features were put on the face using some small clay tools. Eye sockets were made so that different colored clay can be placed inside for eyeballs. Glass beads can be used or any other kind of bead. We have found that eyes look better inside of the clay rather than on top. What students do depends on the type of clay characters that they are building and what expressions they want to create with their characters.

The whole character is comprised of colors of clay representing different sections of the body and the colors of the clothing being worn by the character. For the most part, clay is used for the character and other props are best made out of other lighter materials. Lighter is better, especially if the character has things that have to be picked up or tossed as part of its characterization.

Modeling clay colors can be mixed in the same way similar to mixing paint, that is, blue and yellow clay make green clay. So, that is another advantage of using plasticine clay; it offers the flexibility to create whatever colors wanted for the production. The more one works with clay the softer it becomes; the darker colors can stain the lighter colors. It is important to keep paper towels on the table to clean one's hands by

Steps in Head Production

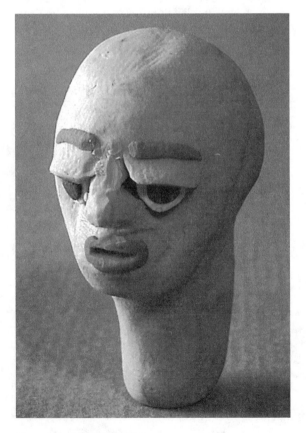

Completed Facial Features

(continued)

BOX 6.1 CONTINUED

wiping the oily material off of them. Then when one goes to work with lighter colors nearby, the lighter colors can be kept pure without staining them with the darker colors.

If while working the clay it becomes too soft, one should place it back into a cool place or a refrigerator. The cold temperature will stiffen the character and make it easier to work with again. It is important to store characters out of areas of direct sunlight and to be cautious about putting figures near areas that have heat such as a heating register. Exposure to heat will quickly make characters soft, limp, and will melt them.

Because it is difficult and time-consuming to mend a character in the middle of the shooting production, it is worth the effort to create well-crafted, flexible figures that will move easily. For example, the neck of a clay character going into the torso, like a peg in a hole, functions longer in production than does a neck in a more permanent attachment. To turn the head, pulling it out and dropping it back down in the preferred position will allow for longer neck life than twisting a clay neck, which will eventually tear.

We've found that once the characters are built and the stage and props are completed that a nice run-through is useful. The run-through involves blocking, how the figures are to be moved in the story. This is a practical exercise that gives the students an opportunity to envision which way the clay figures will be going, how they will be seen, and how they should stand for the camera's point of view.

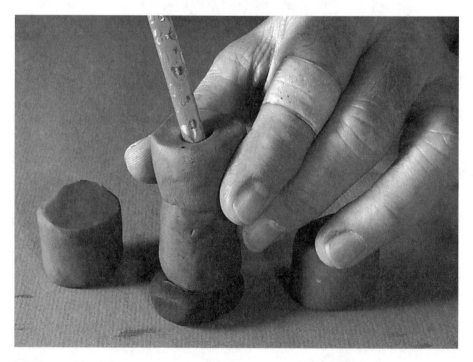

Making a Head Hole

Inserting the Head

Final Construction

(continued)

BOX 6.1   CONTINUED

Completed Character

In preparing to begin shooting the production, it is also important that each student has a good idea of his or her role in this process. This also makes for a better shooting crew. The advance organization of the crew allows shooting at a faster rate, and the name of the game is frames. Filmmakers need to shoot a lot of frames.

Dry run blocking and execution of the story line gives everyone a good sense of what kind of movements are to be made and who is moving which figures. At that point lighting will come into play, because where the figures will be placed on the shooting stage will have been decided.

Sets are created using construction paper, matte board, water-based paints, and markers. Props are often made from clay, are built from scratch using found materials, or can be found in stores in the craft or toy section. Typically, a set will have three walls, much like a set one would see for a live-action film in a studio soundstage.

After the characters, props, and backgrounds are constructed, the set is carefully lit. This can be done with a cheap pair of utility lights from the hardware store, or professional lights with control features can be obtained. This depends largely on the budget or what one has access to, but keep in mind that one feature that sets a film apart from the rest is lighting. Outstanding Claymation films like *Wallace and Grommit* are as painstakingly lit as big-budget live-action films, with numerous, well-placed lighting instruments used to create depth and reality.

Finally, the fast-paced world of filmmaking begins—one frame at a time. We used a digital camcorder with single-frame capability, a Sony VX-1000. Technically, the camera shoots six frames in single-frame mode, which in video terms is one-fifth of a second. (Video records and plays back at a frame rate of thirty frames per second.) This is actually a bit too slow for smooth animation. To compensate for this problem, we used our editing software, *Adobe Premiere,* to increase the frame rate in playing back the animation. This adjustment resulted in faster, smoother motion. With the camera placed on a *sturdy* tripod (emphasis on *sturdy*), the characters are placed on the set and the single-frame button is pressed. The characters are moved slightly—as instructed by the script—and filmed again—and so on; a slow and tedious process indeed. We were fortunate to have an additional camera that allowed us to have two groups filming simultaneously.

Here's a tip for shooting dialogue scenes. Animators typically record their dialogue first, then animate by creating a mouth movement for every sound made from every word. Most school projects such as this one simply do not have time to create animations in this way. An effective technique is to shoot the characters (usually in a close-up shot) with their mouths in various positions of opening and closing. During the editing, the shot can be looped as necessary to fit the amount of dialogue the character has. It's not perfect, but in most cases it gets the job done.

appreciation of the art of animation. Look in audiovisual collections in libraries and colleges or examine the catalogs of distributors who sell or rent artistic and independent works. Also, seek out film festivals that present artistically and historically important works. Independent experimental animators are often artistically ahead of their time. In particular, Stan VanDerBeek experimented with technological advances in filmmaking long before computer-based animation was widely available. He also was the mentor to *Monty Python's Flying Circus* animator Terry Gilliam.

The tools of the multimedia digital era multiply the options of animators who want to color outside the lines; in other words, to create short, personal, expressive, and unconventional works. Multimedia technologies support the artist animator by providing powerful tools for creation, distribution, and criticism. Experimental work caters to artists and innovators with multimedia tools. In that sense, experimental works may include variations of the methods described previously. The technological possibilities of experimental animation have grown to the extent that virtually anyone who wants to experiment creatively with animation is able to do so with readily available tools.

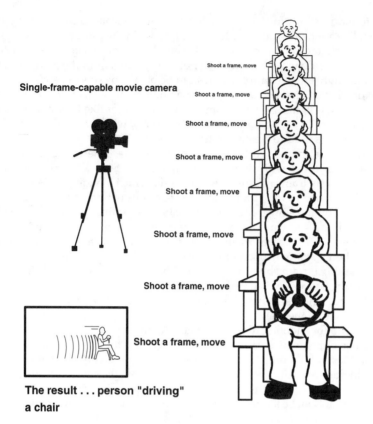

Single-frame-capable movie camera

Shoot a frame, move

Shoot a frame, move

Shoot a frame, move

Shoot a frame, move

Shoot a frame, move

Shoot a frame, move

Shoot a frame, move

Shoot a frame, move

**The result . . . person "driving"
a chair**

FIGURE 6.5   **Pixilation.** The dictionary in *Microsoft Word*
defines *pixilated* as "behaving in a strange or whimsical way."

Direct or Draw on Animation

Using permanent felt-tipped pens to draw directly on clear 16mm or 35mm film
stock and then projecting the results with a movie projector is a traditional animation method. Figure 6.7 illustrates some drawing options.

The nature of this process limits the detail that can be drawn in a small space,
yet the effect has a unique raw energy. Another variation of working or marking
directly on film stock is to scratch on the emulsion side of the black film leader.
Direct animation lends itself well to the abstract or experimental idea described
previously. One problem with this method may be in securing the clear leader and
a movie projector that works. Also, basic film splicing resources may be needed to
splice short films together. An effective way to make direct movies is to transfer the
direct film to a videotape or digital format for editing.

Computer Animation

Much as multi-cel-level animation enhanced and expanded the production of animated films in the 1930s and 1940s, the computer is revolutionizing or, more accu-

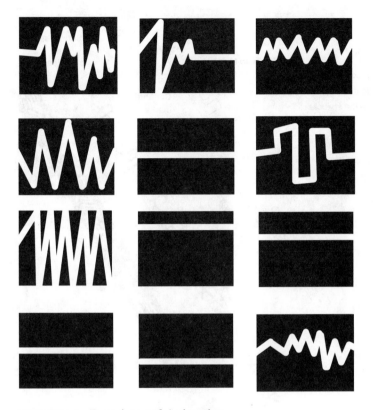

FIGURE 6.6   Experimental Animation

rately perhaps, enhancing and expanding the art form. Using nothing more than off-the-shelf software and ordinary desktop computers, animators, whether in schools or working independently, can create highly expressive and creative works. Figure 6.8 illustrates a typical configuration. Further, entire feature films for theatrical release are made with advanced computers and software. In all cases, the success of the products depends as always on the ideas of the creator, just as it did in 1914 when Winsor McCay released *Gertie the Dinosaur.*

Computer-based animation can be used to make art or to enhance instruction through visualizing complex scientific concepts and principles. The spread of the World Wide Web provides a showcase for all sorts of computer animation. Computer animation software has improved greatly. Powerful yet relatively inexpensive animation packages are available for schools and independent animators. Combining this software with the postproduction and special effects of digital editing systems provides unlimited creative and instructional space for artists, students of all ages, and teachers in any discipline. One of the new generations of computer animation software designed for making animated movies for the Internet is *Macromedia Flash.* This product is highly versatile, even revolutionary,

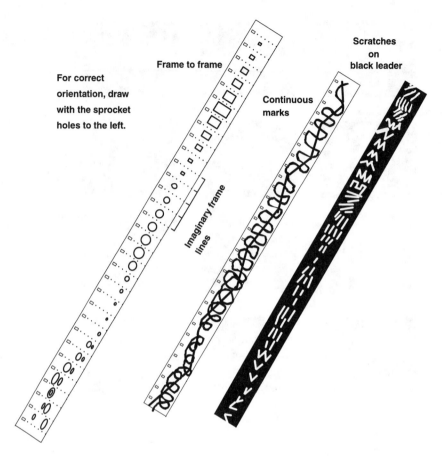

FIGURE 6.7   Direct Animation. Use permanent fine point felt-tipped pens to draw directly on the leader. When projected, the movie plays at twenty-four frames per second.

because of its capability to create highly interactive, high-resolution web pages, movies, and animations in very small Shockwave files. *Flash* takes a while to learn; but the more one uses it, the more intuitive and easy it becomes. Because of its relatively low price and high power, *Flash* is the multimedia program of choice for everyone from professional web designers to school students. Independent animation artists in particular have been drawn to *Flash* because of its conceptual and logical mimicking of earlier forms such as multi-cel-level animation, collage animation, cutout animation, and line animation.

Although computer-based animation is powerful, it is based on the traditions and ideas from the early years of filmmaking. Computer animation does not exist as a completely new phenomenon but rather expands and enhances animation as an art form and teaching tool. After all, the essence of even the most advanced com-

FIGURE 6.8 Graphics Tablet. A graphics tablet provides
expanded artistic and drawing possibilities.

puter films such as *Toy Story* is ideas and characters that come from the blue pencil
drawings of the artists and animators much like Winsor McCay, who created *Gertie*
almost one hundred years ago. The animation activities described in the next section
use all sorts of methods and materials combining old ideas with new technologies.

DRAWING ON THE COMPUTER

Before describing some animation projects, some simple drawing concepts may be
useful to consider. The purpose of these traditional art school projects is to demonstrate the possibility of creating simple drawings for importing and manipulating
in multimedia software. The exercises are not intended to make you an artist or an
illustrator. The point is that anyone with some basic computer graphics software
can apply these concepts to the creation of multimedia products.

Drawing is a useful skill for multimedia designers and producers. The World
Wide Web and software stores are replete with clip art collections and download-
able or importable images and pictures. For many uses, these may work well when
placed into multimedia productions, especially if time is a factor. However, though
some clip art is very good, on the whole it tends to be somewhat impersonal and too
often based on clichés. Thus, in the true spirit of original multimedia production,
consider using original drawings. This is not to say that one needs to be an accom-

plished artist, but that some fundamental drawing skills can relieve the dependence on stick figures and clip art. Some basic notions and ideas can be very useful. Anyone can follow a few fundamental guidelines in order to make simple images that can be manipulated in unlimited ways with multimedia software. (Look at the walking figure in Figure 6.32 (page 184) made with only rectangles and a circle.) The need for drawing and understanding design is another example of the new, multimedia, incorporating the old, drawing. Developing enough confidence in being able to make simple drawings or illustrations is useful to a multimedia designer for several reasons. First, creating a plan or a map or a storyboard before actually using the software often benefits from drawings and illustrations. Second, a simple, even crude image, either drawn on a computer or digitized from a pencil drawing, can be manipulated in unlimited ways. It can be reused, modified, or even animated. Third, basic drawing skills are useful in the creation of animation. Keep in mind that plain and simple drawings can be lively and energetic when animated. Thus, a multimedia producer who may not have great drawing skills may have an exceptional sense of timing, motion, and rhythm.

Some Basic, but Fun, Drawing Ideas

Drawing is the essence or structure of many of the visual arts. Even the spectacular computer-animated features such as *Toy Story* begin as pencil drawings. Although technology enhances the production of such hand-drawn animated features as *Beauty and the Beast*, it cannot replace the touch of the artist and the drawing. In fact, many of the preliminary sketches and drawings of the great animators have a beautiful personal and spontaneous quality that the finished products lack.

In the digital age, drawing is just as important as, if not more important than, ever. Although some multimedia artists specialize in handmade digital animation, all potential multimedia artists will benefit by developing some basic drawing skills. From the cave drawings of Lascaux to this very day or from cave artists to digital artists, the handmade drawing is irreplaceable.

The purpose of the following drawing exercises is not to turn the reader into an artist, but to provide some ideas and exercises that may develop or encourage useful drawing skills. For example, certain students may have a natural talent for drawing, and more than likely they have already mastered drawing on the computer. Thus, these students could be the multimedia project illustrators. Of course, there is always the reliable scanner for digitizing art made from a variety of media.

All potential multimedia producers should try their hands at using the computer as an electronic canvas or drawing pad. Further, these potential multimedia producers should not accept the too often quoted "but I can't draw" or "I'm not creative." Draw anyway.

Some Digital Drawing Tools

The computer as Etch-a-Sketch is not new. Many of the earliest computers in schools came with basic painting and drawing programs. In fact, one of the early programs, *Microsoft Paint,* included under Accessories in Windows, is still very popular and useful. Two early Macintosh drawing and painting programs were *MacPaint* and *MacDraw.*

Modern multimedia production software has multiple features and creative possibilities, yet the painting and drawing functions are pretty much the same as in earlier versions. Note that there is a difference between a paint function and a draw function. A paint program uses "tools" that mimic traditional media to manipulate groups of pixels in painterly fashion, much like putting paint on a canvas. A draw program, alternatively, uses tools to make shapes—circles, squares, polygons, and irregulars—which can be moved around the screen much as an artist would create a collage. Both have advantages and disadvantages. For the exercises in this chapter, a paint program will be needed and/or, bypassing the computer, drawing pens and pencils and paper and/or index cards. Three paint programs will work:

- *Microsoft Paint.* This is a basic but fun and easy-to-use paint program. It is ideal for beginners but can be used for a variety of multimedia needs. *Paint* comes with the Windows operating system.
- *ClarisWorks.* This integrated software package has a paint program that has numerous features and is easy to use.
- *Corel Painter.* This program is very sophisticated software that mimics many conventional painting and drawing tools and processes.

In addition to those, *Macromedia Flash* contains versatile painting tools that, not surprisingly, are especially well suited for creating artwork for use in *Flash. Adobe Photoshop* also contains painting tools.

The primary painting device in these programs is either a mouse or a digital graphics tablet. Of course, a mouse is a routine item on desktop and laptop computers. Some artists may prefer to draw with a mouse, but a more sensitive drawing device is an electronic graphics tablet. Although these tablets can be very large and expensive, smaller reasonably priced ones work very well, especially in school settings. Many multimedia designers prefer the graphics tablet because of the feel and increased sensitivity of the pen. However, this is mostly a personal preference because both the mouse and the tablet allow designers to do the same thing.

The following drawing exercises do not require computers at all. Drawing skills are drawing skills in any medium. That is, one can practice some basic drawing methods on common materials such as pencils and drawing paper. After all, it is the idea that matters most. Besides, some multimedia creators prefer to work in conventional materials, at least initially, and then digitize and import their work into multimedia authoring software where it can be manipulated and modified at will.

Contour Drawing

The line has an honored place in art history. For example, see Henri Matisse's "A Lady with Flowers and Pomegranates" in Figure 6.9.

FIGURE 6.9   *A Lady with Flowers and Pomegranates,* **by Henri Matisse**

The line is also a key element of the study of art from elementary school to graduate school. A popular lesson in the study of drawing is a linear-based technique called contour drawing. The essence of this activity is to observe an object closely and draw its outline or contour. The conventional method for learning contour drawing is to use a sharp soft lead drawing pencil on newsprint. Contour drawing, though only one means of observation, is easily adapted to the creative power of the computer. Figure 6.10 shows a typical contour drawing session with a computer.

Computer drawing programs do a spectacular job with lines. The artist can choose color, width, pen shape, and many other variations. Though fairly simple in concept, the most valuable goal of creating contour drawings is to increase the power of observation as opposed to creating a pretty drawing. Simply put, the process is based on the idea that drawing is seeing. Taking that position as a conceptual framework, follow these steps to practice making contour drawings on a computer:

1. Find a comfortable, well-lit location. Position the computer so that it does not obstruct the view of the artist.
2. Place a common object a few feet away from the computer in an easy-to-see location. Common objects may include a chair, a table, a large lamp, a shoe, a person, or a computer—in other words, virtually anything that can be seen well by the computer artist. Generally, a human-made object works best for contour drawing because of its hard, definitive edges.

Distortion is OK. That is what gives this method its visual interest.

While drawing, try not to look at the monitor. Concentrate on the subject.

FIGURE 6.10   Contour Drawing on the Computer

3. Select a drawing tool—a mouse or a graphics tablet. Open the paint software to a large white, blank "canvas." For starters and simplicity, choose a medium-width black line such as a 4 to 6 point. Choose a paint brush or a pencil. Some software has both choices.

4. Because the essence of drawing, in any medium, is seeing and observing, choose a starting point on the chair, for example. Look at the blank canvas and choose a starting point for the drawing.

5. While intently observing the chair, imagine touching it with a finger while moving along the edges from the starting points of the lines. While doing so, move the mouse or pen along the edges of the chair. Try to keep your focus on the object, not on your drawing. Though it is extremely difficult, try looking at the screen only when you are selecting a starting point for each line. The

drawing will be distorted if this procedure is adhered to. But a drawing is not the point; the point is observation and coordination of the mouse or pen with the eyes.

6. Continue selecting starting points. "Feel" the outline of the object while moving the mouse or pen. Avoid looking at the screen. Concentrate on the subject. Continue this process till the object is complete and the result is an outline representation of the object.

Contour drawings created in this way are often very quirky or odd yet remarkable. The value of this exercise is that the power of observation is reinforced. Thus, virtually anyone, even those who claim they cannot draw, can learn to make respectable contour drawings in this manner. These skills in turn are useful in multimedia applications. With more experience, the artist should eventually find a satisfactory balance between looking at the screen and looking at the object. Thus, the control of the mouse or pen increases while the distortion of the drawings decreases. Just a little practice with this Drawing 101 lesson, mixed with a basic understanding of multimedia software, expands the creative and expressive repertoire.

Now what can one do with the drawings? They may have many possible uses:

1. They may simply be freestanding works of art. Print the better ones and display them. Make a class gallery of computer contour drawings or individual one-person shows of contour drawings.
2. They may replace clip art, especially if the multimedia designers prefer to work with original and unique art. This, of course, is a personal preference of the media designers.
3. They may be imported into a multitude of graphics and multimedia software for editing and modification for use on web pages.
4. When combined in a sequence of other contour drawings, they may be used for creating animated GIFs, *QuickTime* movies, or Shockwave movies.
5. They may be collected and saved as a class clip art collection.
6. Finally, they may be deleted, having served their purpose of reinforcing the powers of observation.

In summation, the contour drawing is fundamental to artistic expression in general and multimedia design and production in particular. A contour drawing may have a life of its own as a freestanding work of art, or it may form the basis of a digital multimedia product. Virtually anyone can learn to make competent and usable contour drawings if willing to concentrate and observe. The next section describes a cousin of the contour drawing, the gesture drawing.

Gesture Drawing

The tools and setup for this type of drawing are the same as for contour drawing. An additional necessity is a human model. If this activity is used with a class, class members can take turns modeling for each other. Figure 6.11 shows a gesture drawing setup.

Look at the
shape, not at
the screen.

FIGURE 6.11   Gesture Drawing on the Computer

Whereas contour drawing is about observation, gesture drawing is about observation and suggestion. The fundamental nature of gesture drawing is the representation of motion. Artists often emphasize some aspect of the human form to suggest what that form is doing rather than what it looks like. A major application of this idea is the depiction or suggestion of action in a storyboard. To conduct this exercise:

1. Ask a student to model.
2. To warm up, have the model hold a pose that suggests or even exaggerates an action, such as in sports or dancing. The model should hold the pose for thirty seconds while the computer artists use their graphics software and their drawing tools to capture the essence of the pose in thirty seconds.

3. Repeat step 2 a desired number of times.
4. By necessity, the artists will have to draw very quickly in order to capture the model's actions, rather than the model's appearance. Using quick strokes or gestures suggests visual rhythm and energy. The drawings will not be of the subject but will be depicted in a few quick strokes of the mouse or pen what the subject is doing. Note that gesture drawing is not the same thing as the action lines that comic book and newspaper cartoonists use.

The first drawings generated by this exercise may look like very informal doodles. However, as the artists continue to observe, the drawings will become more refined.

Variations of this exercise may include longer poses, but not too long. The essence is speed and gesture. The resulting drawings represents the motion of the human form. As with contour drawing, this exercise is about observing.

Gesture drawing has its own peculiar and unique quality. Successful drawings make interesting visualizations of motion; thus they are excellent for planning animation. Again, as was true with contour drawings, gesture drawings are not about results. They are about capturing a moment by visualizing an action or motion.

The combination of these two exercises, contour and gesture, provides practice in using the drawing or painting tools in graphics applications. Contour drawings require patience and concentration. Gesture drawings require action and spontaneity for the model and the artist. Both require accurate observation and both are doable by anyone who wants to learn basic drawing skills. The drawings may have intrinsic value or they may simply serve as practice. Perhaps the most important purpose of these drawing lessons is to increase the power of observation, an essential skill in multimedia design and production. Another rationale for studying these methods is to show that anyone willing to learn some basic skills functions can then use the computer to make useful images.

ANIMATION EXERCISES AND PROJECTS

With just a few basic tools and software ranging from ordinary pencils to digital editing tools, teachers and their students can create lively and highly original animated products. This section describes projects using a variety of methods and materials. Some of the projects do not require any kind of camera. Some require only a computer and software. Other projects require a digital camcorder and digital editing software. Finally, several projects consist of a mixture of materials and methods.

Each animation exercise will be described in the following sequence:

1. Preproduction provides a conceptual framework, relevant supporting information, and materials needed for the project.
2. Production describes the steps required to make the item. This section also includes variations, suggestions, and construction tips and may be organized as Production 1, Production 2, and so on.
3. Postproduction includes items from editing to presentation.

Animation Project 1: The Zoetrope—The Wheel of Life

Preproduction

Concept.   Long before Winsor McCay's work and the motion picture machines of the American Thomas Edison and Louis Luminere of France, devices existed that allowed artists to create illusions of movement. One of the most popular and effective of these was the zoetrope (French for "wheel of life"). This elegantly simple toy consisted of a sequence of illustrations on a strip of paper. When placed in a rotating cylinder or drum with thin slots at regular intervals, the images appeared to move. The zoetrope is still a popular device with which to learn the basics of filmmaking, especially animated filmmaking. Making a nineteenth-century zoetrope with contemporary tools is a challenging and creative project and is an effective starting point to learn the complexities of multimedia production. A zoetrope can be made by hand or by simple computer graphics software, a dynamic mixing of the old with the new.

Materials.   The following items are needed to construct a drum in which to play the zoetrope:

1. A cylindrical box. A forty-two ounce oatmeal box with a flat bottom works well. Others that work with little or no modification are cardboard cylindrical ice cream boxes and peanut boxes. Note that some oatmeal boxes have an extended edge on the bottom and some are flat on the bottom. Use the flat-bottomed one.
2. A "player." This is an old record player or turntable or any device consisting of a spinning disk such as a potter's wheel or free-spinning lazy Susan.
3. A spray can of flat black paint.
4. A hobby knife with a fine sharp blade. For example, an excellent product is an X-Acto with blade number 11.
5. A protractor.

Optional Materials.   Depending on the type of zoetrope being made, choose from the following options:

1. A copier to copy blank zoetropes from this book.
2. A selection of number-two pencils and an assortment of felt-tipped pens of various widths and colors.
3. Scotch tape for taping zoetrope halves together.
4. For computer-drawn zoetropes, graphics software such as *AppleWorks, ClarisWorks, Photoshop,* and a color printer.
5. Other items that may be used to create zoetrope images are image scanners and digital cameras.

Production 1: Zoetrope Player

Figure 6.12 (pages 146–147) shows the anatomy of a typical zoetrope player that is easy to make by following these steps:

1. Obtain a 42-oz. flat-bottomed oatmeal box or a half-gallon ice cream container.
2. Cut the cylindrical box in two. Measure up three inches from the bottom and use a pen knife to cut around the circumference of the box.

3. Cut twelve equally spaced one-inch by one-quarter-inch vertical slots around the cylinder, each one inch from the bottom of the box, and at thirty-degree intervals from the others. Use a protractor to measure the degrees. Cut a small hole (one-quarter inch) in the center of the bottom.
4. Spray the box with cheap flat black spray paint inside and out, top and bottom. Set aside to dry.
5. Make a hole in the exact center of the drum. Be sure the size of the hole matches the size of your player's peg.
6. Place the zoetrope in the drum and spin.

Production 2: Zoetrope Images
There are many ways to make images for zoetropes—from number-two pencils to digital photography. No matter the image-making tools, the concept and process are the same. Zoetrope drawings are based on what animators describe as a cycle.

1 Obtain a forty-two-ounce flat-bottomed oatmeal box or a half-gallon ice cream container.

2 Measure up three inches from the bottom and cut evenly around the circumference.

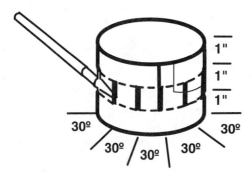

3 Use a pen knife and cut twelve evenly spaced one-inch by one-quarter-inch vertical slots at thirty-degree intervals around the box.

FIGURE 6.12   Zoetrope Player Construction

A cycle is a repeated sequence of drawings that link the first drawing of the cycle with the last drawing of the cycle. When the cycle is filmed or recorded over and over, the action is smooth and continuous. The primary advantage of cycles is that they work very well for repeating continuous actions such as running, rolling wheels, or bouncing balls. Making a successful zoetrope requires that the animator learn the concept of cycles. By doing so, the novice multimedia producer acquires a basic skill that works with all sorts of media from felt-tipped pens to computer animations and even to editing live action.

All that is needed to make a basic zoetrope are the simple materials listed previously. The following steps for producing a simple handmade zoetrope can be adapted as needed.

1. Make a copy of the zoetrope master in Figure 6.13. This blank zoetrope is designed to fit into the player drum described in the previous production step.

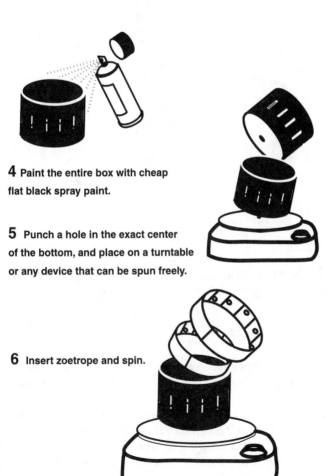

4 Paint the entire box with cheap flat black spray paint.

5 Punch a hole in the exact center of the bottom, and place on a turntable or any device that can be spun freely.

6 Insert zoetrope and spin.

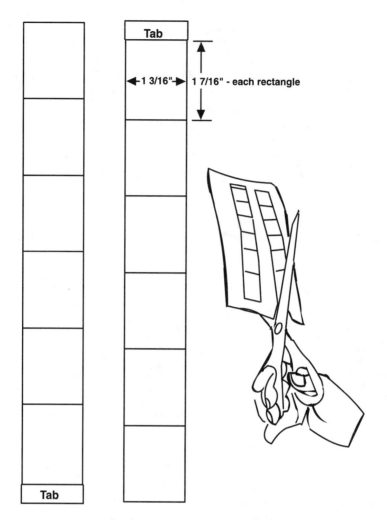

FIGURE 6.13   Zoetrope Master. This zoetrope master is designed to fit the oatmeal-box player of Figure 6.12. Draw horizontally in the frames.

2. After copying the zoetrope master, use a number-two pencil to lightly sketch out a cycle. Be inventive and do not hesitate to exaggerate. Simple ideas work best.

3. Outline the drawings with bold black lines. This helps the viewer see and follow the action while peering through the slots on the cylinder. Thick, solid dark lines, bold colors, and simple graphics and illustrations make the action easier to see. Be sure to use the full frame, and make your images as large as possible. Figure 6.14 shows this process.

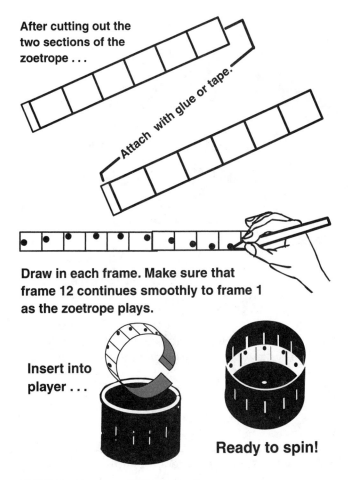

**After cutting out the
two sections of the
zoetrope . . .**

Attach with glue or tape.

**Draw in each frame. Make sure that
frame 12 continues smoothly to frame 1
as the zoetrope plays.**

**Insert into
player . . .**

Ready to spin!

FIGURE 6.14   Assembling a Zoetrope

4. Although color is not necessary to create a successful zoetrope, you may want to add color as accent. Use color sparingly. Generally, too much color obscures the action. Remember that the purpose of a zoetrope is to create an illusion of motion, not to display pretty pictures.
5. When the drawings are completed, tape the two six-frame sections together.
6. See Figure 6.15, and then place your zoetrope in the drum and spin!

These basic steps describe how to make a zoetrope with pencils, pens, and paper. However, other art options are adaptable to the basic production steps.

Computer Drawings.   Using simple computer graphics to make zoetropes has some major advantages. One template can be used over and over. Shapes and colors can

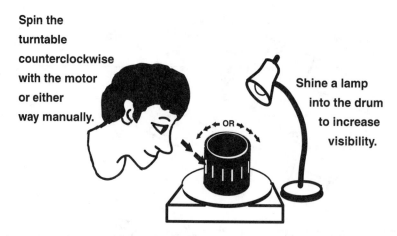

Spin the turntable counterclockwise with the motor or either way manually.

Shine a lamp into the drum to increase visibility.

OR

FIGURE 6.15   Viewing a Zoetrope

be manipulated extensively, thus encouraging experimentation. Computer graphics make very effective abstract or nonrepresentational forms. An inexpensive color printer makes the use of color very easy and effective. Computer-drawn images fit any style of drawing from detailed representational work to free-flowing dances of designs and colors. The basic steps previously presented can be modified for creating a computer zoetrope.

1. Use computer graphics software to draw a blank zoetrope master the same size as the master included in Figure 6.13. Make sure to save the master zoetrope template.
2. Use the software to draw or paint images in the twelve frames. Again, be inventive and do not hesitate to exaggerate. Simple ideas work best. Remember that draw programs create shapes that can be manipulated extensively, thus allowing the artist to move the shapes around and change their colors and sizes. Paint programs move pixels as if they were paint or ink, thus making them very good for freehand work, although the printed resolution will not be as sharp as with draw programs.
3. Print the completed zoetrope, cut it out, tape it together, place it in the drum, and spin.

Digital Images.   Digital and conventional photographs can be used to create interesting and very smooth zoetrope cycles. Interesting, creative, and effective zoetropes can be created using digital cameras. For example, placing a camera on a tripod and shooting a sequence of still images will make a smooth cycle when imported into the zoetrope master. Again, the basic construction steps apply.

1. Use a digital camera to shoot an animated cycle.
2. On your computer, open the zoetrope template drawing.
3. Insert a digital photo in each frame in the sequence they were shot. The photos will need to be resized to fit the dimensions of each zoetrope frame.

4. Print the zoetrope with its newly imported images.
5. Cut out the two parts and tape them together.
6. Place it in the drum and spin!

A variation of the preceding process is to use traditional photos shot with a conventional camera. After the photos have been processed and printed, scan them, save them, and import them into a computer graphic zoetrope template, and follow the same steps as for digital photographs.

Production 3: Ideas to Make a Zoetrope Come to Life

After learning how to make a player drum and zoetropes, consider the following ideas. Use imagination to alter, enhance, adapt, and improve these examples. Figure 6.16 is a set of five zoetrope possibilities.

1 Squash and stretch

2 Gravity—accelerate, decelerate

3 Human motion—from Eadweard Muybridge

4 Dancing graphics

5 Digital photographs

FIGURE 6.16   Sample Zoetropes

Follow the Bouncing and Squashing Ball.   When a ball bounces, it accelerates, decelerates, squashes, and stretches, all of which are used by animators to bring expression and life to their work. Making a ball bounce expressively with a zoetrope is an excellent way to learn about the lively possibilities of animation. Use the twelve-frame zoetrope 1 in Figure 6.16 as a model or guide to making a ball bounce.

Follow the Rolling Ball.   When a ball rolls up a hill, then down the other side, the motion is not constant. Gravity causes the ball—or roller coaster or car or truck—to accelerate rolling down, decelerate going up, and when reaching the peak, accelerate again going down. The cycle is repeated at the next hill. See zoetrope 2 in Figure 6.16 as a model or guide to animate the effects of gravity.

Walking and Running and Flipping.   One of the more challenging aspects of drawn animation is human and animal motion. This includes all kinds of two-legged and four-legged motion cycles for making characters walk, run, jump, skip, hop, and sneak. Making a human motion cycle that is lively and convincing is a very good introduction to basic character animation. There are a couple of excellent sources for models of human and animal movements that can be adapted to the individual styles of animators. These are Preston Blair's classic work *Cartoon Animation* and *The Human Figure in Motion* by Eadweard Muybridge. Zoetrope 3 in Figure 6.16 is a flipping man based on Muybridge's work.

Make a Choreography of Graphics.   There is a long tradition of abstract or nonrepresentational filmmaking. This idea works very well for making zoetropes that are seen as dances of shapes, color, and space. Further, making this kind of a zoetrope works well whether using a computer or pencils and pens. Of course, this is limited only by the animator's imagination, and this approach works well for people who are not comfortable with their representational rendering skills. Zoetrope 4 in Figure 6.16 is an example of this method.

A Rotating Object.   Using the digital photography method previously described, select an object, such as zoetrope 5, the toy car in Figure 6.16. This method is an interesting combination of stop motion combined with the principle of the zoetrope.

Postproduction: Playing a Zoetrope
Playing a zoetrope requires that the drum be placed on a device that spins freely. No matter the technique used to make zoetropes, they all are played the same way. Ideally, an old turntable works well. A motorized device also works as well as a manually operated one. The advantage of a manually spun one is that the zoetrope images can be designed to operate clockwise or counterclockwise. Also, a clip-on or gooseneck lamp shining into the drum helps illuminate the images, making them easier to view. Figure 6.15 shows a typical zoetrope setup.

Zoetrope Summary
The preceding ideas are simply starting points. Anything that can be drawn or photographed can be given life on a zoetrope, if one is creative and inventive. Making a

zoetrope has instructional and educational values. The maker is introduced to basic animation theory, technique, and skills that can be applied to the creation of motion in any digital medium. Further, making a successful zoetrope requires judgment, experimentation, and a willingness to try and retry. Finally, this activity encourages students to integrate old tools with new tools expressively and creatively.

Animation Project 2: The Flip Book—
Movies to Carry in Your Pocket

Another popular cameraless movie production technique is the flip book made up of stacks of cards and operated by the thumb. Figure 6.17 illustrates typical flip book configurations. Flip books come in countless variations. Although some flip books are published by artists and some by studios as feature tie-ins, most are homemade.

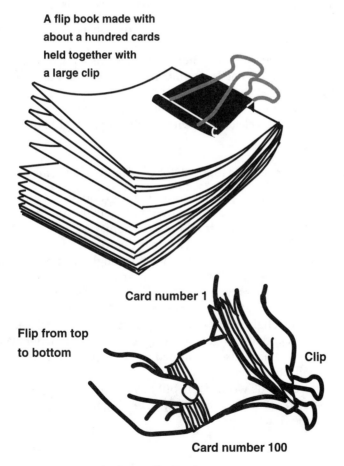

A flip book made with about a hundred cards held together with a large clip

Card number 1

Flip from top to bottom

Clip

Card number 100

FIGURE 6.17   Playing a Flip Book

Preproduction

Concept.   When making a flip book, the artist is creating a traditional form of animation called line animation. McCay's *Gertie the Dinosaur* was made with black ink lines on white cards, and contemporary animators use pencils and paper to design the artwork that will be the basis of big-budget studio animated features. By creating a flip book, the artist is exploring, experimenting with, and learning about the unlimited possibilities of the art of animation. As with the zoetrope, the artwork from a flip book can be digitized for use in computer moviemaking. The following section describes a simple method for constructing a flip book, which can easily be converted to animated computer graphics.

Materials.   Flip books are made with everything from little paper tablets to index cards. Even old books that are to be discarded can be used to make flip books. The following materials can be used to make the flip books described in this section. As with all projects in this book, there are many variations and adaptations. Figure 6.18 shows a sequence of flip book drawings on index cards.

1. Three- by five-inch unruled white index cards. Generally, a hundred-card pack works well for one flip book.
2. A large clip to hold the cards together while they are being flipped.
3. A selection of pens and pencils—number-two pencils and an assortment of felt-tipped pens—in varying widths and colors.
4. A light box for tracing—such as a photographic slide viewer, stage of an overhead projector, or a clear glass window during daylight hours.

Production

Follow these steps to make a basic flipbook for playing with a thumb.

1. Use the three by five unruled index cards and draw on them vertically. Use a number-two lead pencil to lightly draw rough versions on the cards. Most flip books are designed to play from top to bottom.
2. Place the cards on a light box for tracing in order to establish the correct relationships between drawings. That is, tracing through the index cards allows the animator to register the drawings in order to maintain consistent sizes and positions. A clear glass with an exterior view works well too. Remember when tracing to line up all corners and edges of the cards. With either the light box or window, light number-two pencil lines are easy to see.
3. Flip the cards back and forth while working to preview the action. When satisfied with the movement, use felt-tipped pens to color each card. Use color economically, yet expressively.
4. Around a hundred cards works well, but fewer will work depending on the desired action. After creating a smoothly operating flip book, use a large clip to combine all the cards.

Postproduction

As with the zoetrope, there are limitless variations. Further, the individual cards of the flip book are ready for converting individual digital images for use in creating

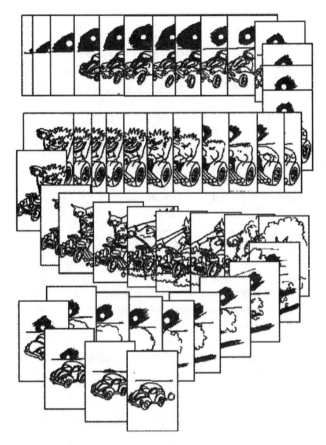

**FIGURE 6.18   Flip Book Made with Three by Five
Unruled Index Cards**

animated GIFs. Creating a flip book is a quick yet very effective way to learn to animate. Skills and practice derived from making flip books can be carried over into
working with computer animation software. In particular, creating a flip book can
be the first step in producing animation for multimedia products and web pages.

Animation Project 3: Drawing the Line—Animated GIFs

A GIF (graphical interchange format) is a graphics file used on web pages mostly for
artwork—drawings, computer graphics, and various illustrations. An animated GIF
consists of a series of still GIF images placed in a sequence by special GIF-building
software. The animated GIF plays when placed on a web page or in multimedia production software. These silent animations most often appear as decorations, design
elements, visual accents, or even animated bullets. The following section will
describe ways to create art for animated GIFs for use as stand-alone movies, web
page elements, or components to be used with other multimedia software.

Preproduction

Concept.   GIF-building software is relatively inexpensive and can be downloaded from the World Wide Web from a number of sites. Some GIF-building programs are inexpensive shareware, some are from software companies, and a few are free-ware. An example of an excellent one for PCs is *Ulead GIF Animator.* With this par-ticular GIF builder and others, the animator can import many types of digital images, place them in any desired sequence, and designate frame rates, loops, and so on. Also, many video effects are available to use as transitions between images. Having a good GIF builder is like having a little animation studio in the computer that provides a practical and inexpensive way to learn about animation. There are several popular multimedia production and graphics editing software that contain animated GIF-building capability. Three popular examples are *Paintshop Pro, Adobe Photoshop,* and *Macromedia Flash.* Of course, some GIF builders are simple and oth-ers are more sophisticated. Some animated GIFs may consist of just a few drawings that cycle continuously, and others may contain many images created by a variety of methods that tell a story or express an idea. Animated GIFs may also be saved, exported, and/or converted to a variety of movie files. Many animated GIFs can be found in clip art collections, and some free ones are available on the World Wide Web. However, making your own has special satisfaction and provides an excel-lent opportunity to further exploit the computer as a creative and expressive tool.

Materials.   Most images that can be created and saved as graphics files can be used to make animated GIFs. These are some materials that will be needed:

1. A desktop or laptop computer, but not necessarily the biggest and most pow-erful because making small animated GIFs does not require a lot of memory and storage space.
2. GIF-building software as described previously.
3. Digitizing resources such as a scanner, a digital camera, and graphics soft-ware. These are necessary to convert images to individual still image GIF files that can be placed in the GIF builder and exported as an animated GIF, for example, scanning the cards of the flip book described in the previous proj-ect. Some GIF builders will accept many kinds of files, such as PICT, TIFF, and JPEG, and convert them within the software.
4. Drawing and painting resources—graphics software, index cards, pencils, felt-tipped pens. Art for animated GIFs can be made with many types of media.

Production 1: Animated GIFs from Handmade, Digitized Art

Begin exploring the capability of this simple computer animation method by fol-lowing, adapting, or modifying these steps to create animated GIFs from hand-drawn art:

1. Use index cards to draw an animated cycle, as with a zoetrope, or an ani-mated sequence as with the flip book.

2. Convert the art to digital images. Using a flatbed scanner, scan and save each card as a graphic file, being careful to place, or register, each one in exactly the same position, for example, in a corner. Scan each card at 72 to 96 dpi, exactly as it will appear in the completed animated GIF.

3. When the images are scanned and saved, following the procedures specified by the animated GIF-building software, insert, import, or cut and paste them into the GIF-building software. If necessary, use a graphic editing program such as *Photoshop* to modify, crop, or resize the scanned images. Remember that the frames' dimensions must all be the same.

4. Manipulate the images using the animated GIF builder's features. The animator now has a great amount of control over the images: frames per second, cuts, dissolves, fades, image manipulation, and others. Try and retry. Save several versions. All GIF builders share some basic functions. Explore features and operating instructions by referring to tutorials that are included with the software.

5. Save the movie as a conventional GIF file. Depending on the software, the movie can be optimized for use in a web page. If many images are scanned (one hundred or more), through trial and error, the animator may decide to use only half of them, such as every other one, thus achieving a smooth movement with a smaller file size. Also, an animated GIF can be converted to movie formats such as *QuickTime* for further editing with sound.

6. Treat the animated GIFs exactly as GIFs when placing them in web pages.

Figure 6.19 summarizes the preceding steps.

Production 2: Animated GIFs from Computer Graphics
Another task closely related to the preceding project is to create animated GIFs using computer graphics software. Instead of drawing and scanning, the animator uses graphics software to draw or paint the images. Create an image, save it, change the image or create another one, save it, change it again, save it, change again, save it, and so on until you have built a sequence of images to place into a GIF builder by inserting or pasting. Here are the necessary steps, also illustrated in Figure 6.20.

1. Open a graphics software program, such as *ClarisWorks Drawing.*

2. Draw a series of squares—between six and twelve works well—about one-by one-inch square. These will be the frames of the animated GIF movie. From the center of each square, a series of smaller squares were drawn, each a little larger. If creating a cycling motion, design the graphics so that frame 1 smoothly follows frame 12—or the last frame of the cycle—and begins the cycle over.

3. Select frame 1 (it may need to be grouped if using a draw program). Copy it, and paste it in the first frame of a GIF builder.

4. Copy frame 2 and paste in the GIF builder. Continue this sequence until all frames are complete.

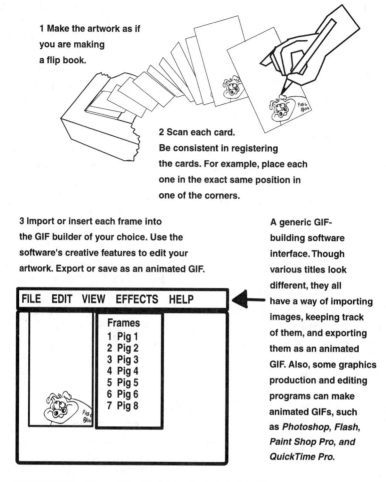

1 Make the artwork as if you are making a flip book.

2 Scan each card. Be consistent in registering the cards. For example, place each one in the exact same position in one of the corners.

3 Import or insert each frame into the GIF builder of your choice. Use the software's creative features to edit your artwork. Export or save as an animated GIF.

A generic GIF-building software interface. Though various titles look different, they all have a way of importing images, keeping track of them, and exporting them as an animated GIF. Also, some graphics production and editing programs can make animated GIFs, such as *Photoshop*, *Flash*, *Paint Shop Pro*, and *QuickTime Pro*.

FILE   EDIT   VIEW   EFFECTS   HELP

Frames
1 Pig 1
2 Pig 2
3 Pig 3
4 Pig 4
5 Pig 5
6 Pig 6
7 Pig 8

FIGURE 6.19   From Flip Book to Animated GIF

5. When the images have been copied and pasted consecutively into the GIF builder, save the movie as an animated GIF that can be exported to other software or placed onto a web page. Set the movie to loop.

This process demonstrates the possibility of using simple, inexpensive software to create lively designs that will add color and interest to web pages. For these tasks, all that was needed was basic GIF-building software and drawing or painting graphics software. Even with the limitations of these resources, the animated possibilities are endless.

Postproduction

Simple is better. The animated GIF, though a staple of the World Wide Web, is intended to be a simple and easy way to create animated images for web pages.

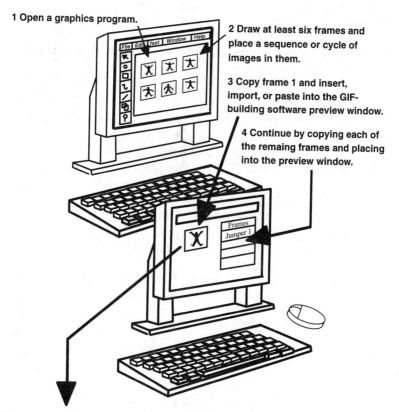

1 Open a graphics program.

2 Draw at least six frames and place a sequence or cycle of images in them.

3 Copy frame 1 and insert, import, or paste into the GIF-building software preview window.

4 Continue by copying each of the remaing frames and placing into the preview window.

5 Use the GIF-building software to arrange, rearrange, or edit the sequence of images. For a repeating cycle, set the GIF to loop. Save the animated GIF for use with other multimedia software.

FIGURE 6.20   The Basic Steps for Producing Simple Animated GIFs

Therefore, most animated GIFs are very small and are intended mainly for decoration or entertainment. However, longer animated GIFs with lots of effects can be made and exported for the addition of sound and other elements. Animated GIFs can also become elements of more sophisticated productions using software such as *Flash.* The major advantage of the animated GIF is its simplicity. In fact, making a number of little animated GIFs is an easy and fun way to learn about animation.

Animation Project 4: Direct Animation— Making Your Marks on Film

Direct animation is a somewhat unusual animation method, but some accomplished animation artists have made stunning movies with it, the most notable being Norman McLaren. He worked directly on clear 35mm motion picture stock. His best-known work of the direct method is the short film *Hen Hop.*

Preproduction

Concept.   Simply stated, direct animation is the process of marking directly on the film by either drawing on clear leader or scratching on black leader.

Materials.   All that is needed for making this kind of movie is the following:

1. Clear or black film leader, either 16mm or 35mm depending on the process. Leader may be purchased in 1,000-foot spools for around $30 for clear or black. One source is RTI and the web address is www.discchek.com.
2. Some permanent fine point felt-tipped pens for clear leader or some fine pointed scratching tools for black leader.
3. A 16mm projector for projection or funds for a film-to-tape transfer for either 16mm or 35mm film. Video postproduction companies can transfer film formats to any video format, analog or digital.
4. A film splicer and splicing tape. This is a handy tool, though not crucial.

Production

Review Figure 6.7 (page 136). Figure 6.21 illustrates the process of playing a direct movie. After acquiring the leader, follow these steps:

1. Draw on the clear leader with the permanent felt-tipped pens. When doing this as a class or group activity, cut the film into strips of about three feet each and give each participant a strip. In order to maintain a correct orientation for the projector, draw with the sprocket holes to the left. Begin on frame 1, which will be the top frame.
2. There are two basic approaches to marking on the film.
   - One is to work frame by frame in the blank area between the sprocket holes. Imagine a line running horizontally across the leader as if it were coming out of the sprocket hole. Drawing frame by frame can be tedious, but this method captures the essence of animation as consisting of multiple still images.
   - Another choice is to make arbitrary marks and designs directly on the leader without regard to individual frames. For example, draw a long vertical line that may run the full length of the film.
3. If the leader is transferred to a video format, edit it using digital editing software and processes described elsewhere in this book.

Postproduction

Direct animation onto film leader is a creative procedure resulting in a movie that is spontaneous, energetic, and fun to watch. Further, the animators see the film grow as they work frame by frame, thus experiencing the nature of moviemaking. Because of the necessity of drawing very small images, direct animation is usually a dance of nonrepresentational shapes and colors. The primitiveness of this process is its strength, and the visual energy of the constant fluctuation is its appeal. A direct movie makes a dynamic presentation when projected on a large screen in a dark room, especially with energetic music playing on an audio CD.

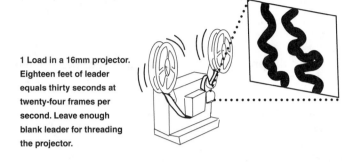

1 Load in a 16mm projector. Eighteen feet of leader equals thirty seconds at twenty-four frames per second. Leave enough blank leader for threading the projector.

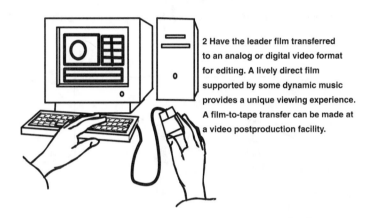

2 Have the leader film transferred to an analog or digital video format for editing. A lively direct film supported by some dynamic music provides a unique viewing experience. A film-to-tape transfer can be made at a video postproduction facility.

FIGURE 6.21   Direct Film Projection and Postproduction

Animation Project 5: Motion from Still Images—A Rotating Portrait

Although scanned hand-drawn art makes very effective animated GIFs, digital photos provide a live-action alternative. Using a common digital still camera or a still photo function on a digital camcorder, one can take a series of pictures, place them in sequence, and animate them.

Preproduction
Concept.   If done well and creatively, the effect of this technique is similar to the traditional animation method called pixilation, as described earlier in this chapter.

Materials.   Items needed for this exercise are similar to those of previous projects:

1. A digital camera to shoot a sequence or cycle of portraits. Another possibility is to use a conventional camera and scan prints or have a disk made when they are processed.

2. A tripod for the firm camera support that is crucial for this exercise.
3. A computer with graphics software with animation capability.

Production

Figure 6.22 illustrates the process of using a digital still camera to make animated GIFs.

1. Place a camera on a tripod. Frame a model. Either a close-up or a wide shot will do. Select a simple, uncluttered background and a space with even lighting.
2. Have a model or subject provide a series of poses, holding each pose long enough to shoot one still picture—pose, shoot, pose, shoot, pose, shoot, and so forth. For example, have the model rotate thirty degrees clockwise, take a picture, rotate thirty degrees clockwise, take a picture. Continue until twelve pictures have been made.

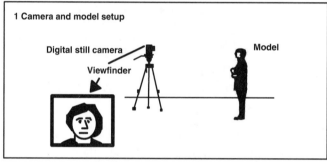

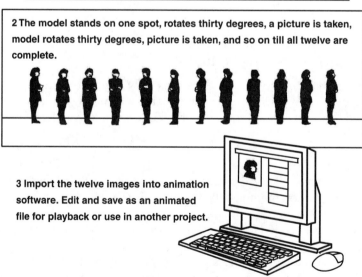

FIGURE 6.22   A Rotating Portrait

3. If using a digital camera, simply import the images into a GIF builder, or if photographic prints were made, scan those and import them into the GIF-building software. When the photos are the software, animate them using several features such as frame rate, loops, video effects, and filters. If done carefully, the subject will appear to rotate smoothly over and over.

Postproduction

The possibilities for making this kind of animated GIF are unlimited. For example, a series of still images of an erupting geyser can be used to create an animated GIF that simulates the eruption. Remember that graphics, especially large ones, use a lot of memory. Therefore, this project and its variations will work better with smaller images, for example, three by five inches or smaller.

Animation Project 6: Constructing and Operating an Animation Stand for a Digital Camera

Historically, animation was made with motion picture cameras using either 16mm or 35mm film. These cameras were capable of exposing one frame at a time. Thus, an animator could place a drawing under the camera and expose one frame, which was usually one-twenty-fourth of a second, remove it, place another picture, expose a frame, and so on. This resulted in twenty-four pictures or frames per second. When projected, the movement of the film through a projector gave the still pictures an illusion of motion. Some animators shot two frames per drawing, thus cutting in half the number needed to achieve smooth motion. The animation stands could be very simple, consisting of a camera mounted on some kind of photographic copy stand, or they could be very complex and as tall as a two-story building to allow for a lot of camera movement. This was the primary production method used by the major studios such as Walt Disney and Max Fleischer. Simpler setups were used by independent filmmakers, such as a 16mm camera mounted on a makeshift animation stand of some sort. Even in the digital era, creating animated movies on "real" film is still very common and popular because film has a special aesthetic quality that appeals to media producers.

Preproduction

Concept. In the traditional method, after the film was exposed in the animation camera, it was processed and then went through the complex sequence of editing, matching, and release printing resulting in a cartoon or a movie reel. Even though film animation is still common, the film is usually transferred to a digital or high-end analog video format for editing. This is much less expensive and far more flexible because a digitally edited master can be converted to any media format from small files for use on the World Wide Web to videocassettes and DVDs. Producing an animated film using original artwork and a camera is thus expensive and complex. Although its form is relatively simple, creating hundreds of drawings for even a very short film takes a long attention span and a serious commitment of time and effort.

That is why most school students never have the opportunity, or desire, to try this unique art form. Most are content to sit and watch animation in a theater or on television. There are those, however, who want to *create* animated films, and the growing quantity and quality of digital media production tools makes this possible. More than likely, these students have been inspired or stimulated by the animation they have seen in the mass media—music videos, television programs, the World Wide Web, television commercials, computer animation, video games, and feature films.

Materials.   Creating an animation stand for use with a digital video camera is very simple, requiring just a few basic items. Figure 6.23 illustrates two popular methods for improvising animation stands.

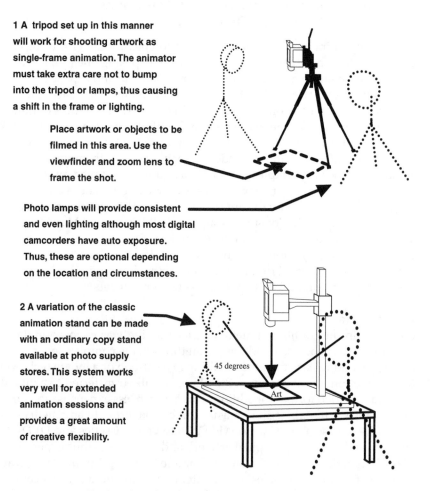

1 A tripod set up in this manner will work for shooting artwork as single-frame animation. The animator must take extra care not to bump into the tripod or lamps, thus causing a shift in the frame or lighting.

Place artwork or objects to be filmed in this area. Use the viewfinder and zoom lens to frame the shot.

Photo lamps will provide consistent and even lighting although most digital camcorders have auto exposure. Thus, these are optional depending on the location and circumstances.

2 A variation of the classic animation stand can be made with an ordinary copy stand available at photo supply stores. This system works very well for extended animation sessions and provides a great amount of creative flexibility.

45 degrees

Art

FIGURE 6.23   Two Animation Stands for Digital Animation

1. A digital camcorder with a "photo" or "digital still" feature. Most digital camcorders have this function but some models do not. In fact, the digital still function may actually be a several-second recording of a frozen image. Some digital camcorders have a true single-frame function. Very few analog camcorders have this feature. A digital still camera will work although its image-storing capacity will be much less than that of a digital camcorder.

2. A set of photo lamps is helpful. However, any evenly lit location in which the stand can be placed will work. The photo lamps provide more control. Experimentation and camera testing are the best ways to achieve a successful setup.

3. A sturdy tripod. The most fundamental way is to mount the camera on a very sturdy tripod and simply frame the artwork through the viewfinder. This will work by placing the artwork or stage on the floor and setting up the tripod to shoot down at it. Also, placing the artwork on a wall or bulletin board will work. The setup of the tripod and camera in relation to the artwork depends on the nature of the project. Whichever way is chosen, an evenly lit surface for the artwork is crucial for obtaining quality results. Digital camcorders have automatically adjusting exposures, but exposures may also be set manually.

4. Copy stand. The best way to improvise a digital camcorder animation stand is to use a common photographic copy stand. Some of these come with mounted lights. This tool is a routine item found in most educational media centers or photographic labs. The camera mounts to the copy stand parallel to the surface or stage. The artwork is then positioned for filming. The camera's viewfinder and the copy stand's column can be adjusted to fit the art's format. Remember that the artwork will appear upside down to the camera operator when oriented correctly to the camera. An inexpensive pair of hardware utility lights works well for achieving an evenly lit surface.

5. A registration system. For smooth action, it is crucial that the sequence of cards or paper need to be registered consistently. (Figure 6.25, p. 169, illustrates two methods for registering artwork: one made from poster board and one that uses a peg bar.)

6. A computer equipped with digital editing software. Make sure the computer is capable of importing and storing digital video.

Having set up or improvised an animation stand, anything that can be placed on the stage under the camera can be animated, including drawings on index cards, punched bond animation paper, cutout characters, collages, and objects.

Production
Whether using a tripod or a copy stand, the most important consideration is that the camera's lens be exactly parallel to the working surface. When taping artwork, a sturdy mount is crucial. Here are the steps for operating an improvised animation stand:

1. Using the copy stand's or tripod's adjustments along with the zoom lens, frame the work surface through either the LCD viewfinder or the eyepiece.

2. Place a piece of the artwork under the camera and adjust it in the frame. (The next project describes ways to register the art from frame to frame, thus maintaining a smooth flow of animation.)
3. Check the light on the working surface. If using photo lamps, place one on each side of the surface at forty-five-degree angles. An evenly lit taping or recording surface is vital to achieving high-quality results.
4. Note that the correct orientation of the artwork to the camera will be upside down to the camera operator.

Setting up and adjusting the camcorder for animating artwork requires experimentation. While setting up, shoot a few frames and preview them using the VCR function.

Postproduction

The major advantage of this process is that the animation artists and camera operators, usually one and the same, have a real animation experience. The experience of creating artwork and "filming" (taping) it on an animation stand is the essence of animated movie production. Another advantage is that the animators can see their own highly personal work come to life. Handmade artwork is unique to each animator's style. In addition, the animators will be working with and manipulating real physical images with a variety of materials that they can touch and see. This method is an ideal mixture of animation history and tradition with the considerable creative and production advantages of digital production technologies.

Even a basic animation stand will provide an opportunity to explore all sorts of animation methods and techniques. In particular, using a digital camcorder stand is essentially the same filming method that animators have been using for almost a century. Of course, the technology is radically different. Usually, an animation stand is ideal for working with "traditional" materials such as paper, pencils, paint, felt-tipped pens, magazine cutouts, ink, or most any flat artwork. The next section describes basic animation projects using a sturdily mounted camera and simple art materials. These ideas and techniques reinforce the merger of time-honored animation practices with the practical and creative possibilities of digital media production technology.

Animation Project 7: Crossing Index Cards with a Digital Video Camera

The concept and process of line animation as a production method was introduced in earlier projects dealing with zoetropes, flip books, and animated GIFs. Line animation consists of making complete drawings usually on cards or bond paper in sequence and registration and then photographing each with a film or digital camcorder.

Preproduction

Concept.   Line animation is usually thought of as being useful mostly for planning and designing the "rough" artwork that will be cleaned up and converted to transparent "cels" (acetate) for filming. Over the years, and with an increased interest in independent filmmaking, line animation has become an accepted technique in and of itself. The special aesthetic quality and the possibilities of creating visually exciting animation with relatively inexpensive materials have made this technique especially popular with independent filmmakers and students. Two inexpensive methods for students to learn animation while producing their own films are to use five- by eight-inch index cards or specially punched animation paper. Figure 6.24 shows how index card movies are filmed.

Materials.   These materials are readily available, inexpensive, and the index cards are just thin enough to trace through because each drawing will need to be placed in relationship to the previous one.

1. Five- by eight-inch unruled index cards. This is a good, practical size that films or tapes very well. Nine- by twelve-inch Acme punched bond animation paper with Acme peg bars also works well. This more expensive option adds flexibility and ease of filming. The paper is available from Cartoon Colour in 500-sheet packets.

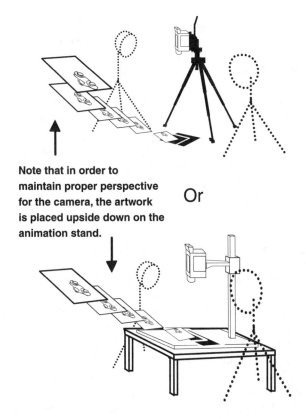

Note that in order to maintain proper perspective for the camera, the artwork is placed upside down on the animation stand.

Or

FIGURE 6.24   Taping Line Art on Index Cards with a Digital Camcorder

2. An assortment of pencils and pens will be needed.
3. Light boxes or a room with windows.
4. Black matte board to construct a registration board.
5. A digital camcorder and copy stand or a tripod.
6. A computer with digital editing software.

Production
Use the unruled index cards to, in effect, make a flip book. Draw on a horizontal format to match the aspect ratio of the camera. Work toward the center of the cards to provide some framing margins when the cards are shot on the animation stand.

1. Draw lightly with a number-two pencil to work out the animation and drawings. Remember that the more drawings you make, the smoother the animated motion will be. As a rule of thumb, think of creating 15 drawings for 1 second of video. So, for a 10-second animated movie, make 150 drawings. Also remember that animators often repeat artwork in cycles and some hold a shot or picture for several frames, especially for titles or written information. As was suggested with flip book construction, to enhance tracing, hold the cards against a window while drawing, use a light box or the stage of an overhead projector.
2. Maintain registration from card to card by simply laying one card on another. For shooting index cards, a simple registration device should be constructed out of black matte board and taped down firmly for filming the art. Any material or variation will work as long as the artwork maintains registration during filming.
3. The traditional method for line animation is to use specially punched tracing paper or bond paper. The punches in the paper are designed for placing over pegs that keep the artwork positioned correctly. The punched bond paper comes in nine by twelve 500-sheet packages and plastic peg bars can be purchased very inexpensively from Cartoon Colour (www.cartooncolour.com). They are ideal for creating line animation. The peg bar can be taped to the animation or copy stand, and each punched sheet placed on the pegs and filmed or recorded. This process makes a very nice line animation.

When working with school students for limited periods of time, it may be impractical to expect them to produce hundreds of drawings for an animated movie lasting just a few seconds. Therefore, in either the shooting phase or the editing phase, experiment with fewer frames per second. Also, frame rate options vary depending on a camera's features. For example, some digital cameras, when set in the still photo mode, will record several seconds of an image. In this case, the frame rate of the animation can be chosen at the editing phase by simply deleting the excess frames. This may seem awkward and time-consuming but is a very effective way to create digital animated movies. Further, some digital camcorders, as mentioned previously, have a single-frame option, though in reality the camera may record six frames, or about one-fifth of a second. No matter the features of the camera, from basic to sophisticated, the purpose is to record individual pieces of art. When edited, this artwork can be manipulated in many ways in order to create an animated movie.

Postproduction

This technique is a merging of the old and the new. The old being the process of making a movie by hand one picture at a time. Traditionally, the completed artwork was then filmed on motion picture film stock in a 16mm or 35mm camera. This was an expensive and time-consuming process, although the results could be very impressive.

The new part of this process is how the movie is filmed and edited. Chapter 5 presented skills and processes for making and editing digital live-action movies. Most of the process for animation is the same, the major difference being how the images are created.

Another consideration for creating line animation is registering the artwork in order to be consistent from frame to frame. Animators use several methods for this. For an index card film, making a simple copy board out of black poster board works well. The best way to describe the steps in this process is by following the illustrations in Figure 6.25.

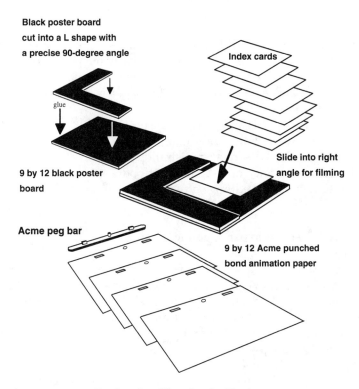

FIGURE 6.25   Registering Line Art for Taping

Learning the skills of animation is an intensely hands-on process, which can be accomplished in many ways. There are books such as *The Animator's Survival Kit* by Richard Williams and *Cartoon Animation* by master animator Preston Blair. Some group activities can also enhance the process of learning animation. The following exercises are adaptations of some group projects that are used to teach animation. No matter the materials, tools, or resources from 16mm film to digital video to *Toy Story*, bringing life to animated movies requires practice. The following project ideas require an animation stand such as the one described previously or a tripod for stop motion animation.

Animation Project 8: Linear Portraits

Preproduction

Concept. This project is a popular animation activity based on the use of index cards. It is similar to the process of creating a flip book described previously in this chapter. Be sure that the artwork is created horizontally in order to have a similar frame ratio as the camera's viewfinder. Refer to Figure 6.26 to get a visual idea of how this project works.

Materials. Because this is a variation of line animation as described in Project 7, the same materials will be used:

1. Five- by eight-inch unruled index cards. This is a good, practical size that films or tapes very well. Nine- by twelve-inch Acme punched bond animation paper with Acme peg bars also works well. This more expensive option adds flexibility and ease of filming. The paper is available from Cartoon Colour in 500-sheet packets.
2. An assortment of pencils and pens will be needed.
3. Light boxes or a room with windows.
4. Black matte board to construct a registration board.
5. A digital camcorder and copy stand or a tripod.
6. A computer with digital editing software.

Production

Follow or adapt these steps in participating in this project.

1. Each participant draws a simple line or contour portrait of each of the other participants. These drawings become the key frames for this animation project.
2. Draw "in-betweens" on additional cards between the key frames. These in-between drawings are used to create transitions from one key frame portrait to the next. For example, portrait 1 key frame drawing is followed by six drawings that gradually change to portrait 2 key frame drawing, followed by six drawings that gradually change to portrait 3 key frame drawing, followed by six drawings, and so on until the whole set is complete. Continue through all the portraits.

FIGURE 6.26 Linear Portraits

3. After completing the desired number of drawings, set up a digital video camera and a registration system on an animation stand, or set up a sturdy tripod in a way that allows framing the artwork. Make a registration device for the cards as illustrated in Figure 6.25 and tape it down. Use the zoom lens to crop the artwork.

4. Place a card under the camera, record it, place the next one, record it, place the next one, record it, and so on until all of the cards have been recorded. This process requires concentration and extra care in not moving or hitting the animation stand or tripod while recording. Recording or filming depends on the capabilities of the digital camera as described in previous sections. Some are able to record a true single frame while others record several frames

and still others have a still photo option that records several seconds of a frozen image. No matter how the frames are recorded, digital editing software will allow numerous combinations of speed or delay time per frame and multiple use of the same images.

Postproduction

The following steps will bring the portraits to life:

1. Connect the camcorder to a multimedia computer and import the filmed artwork. Depending on how the cards were recorded, the pictures may not need much editing though even basic digital editing software allows unlimited creative possibilities.
2. For this project, digital transitions may be needed only for the beginning and ending because the purpose of this activity is to draw the transitions or morphs. Edit all of the participant's movies together, thus making a class or group film that can be exported in a number of formats.
3. Add sound effects and music. There are many sources for free digital sounds that work with editing software. They can be downloaded from the World Wide Web, digital sound libraries can be purchased for digital editing, or sounds may be recorded with a digital camera or through the computer. Sound quality and sound design are crucial for animation so be creative in choosing sound. To be effective, music and effects can be done very simply.

This project is valuable because it introduces the participants to the fundamental animation concept of key frame drawings and in-between drawings. This concept is especially important to understand because some important computer-based animation software, such as *Flash*, is based on this concept. As with any animation project, the variations of this activity are endless and may be adapted to selected audiences, available resources, and educational goals.

Drawing faces on index cards, drawing transitions between those faces, using a digital camcorder to record them in sequence, and using digital editing software to make a complete movie are the major animation steps, from start to finish. Building on these experiences, the participants can conceptualize, plan, and produce many variations of the process.

Animation Project 9: Moving Abstractions

Preproduction

Concept.   Successful and visually interesting movies do not necessarily need to be produced with slickly rendered drawings. Dancing shapes and colors choreographed in time and space and accompanied by synchronized sounds and music can be visually exciting to watch and fun to produce. A successful abstract or nonobjective film is based on one of the more important elements of animation—rhythm. For example, draw a shape in the center of a card or paper. Then make twelve additional drawings making the shape evolve into another design or object.

That object can then evolve in twelve different drawings back to the original shape. This process is then repeated with additional drawings; the result is a shape that evolves into something else in one second, changes back to a square in one second, and then the process is repeated over and over with unlimited possibilities of objects, shapes, or designs. A film produced this way will have a pleasing pace or rhythm. Figure 6.27 illustrates a rhythmic pattern.

There are endless variations of this concept such as using computer animation software, or scanning the drawings and placing them in animation software such as GIF builders. Another variation would be simply to begin drawing with no particular idea or place to go. Just let the move come to you, so to speak.

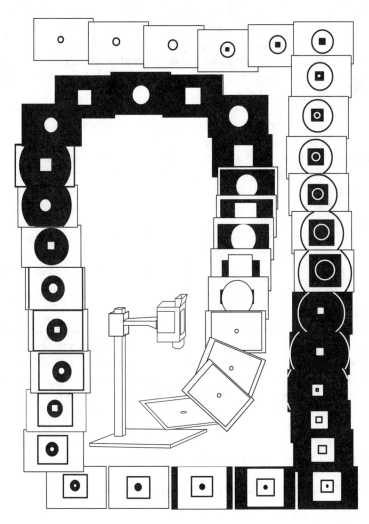

FIGURE 6.27   **An Abstract Movie**

Materials.   This project requires the same materials as the previous project:

1. Five- by eight-inch unruled index cards or nine- by twelve-inch Acme punched bond animation paper with Acme peg bars.
2. An assortment of pencils and pens will be needed.
3. Light boxes or a room with windows.
4. Black matte board to construct a registration board.
5. A digital camcorder and copy stand or a tripod.

Production
Follow these steps:

1. Begin by drawing a simple outline shape on the first card. Draw it lightly with a pencil. Also, begin numbering the cards. A small, very lightly written number in the lower right corner works well. This is especially important as the number of cards begins to swell.
2. Draw exactly the same shape in the same location on card 13. Cards 1 and 13 are called "key frames" because these frames contain starting and stopping points of complete actions.
3. On the eleven cards between 1 and 13, make drawings that cause the shape on card 1 to change radically but smoothly into other shapes, then change smoothly back to the first shape.
4. Follow this process for the desired number of seconds for a movie. For example, a ten-second movie made this way would consist of one basic shape pulsating, changing, dancing yet every twelve frames returning to the starting shape.
5. After creating a stack of drawings in pencil, go back and color each one. Bold, simple colors work well.
6. Film the drawings on the animation stand. Or, they can be scanned for import into animation software.
7. Using selected software, postproduce the movie with sound, music, and transitions.

Postproduction
This method provides a starting point for the creation of abstract or nonrepresentational animated movies. This systematic approach will provide a pleasing visual rhythm of constantly changing shapes. There are unlimited possibilities for creating this type of animation, so experiment. The idea of creating abstract movies is very old, yet still captures the imaginations of artists and animators. Combined with the capability of digital production tools, the creative possibilities are limitless. This method is ideal for adapting to the talents, interests, and confidence of individual animators who believe or may say, "I can't draw." The ability to render "realistic" drawings is not necessary for success with this type of animation.

Animation Project 10: A Very Short Story

Traditionally, storytelling is the most popular style in animated films because everybody likes stories. A seven-minute Bugs Bunny or Pluto cartoon for example is a story. A feature such as *Bambi* is a story.

Preproduction

Concept. When the animators have a sense of animation and a familiarity of the process and materials, developing a little story is much less intimidating. A story does not need to be long because little gags, sketches, or sequences based on simple visual ideas and actions need be only a few seconds each. Simple line animation works well for animated storytelling. Figure 6.28 illustrates a very short story made on index cards.

Materials. Again, line animation materials are all that is needed:

1. Five- by eight-inch unruled index cards or nine- by twelve-inch Acme punched bond animation paper with Acme peg bars.
2. An assortment of pencils and pens will be needed.

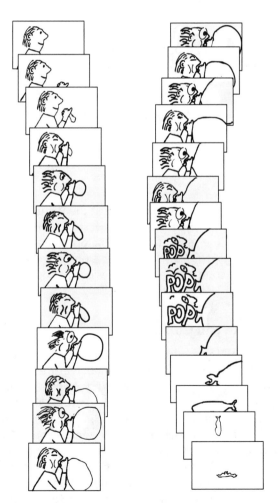

FIGURE 6.28 A Very, Very Short Story

3. Light boxes or a room with windows.
4. Black matte board to construct a registration board.
5. A digital camcorder and copy stand or a tripod.
6. A computer with digital editing software.

Planning. Storytelling animation requires careful planning, so be sure to write down or brainstorm ideas as simple scripts or descriptions of the action in a proposed movie. The point of using animation for storytelling is to entertain, so the ideas are usually funny and have surprise endings.

Production
1. Write some scripts or descriptions of animation ideas that may make interesting little stories. These should be simple and short, and lend themselves to visual action, but most important, they should have surprising and funny or entertaining endings.
2. Storyboard some of these scripts using the method described in Chapter 5. As a reminder, a storyboard is a series of simple sketches of each scene or shot in a proposed film and serves as a guide to creating the artwork.
3. As with other line animation techniques and materials, use the art materials and index cards to tell the story. Effective animation for storytelling often is based on action. Think about exaggerated and expressive movements and interesting and unusual angles of view.
4. Digitally film the artwork using the animation stand and techniques as you did in the previous projects.

Postproduction
Import the images into digital editing software and edit the images in the correct sequence. Add sound, music, and other effects. This storytelling or narrative approach to animation requires the animators to develop characters and bring them to life. These movies may be group or class projects or the work of individual animators. Several five- to ten-second animated movies edited together can create an entertaining little film festival.

Animation Project 11: Cutout and Collage

An old yet very effective method for producing animated movies is cutout or collage animation. As a matter of fact, the first animated feature film was Lotte Reiniger's silhouette cutout film *The Adventures of Prince Achmed* in 1926. One of the most important animation artists of the twentieth century, she continued to work with this method till her death in 1981. In 1973, animator Frank Mouris received an Academy Award for his short *Frank Film,* which consisted of thousands of manipulated cutouts from magazines and catalogs. Another notable accomplishment with cutout animation was Terry Gilliam's animations for *Monty Python's Flying Circus.* Early versions of the popular television series *South Park* were made with cutouts, although the producers had to switch to cutout-mimicking computer animation software in order to keep up with production demands as a result of the show's popularity. Another showcase for outstanding cutout animation is *Sesame Street*, which frequently uses the work of independent animation artists.

Preproduction

Concept.   From the silent era of the 1920s to the modern digital age, cutout animation continues to be popular and is in fact enhanced by newer technologies. The major expressive advantage of this technique is in the unique visual and aesthetic quality of two-dimensional cutouts. Figure 6.29 illustrates the process of cutout animation.

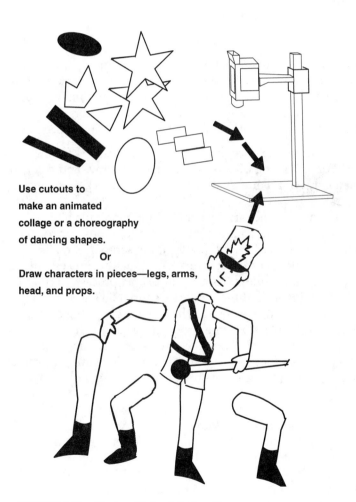

Use cutouts to make an animated collage or a choreography of dancing shapes.

Or

Draw characters in pieces—legs, arms, head, and props.

FIGURE 6.29   Taping Cutout Animation

Materials.   Cutouts can either be drawn or taken from magazines, photographs, newspapers, and other printed resources. They are then placed on the animation stand or under a tripod and manipulated frame by frame. The list of materials needed follows:

1. An animation stand and digital camera as previously described.
2. Old magazines, newspapers, posters, postcards, greeting cards, books, wrapping paper, advertisements, wallpaper samples, and so forth for cutting out and animating.
3. Art materials for drawing images that will be cut out and animated. Many cutout animated films use art created by artists for specific movies.
4. Scissors and knives such as matte knives or hobby knives. Depending on the nature of the work, the animator needs to cut out images and shapes from a variety of sources and materials.
5. A computer with digital editing software.

Production
Filming or recording cutout animation is similar to filming or recording line animation. The setup is the same whether with a tripod or a copy stand. The major difference is in how the artwork is recorded. The process of filming cutout animation takes concentration and patience. Further, cutout animation production requires practice and experimentation. The following steps explain the process:

1. Acquire the artwork. For collage animation, cut images from various printed sources. For animating objects and characters, draw and color the artwork and then cut it out. For ease of handling, card stock or heavyweight paper works best.
2. On the animation stand, arrange, move, and manipulate the artwork for the desired effects and motion. For example, add, reposition, or remove items. Shoot a frame, or record a still photo of the setup. Next, add, reposition, or remove items and record that setup. Continue this process until the movie, scene, or shot is complete. As a result of this process, accumulate enough frames for editing later. If the artwork does not lie flat, you can place a piece of clear glass over it. However, when using glass, fingerprints, dust, and reflections on the glass become problems. That is why using heavyweight paper or card stock is an advantage. An animation surface of nine by twelve inches is sufficient for most cutout animation. However, the camera may be adjusted according to the nature of the artwork being filmed.

Postproduction
Import the tape into the graphics editing software. Add music, sound effects, transitions, titles, and other effects for a complete project. Cutout animation has distinct advantages, but it is also more difficult to film than simply replacing line drawings on cards or paper on the animation stand. The versatility of cutout animation is its major advantage. For example, this method works for creating characters that walk and talk as well as for abstract movies.

Animation Project 12: Stop Motion/Object Animation

Animating objects is another method of unlimited potential. Nearly any objects can be animated: characters made of clay (such as Gumby) or a variety of materials such as table tennis balls, heavy wire, cardboard, painted blocks of wood, tools, people, even little characters made of anything the imagination can improvise. Figure 6.30 illustrates a stop motion setup.

Stop motion dinosaurs appeared in movies of the silent era, and in 1933 the stop motion animated movie *King Kong* appeared. Many years later, the technique continues to entertain. The movie by animators Peter Lord and Nick Parks, *Chicken Run,* for example, was made with an almost unlimited palette of clay, objects, and materials. Though *Chicken Run* is an instance of big-budget feature film production, stop motion animation is a good choice for low-budget or even no-budget movies. Because most anything that can be framed in a camera's viewfinder may be filmed, the conception of stop motion or object or even clay animation (often referred to as Claymation) is very broad. The mind-boggling stop motion feature *Koyanisqatsi* was made with motion picture cameras that photographed a single frame at designated intervals. One particularly memorable series is the stop motion sequence or time-lapse wide angle scene of a few hours in Grand Central Station presented in about a minute. The pixilated motion of thousands of people as they scurry about reinforces the movie's theme and title translation of "life out of balance." Stop motion can also be as simple as animating some objects on a tabletop or using a sequence of still photos to make a zoetrope, as described previously.

Other variations of stop motion also exist, including time-lapse photography. This process is often associated with drastically compressing time in order to show the blooming of a flower in just a few seconds. Still another variation of stop motion animation is often called pixilation. This process animates human motions

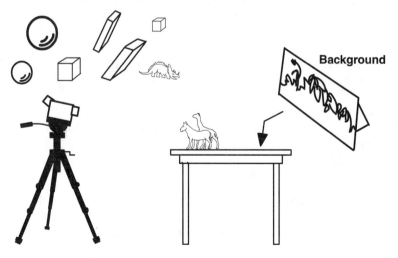

FIGURE 6.30   Taping Stop Motion

and actions as single frames, thus suggesting pixie-like actions and appearances. This process is how an animator can create the illusion of many people getting out of a small car, for example. As mentioned earlier in this chapter, the Canadian animator Norman McLaren created the pixilated movie *Neighbors* in the early 1950s. This movie stands as one of the all-time great stop motion short works. Although the stop motion method McLaren used was fascinating to watch, the real power of *Neighbors* was its universal message of love thy neighbor.

Preproduction

Concept.   As the technology of computer-based digital media production improves, 3-D computer animation software allows animators to create what appears as traditional stop motion movies. Look at *Toy Story,* for example, or most anything the famous computer animation studio Pixar creates. Viewers will continue to wonder if what they see is computer rendered or stop motion. Further, modern digital camcorders and supporting digital editing resources provide a tremendous opportunity for students and teachers to experiment with the expressive qualities of this method. An unlimited variety of objects and materials can be animated in stop motion fashion on an animation stand much the same way as with cutout animation.

Materials.   Getting started in stop motion animation requires only the following few items:

1. A digital camcorder. A photo still or single-frame option is helpful, but single frames can also be extracted from full-motion video in the editing step.
2. A tripod.
3. Photo lamps are useful for lighting stop motion sets, although they may not be necessary depending on available light and location.
4. Depending on the nature of the project, an assortment of objects and materials. Due to the nature of this process, virtually anything can be animated from clay to people.

For the novice stop motion animator, simple objects such as colored blocks of wood or even a chess set make interesting subjects.

Production

The following steps describe a stop motion setup using a tripod and camera. This combination has powerful animation potential because of the flexibility it provides, plus the concept is a natural adaptation to modern digital technology. To set up for simple object animation:

1. Select some objects that are easy to move, such as a set of child's wooden blocks.
2. Locate a surface on which the objects to be animated will appear, a tabletop, for example. This area, or stage, is where the action will take place. Some stop motion films require rather elaborate sets.

3. Place the camera on the tripod and frame the set. Make sure the tripod is in a location that protects it from being bumped. An accidental camera position change will ruin a carefully planned and filmed shot.
4. Place and adjust lights to achieve a desired effect. Be aware of shadows and light direction.
5. Begin by shooting several seconds of frames before the action starts. Then move the object, such as a block, a short distance, and record a still picture. Move it again and shoot another still picture. Continue this process with other objects and actions. After a shot, select the VCR option on the camera and play it back to evaluate the shot. Some stop motion animators work by instinct by letting their eyes and hands determine how much to move an element. Others create templates or other devices to mark positions.
6. Import the video into a digital editing system.

Postproduction

Stop motion animation, although simple in concept, is a highly specialized process. Stop motion animators are no different than other artists in that they all have individual and personal working styles. Stop motion films may be elegantly simple or exceedingly complex, requiring the skills of many people. However, this process also works well with very young animators who can write stories, create clay characters, build sets, and film their work. Box 6.1, Neighborhood Stories: A Case Study in Claymation by animation artists Ron Schildknecht and Ruben Moreno, shows what fifth graders can do with stop motion animation.

Animation Project 13: Multiple-Cel-Level Animation

Preproduction

Concept.   This classical style of animation, the backbone of studio animation for many years, is a very expensive and time-consuming process that requires precision, specialized materials, patience, and a lot of time. Cel animation is being replaced by technological computer-based processes that retain the handmade look yet allow animators to use a much richer palette of colors and effects. That is, in the case of a Disney feature, such as *Beauty and the Beast,* the characters and their actions were created by animators using punched bond paper, animation disks on light boards, and blue pencils. However, instead of the traditional expensive and tedious process of painting and filming hundreds of thousands of cels, the art was converted to digital images for editing, coloring, postproduction, and transfer to film for theaters.

Materials.   Cel animation can be created with the traditional method using punched bond paper and clear acetate cels or clear sheets of acetate. Special acrylic paint is needed to paint the cels. The artwork is then filmed on the digital animation stand and postproduced. To conduct a simple cel animation experiment using a digital camcorder, refer to Figure 6.31.

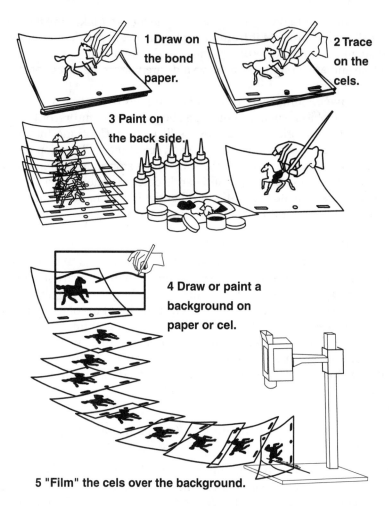

FIGURE 6.31   Classic Cel Animation

A basic, or beginning set of materials will be needed:

1. Nine- by twelve-inch punched bond animation paper.
2. Acme or Oxberry peg bars for registering the drawings.
3. Pencils for roughing out the actions on the bond paper.
4. Acetate ink for tracing the cleaned-up drawings onto the cels.
5. Nine- by twelve-inch acetate cels.
6. Acrylic animation colors—a basic set of primary colors, secondary colors, with larger bottles of black and white.
7. White gloves for handling the cels.
8. Canned air for blowing dust off of the cels while filming.

9. A shadow guard for mounting over the camera lens to avoid reflections.
10. An isolated space in which to film.
11. A digital camcorder and animation stand.

Production

Again, Figure 6.31 presents the steps for creating cel animation. Look at that illustration and follow these steps:

1. Create a very short line-animated cycle of about twelve to fifteen frames. Use a pencil and the animation bond paper for this task. Use a light board for tracing.
2. When finished—the cycle is smooth—place bond paper drawing number 1 on the peg bar. Place a clear cel on top of it on the peg bars, and trace the image onto the cel using acetate ink or a high-quality black permanent felt-tipped pen. Repeat this process for all drawings in the cycle. Handle the artwork with the white gloves.
3. When the ink is dry, paint the traced images from the backside, or opposite the inked side. This may require mixing the acrylic cel paints to the desired colors. Handle the artwork with white gloves. Do not stack the cels before the paint is dry. When the paint is dry, store the cels with the tissue paper between each one.
4. Create a background using conventional art materials and paper.
5. Shoot the artwork with the digital camcorder on the animation stand.

Postproduction

Follow the conventional digital postproduction process—editing, sounds, and transition effects. Cel animation, although beautiful to watch, can be difficult and impractical to produce in large quantities. However, the creation of a short cel-animated movie provides insight into the complexities and history of animation as an art form.

Animation Project 14: Learning to Walk and Talk

Preproduction

Concept.   One real thrill of creating animation is to see a character "come to life." This project will describe two ways to do that. One is through the creation of what animators call a walk cycle, which can be repeated over and over, and the other is by making a character talk with lip synchronization.

Materials.   The major component of this two-part project is the software. Therefore, the following will be needed:

1. A computer with as much RAM as possible.
2. *Macromedia Flash* is a highly versatile product for creating smooth high-resolution animation, among many other possibilities. Participating in this two-part project requires at least an entry-level understanding of *Macromedia*

Flash. Again, this can be achieved by opening *Flash* and selecting *Help + Lessons.*

3. Depending on one's drawing style, such items as an image scanner, pencils, felt-tipped pens, and drawing paper may be needed.
4. Illustrations or photographs of models of walk cycles and mouth shapes. Sources for these include *Cartoon Animation* by Preston Blair, *The Human Figure in Motion* by Eadweard Muybridge, and *The Animation Book* by Kit Laybourne.

Figure 6.32 is a generic model made from a synthesis of various walk cycles. Figure 6.33 is a generic set of commonly used animation mouth shapes.

Production 1: Walking

This part of the project makes a simple character that walks across a computer screen. As with all multimedia projects, there are numerous ways to do this. *Flash* again is a good choice because, as an animation tool, it is self-contained. That is,

A two-legged eight-frame walk cycle

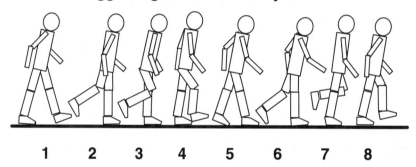

| 1 | 2 | 3 | 4 | 5 | 6 | 7 | 8 |

A four-legged eight-frame walk cycle

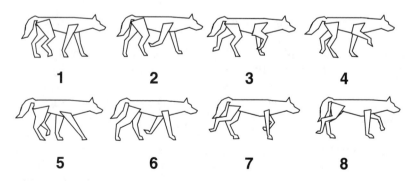

FIGURE 6.32   Walk Cycle Samples—Two Legged and Four Legged

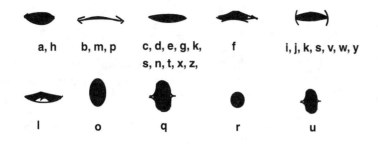

a, h   b, m, p   c, d, e, g, k,   f   i, j, k, s, v, w, y
s, n, t, x, z,

l   o   q   r   u

The above used in a simple statement . . .

H   o   w   a   r   e   you?

FIGURE 6.33   Generic Mouth Shapes

after some practice and learning with this package, it has enough built-in features to create lively and highly original animated characters. However, the project can be adapted to other software such as *Macromedia Director* or even *Adobe Photoshop,* both of which have animation capabilities. Also, a variation of this process is to make the drawings for the cycle on index cards, cut them out, scan them or film them with a digital camera either on digital videotape or as digital stills, then import them into moviemaking software such as *Flash,* GIF-building software, or even *QuickTime Pro.*

The essence of this project is in using the drawing tools in *Flash* to create a cycle that is a two-legged character walking. Follow, or adapt these steps:

1. If necessary, review the drawing tool functions in *Flash* lessons.
2. Locate and study a generic walk cycle. Some can be made up of as few as four drawings or as many as sixteen. Examine Figure 6.32. These are generic repeating cycles of eight separate drawings. When these or similar drawings are placed in individual key frames in *Flash,* the character walks. Refer to *Cartoon Animation* by Preston Blair for walk cycle guides. Also, a Web search may yield examples.
3. Open *Flash* and select *Insert.* Insert eight consecutive *Blank Keyframes* on Layer 1.
4. Select *Modify + Movie* (or *Document*). This opens the *Movie Properties* box. Choose a white background and set the horizontal and vertical dimensions. Note that the default dimensions of 550 pixels by 400 pixels work well for this project.

5. From the *Tools* menu, select the *Pencil* tool, and draw in the *Straighten* mode. However, to fit a particular drawing style, choose the *Smooth* mode or choose the *Brush* tool. Under *Window* select *Panels + Stroke*. Set the *Stroke* at a height of 2, and select black or make alternate choices for desired thickness and color.
6. Using the previously described setup, draw a character in frame 1 in the same position as drawing 1 in the walk cycle in Figure 6.32. Engage the *Onion Skin* option and set it to reveal drawing 1.
7. Select *Key Frame* two; make sure the *Onion Skin* option is chosen and set to show the previous frame. Use the drawing tools to trace drawing 1, except for the arms and legs positions, which will be different or changed in drawing 2. See position 2 in Figure 6.32. Continuing to use the *Pencil* Tool, draw the new positions in frames 2 through 8.
8. When the eight positions have been drawn and placed in the eight *Key Frames*, select each and convert it to a symbol (*Insert + Convert to Symbol + Graphic*). This places the eight drawings as symbols in the Library (*Window + Library*) that can be dragged into the *Flash* program. For example, using the *Onion Skin* selection, the drawings may be placed in such a way as to make the character walk across the screen. Or they may be placed on top of one another on separate frames to make the character walk in place. Select *Insert + Layer* to add a background layer below the walk cycle. Using *Flash*'s drawing tools, create a background the same size as the frame. Select the background graphic you have drawn and select *Insert + Convert to Symbol + Graphic*.
9. Play the walk cycle over and over, adjusting it to make it as smooth as possible.

From these steps, you can go on to experiment with variations of walk cycles such as running, flipping, sneaking, jumping, and strutting as well as four-legged cycles. Figure 6.32 also illustrates a sample four-legged cycle. Examples of these are provided in the references cited in this section. Creating a repeating motion cycle is a fundamental skill in character animation. The trial and error, playing, adjusting, and replaying required to create a smooth cycle are the essence of handmade animation whether on a computer or on index cards.

The two-legged walker in Figure 6.32 is made of simple shapes. Be more inventive. Create a unique character and use the model for leg and arm positions.

Finally, remember that experimentation is the best way to learn to create repeating animated cycles. The nature of digital multimedia tools enhances the learning of this skill because it allows instant feedback for analysis and adjustment. Although drawing skills can be useful, they are not crucial. The key aspect of expressive character animation is expressive movement. Thus, very simple images that move smoothly and convincingly make more successful animated movies than slickly drawn ones that are stiff and lifeless.

Production 2: Talking
Animators have known how to make characters speak since the first sound motion pictures were released. Although Disney's *Steamboat Willy* is often considered the

first sound cartoon, the Fleischer Studios created lip-synchronized sound experimental cartoons years before. Nothing does more to bring animated characters to life than making them speak. One cannot imagine a silent Bugs or Daffy or Donald. The control and manipulation of sound is a fundamental multimedia skill. Although sound design and editing can be very complex, only a few basic skills and concepts are needed to integrate sound successfully with digitally animated movies.

Multimedia software makes lip synchronization a simple matter of matching drawings of consonant and vowel mouth shapes to recorded voices. Like learning to create walk cycles, learning how to match sounds with images is also an experimental process, a regime of trying and retrying. Keep in mind that there are multiple variations of this process and various multimedia software packages make it possible. For the sake of consistency and specificity, the following lip-sync directions are based on *Flash.* As with previous directions, these concepts and ideas can be adapted to various software and media. Continuing with *Flash* as the multimedia software of choice because of its versatility, follow these steps to make a character "talk."

The following steps are divided into setup and drawing.

SETTING UP BEFORE DRAWING

1. Open a new *Flash* screen. Leave the frame at 550 pixels by 400pixels.
2. Select or record a sound file of a short statement or sentence that a character will speak. This sound file may be recorded directly onto the hard drive of the computer and converted to a sound file such as AIF for Macintosh or WAV for Windows. Various multimedia software packages record, edit, and convert sound such as music, voice, and effects. An excellent sound editing title is *SmartSound.*
3. After recording or selecting, editing, converting, and saving the statement as the appropriate sound file, select *File + Import.* This places the sound file in *Flash's* Library.
4. Open the Library (*Window + Library*), and drag the sound file onto the first *Keyframe* of *Layer One.*
5. Estimate the length of the recorded statement, and insert a *Keyframe* on *Layer 1* at the correct distance from the first *Key Frame.* For example, if the animation is set to play at twelve frames per second, and the recorded statement is two seconds long, insert a *Keyframe* on frame 24 or even 30 to provide a little working space. Notice the pattern of the sound is visible in the layer.
6. Next, select *Window + Panels + Sound.* The sound panel will appear with the file name of the recorded sound. Locate *Sync* and select *Stream.* A streaming sound in *Flash* allows the producer to listen to each syllable of the spoken statement. This basic setup is now ready for creating the drawings that will be synchronized with the sound.

DRAWING IN SYNC

1. Insert a layer under the Sound layer. Label it as the Mouth layer; label the one with the voice the Sound layer.
2. Insert a third layer and label it Head. There should now be three layers from top to bottom. Layer 1 is Voice, Layer 2 is Mouth, and Layer 3 is Head.

3. Choose a drawing tool, pen or brush, and draw a human head on the bottom layer, which should be labeled as Head. For example, choose the pencil with the smooth mode. Choose *Window + Panels + Stroke* and select a line width and line color. A fairly thick—4 point—black line works best.

4. Draw a large simple contour drawing of the head. Leave the mouth off. Add detail and color as desired.

5. Animators use or adapt standard mouth shapes for vowels and consonants. See the ones in Figure 6.33. Based on these, use a pencil to draw each of the basic mouth shapes. Select all of the Head and choose *Insert + Convert to Symbol* and convert it to a graphic symbol. Next, *Insert + Keyframe* on frame 1 of the second, or Mouth, layer. In that *Keyframe,* draw a mouth shape—refer to Figure 6.33—that matches the first syllable of the first word. Notice that the shape may be needed over several frames. Continue to read the soundtrack by moving back and forth while listening to the voice. Create mouth shapes that match the syllables of the voice. After drawing a mouth, circle it with the *Lasso* Tool then select *Insert + Convert to Symbol.* The mouth shape will be placed in the Library for repeated uses. Repeat this procedure for each mouth shape.

6. Select *Window + Library.* Matching the mouth shapes to the voice pattern is simply a matter of dragging the Play Head over the voice pattern and inserting *Keyframes* on the mouth level. Place the mouth shapes in matching *Keyframes.* This is a trial-and-error process but *Flash* symbols make it relatively easy. Also experiment with other symbols, such as eyelids.

7. To make the movie start, play and return to the first frame. Add a *Button* and a *Frame Action.* To do so, select *Window + Common Libraries + Buttons.* Choose a premade button, and drag it onto the first frame of the Head layer. Select *Windows + Actions* and select the action *Play.* Place the *Frame Action* Stop in the first frame on the Head layer. Insert a new *Keyframe* as the last frame on the head layer and insert the *Frame Action* Go to Frame 1 and Stop.

8. The final step is to select *File + Export Movie* to make a Shockwave (swf) file that will play in a *Flash Player.* When posting the Shockwave file to a web site, any modern Web browser with a *Flash Player* plug-in—virtually all of them— can play it. Note that *Flash* also provides the options to publish the movie as HTML, *QuickTime,* or other file types.

Postproduction: Walking and Talking

In creating animated movies, no other experience is more exciting or fulfilling than to see a character talk or sing. Although this does take some practice, digital media production tools make it possible. The previous steps accompanied by the illustrations and the *Help* menu in *Flash* are a starting point from which to venture into more ambitious experiments. As users learn more about *Flash,* the more they will develop their own unique ways of using it to create illusions of life.

Animation Project 15: Digital Doodling

Preproduction

Concept. Following the tradition of abstract animation, this project describes how to create a computer-animated movie from repeated frames of random shapes, colors, and lines. In this process, there is no attempt to make smooth, continuous motion. Rather, each frame is created much as one doodles. The result is a very fast-paced sequence of shapes, colors, and lines—each one totally unique and unrelated to the others. The crude but energetic visual impact can be reinforced by selecting accompanying sound effects and music.

Materials.   This idea adapts well to the creation of a movie of marks, or an animated visual chant. This project has several advantages: it does not require expensive software, it does not require representational illustration, and it happens quickly. An animator can create a movie in a very short time. The following materials are needed:

1. A PC or Windows computer is required. Of course, the idea may be adapted to other hardware, software, and operating systems.
2. The software needed is *QuickTime Pro* and drawing or painting software such as *ClarisWorks* or *Microsoft Paint*. The concept, however, can be adapted to other graphics software such as *Macromedia Flash*.

Production
This step is where the "doodling" becomes a movie.

1. Open the *QuickTime Player.* Note that the *QuickTime Player* is a free download. To acquire additional editing features, download, for a fee, *QuickTime Pro*. Open *QuickTime Pro*, and save as Chant.
2. In *Microsoft Windows*, select *Start + Programs + Accessories + Paint*.
3. In *Paint*, select *Images + Attribute* and set the frame size at 3 inches high by 2 inches wide.
4. On the three by two frame, make some repeated marks. Use the software's painting tools—*Brush, Pencil, Fill, Spray*, and shapes.
5. When the frame is filled up with repeated marks, select *Edit + Select All + Copy*.
6. Return to the *QuickTime Player;* select *Edit + Paste*.
7. Return to *Paint*, delete the previous marks, draw some more, choose *Edit + Select All + Copy*, return to *QuickTime Player*, and *Paste*.
8. Repeat that process for as many frames as desired. For example, making a five-second movie will require sixty frames running at twelve frames per second.
9. Remember to save the movie frequently.

Thus, *QuickTime* allows the animator to build a movie simply by drawing, cutting, and pasting into the *QuickTime Player.* This can be a long and tedious process if one desires a longer movie. However, several short movies may be edited together as a class project. To do basic editing in *QuickTime Pro*, follow the same procedure. Select an entire movie, copy it, and paste it into a *QuickTime Player.* The short movies of an entire class can be sequenced in this manner, yielding a good length. So, fifteen 5-second movies turn out to be a good length. The visual effects are psychedelic and stimulating works of very fast-paced rhythm. Once the technique is mastered, the animator may try some varying effects such as using the same image twice, one as it was drawn and one inverted. Further, an animator who likes to draw characters can also use this method to create lively and active human and animal forms. Although a movie compiled from several short movies may be interesting in and of itself, sound can add another dimension to the experience of creating and watching the movie.

Postproduction

In this project, the sound is added in postproduction. The choice of sound is based on the visual character of the movie. Follow these steps:

1. Acquire or record a sound file. Common sound files are AIF and WAV. Sound effects and music are available from commercially produced CD-ROMs, from clip art collections, and from the Internet. *QuickTime Pro* can record sound from an audio CD by simply selecting *File + Import* in *QuickTime Pro*. *Quick-Time Pro* also provides very basic sound editing for the recorded music

2. If using a WAV file, simply open the file in a separate *QuickTime Player*. From *Edit,* choose *Select All + Copy.* Select the *QuickTime Player* that has the movie to which the sound will be added. Select *Edit + Add.* Click on the movie player and select *Paste.* This puts the soundtrack next to the pictures. If the sound selection is longer than the movie, gray frames will be added. In that case, another option is to select *Edit + Add Scaled.* This matches the length of the music to the length of the pictures. Be warned, though, that if they are radically longer or shorter than each other, the sound will be drastically distorted. Note that a WAV file must be converted to an AIF file for import into *QuickTime* on a *Macintosh. QuickTime Player (Pro)* can convert and export a sound file as AIF.

3. With the sound added, save the movie by selecting *File + Save As.* Give it a name and select *Make Movie Self-Contained.*

This project needs only basic, inexpensive software to complete. However, with patience and practice, the creative results can be far more than basic. Virtually anyone can succeed with this process. As described, putting several of these short movies together following the procedures described makes a lively and entertaining class or group project. This idea is also adaptable to other software packages. The key to do so has more to do with the concept than with the software. A digital visual chant is a terrific example of the historical and artistic heritage of abstract animation production.

Students in elementary school to university graduate students will derive satisfaction from this simple project. In fact, some may be mesmerized by the process of choreographing sound, shapes, colors, motion, space, and rhythm. Possibly the most valuable advantage of this project is that a student animator cannot opt out because "I can't draw."

Animation Project 16: Rotoscoping

Preproduction

Concept.   An interesting digital variation of an old animation method called rotoscoping can be accomplished with multimedia and graphics software such as *Flash* and *Photoshop* or any graphic software that uses layers, thus allowing an artist to trace. A dramatic use of this method done with ink and cels on film is the Fleischer Studios' feature film of 1939, *Gulliver's Travels*.

Materials.   Items needed for this project include the following:

1. *Macromedia Flash*. This software is ideal for this project because of the manner in which it uses *Key Frames* and *Layers*.
2. Images to be rotoscoped may be a sequence of digital stills shot specifically for this project, or a digital video sequence may be imported.

Production
This can be a tedious process, but the result will be worth the patience and effort.

1. Open *Flash* and leave the movie size at the default size—550 pixels wide by 400 pixels tall.
2. *Import* the sequence to rotoscope. See that the imported sequence is on *Frame one* of *Layer 1*. For this project, use a *QuickTime Movie* file created in *QuickTime Pro*. A *QuickTime Movie* can be created by shooting a sequence with a digital camcorder. Import the video into digital editing software. Edit the sequence to rotoscope and export it as a *QuickTime Movie*. For this project, a short sequence of two to four seconds is recommended.
3. On *Layer One*, insert a *Frame* at the end of the movie sequence. For example, if the sequence is two seconds long and *Flash* is set to play twelve frames per second, insert a *Frame* at frame 24 on the first layer. After doing this, the movie can then be played back and forth.
4. Select *Insert + Layer*. This places an empty layer above the movie.
5. Select *Insert + Keyframe* and insert an appropriate number of *Keyframes,* beginning at frame 1 to cover the length of the movie. For example, for two seconds, insert twenty-four *Keyframes*.
6. Select *Layer 1,* the one with the movie, and lock it.
7. Begin tracing by selecting *Keyframe 1 + Layer 2*. Select the *Pencil* tool + *Smooth* and select *Window + Panels + Stroke*. Choose a stroke width with black as the color.
8. Using the *Pencil* tool, trace the first frame. To check the drawing, select *Hide, Layer 1*. Check the drawing, then choose *Show Layer 1*.
9. When that drawing is complete, select *Keyframe 2 + Layer 2,* and trace that drawing. Continue this process until all of the drawings have been traced.
10. When satisfied with the sequence of traced drawings, delete *Layer 1*—the movie layer.
11. Now go back and modify the drawings by adding color, changing sizes, placing the images in various locations in the frames, or making other creative modifications.

Postproduction
Depending on the use or destination of your completed rotoscoped sequence, it can be exported as a number of file types from *Flash Player* to animated GIFs for use

with other software. Of course, the rotoscoped sequence may be part of a *Flash* production in which case it can be converted to a *Movie Clip Symbol* for use throughout the producton.

As has been mentioned previously, learning multimedia software requires experimentation. This is especially important in learning animation. Multimedia animators tend to develop personal styles and preferences for the way they use the software.

Some Final Thoughts about Animation

Planning and Postproduction

A very carefully planned animated movie shot with a digital camcorder or created in software such as *Flash* may need only some basic editing and minimal postproduction: transitions, titles, music, and sound effects. Typically, though by all means not always, carefully planned and shot animated films do not require a lot of editing because of the nature of animation production. For example, artwork production is so time-consuming that usually just enough is created to cover the idea or story of the movie. Therefore, most of the animation is used in a final version, whereas in a live-action video, the filmmaker may shoot three or four or more times more video than needed. Due to the variety of digital camcorders and their many features, some may not be able to record a single frame. Some may record a burst of six frames, for example, or some will record or freeze a few seconds of a still picture when in the photo still mode. Either way, digital animation software is capable of removing single frames, which then can be used to create the movie frame by frame. In this process of animation production, the computer serves as everything from a motion picture lab to the distributor. Another major advantage of digital animation production is that gratification is not deferred. The filmmaker can check all aspects of production and test the animation movement frequently.

Sound Design and Editing

Sound design and editing are crucial components of animated film production. In fact, one may even make a case that the quality of a finished animated movie depends more on sound than any other element including the animation. Even simple cartoon sound effects can bring a movie to life. Digital editing software provides a lot of flexibility in combining sound effects and music with the edited images and is done much the same way as editing the images. Digital sounds come from many sources. Some clip art collections have music and effects, sound libraries of digitized sounds are available, and sound can be recorded from audio CDs. Perhaps the most original way to obtain sound effects is to make them yourself. This is called Foley art in feature film production, and the easiest way to do it is simply to cover the digital camcorders, use the camera to record sounds, and then import those sounds along with the video.

Be warned that creating digital animated movies can be addictive. There is always something else to try. One idea leads to another. Creating "life" with still pictures and inanimate objects appeals to modern animators of all ages as it did to

Winsor McCay in 1914; only the tools are different. Digital animation provides numerous opportunities for students and teachers to expand the notion of instructional technology as a medium of construction, originality, and self-expression. The computer becomes much more than a dispenser of isolated facts and information. It is not too difficult to imagine the excitement of the pioneers of the motion picture huddled around a big loud projector in a darkened room watching shadows flicker on a white sheet. Neither is it too difficult to imagine a group of students gathered around a computer spellbound by the little flickering images they have just brought to life.

Summarizing Animation Production: A New Generation
From zoetropes to digital camcorders, the art of animation continues to grow, entertain, and fascinate. The potent combination of the traditions and methods of animation with a new generation of computer software stimulates and expands that growth. For example, *Macromedia Flash* together with the rise of the World Wide Web makes the art form of animation more accessible than ever, not only as entertainment or amusement but also as a robust and lively means of individual expression. A powerful yet inexpensive desktop or laptop computer with a couple of reasonably priced graphics and animation software packages, in a word, replaces many of the expensive tools of traditional animation—except, of course for originality and ideas. The most significant advance as a result of this evolution of the art form is its accessibility to students and teachers at all levels. Software such as *Flash* borrows many of the terms and concepts practiced and used by generations of animators. For example, *Flash* uses *Keyframes* as a basis of designing actions and *Tweens*—short for "in-betweens"—for automatically creating drawings in between *Keyframes*. Other terms used to mimic the tools of traditional animation are *Layers, Onion Skin* (tracing paper), *Ink,* and *Movie.* With *Flash,* the animator literally builds a movie frame by frame. Gratification is not deferred because playback and analysis of the ongoing work are instantaneous. Further, the possibilities and choices of how to create and manipulate the artwork are infinite.

INFORMATION SOURCES AND IDEAS
FOR LEARNING ABOUT ANIMATION

Acquiring computers, cameras, and software to create a digital animation suite is only the first step. How do aspiring and veteran animators learn and develop new skills and ideas? Where can they see the work of independent animators and where can they present their own work? What are some sources of motivation and inspiration? The following sections may at least provide a starting point for answering some of those questions.

From Winsor McCay to Pixar, the ultimate goal of animators has been and is to create life or, more accurately, the illusion of life. Animation did not achieve respect and recognition as a media production genre till animators and studios demonstrated that they could create characters that lived, not just moved. That quest is no different in the early twenty-first century than it was in the early twentieth century. Animators using the very latest and most powerful digital tools seek the same thing as McCay did—life. Thus, character animation remains the backbone of the art form. The following resources will help a novice animator explore the possibilities of character animation.

Books for Learning Character Animation, History of Animation, and How to Animate

1. *The Animation Book* by Kit Laybourne. This classic work covers all aspects of animation. This book, first published in 1979, provides the most comprehensive introduction for those who want to make animated movies from zoetropes to 3-D digital. A notable strength of *The Animation Book* is its emphasis on independent animation. The latest edition was published in 1998.

2. *Cartoon Animation* by Preston Blair, an animator and cartoon director at MGM for many years. This is a classic work on the subject of character animation. It has been through several editions and contains a wealth of practical ideas about animating people and animals. Of particular value are the numerous guides for creating walking and running cycles for two-legged and four-legged creatures. His concepts work well for novices and veterans and for school use, and his concepts are a perfect fit for computer-based animation.

3. *The Human Figure in Motion* by Eadweard Muybridge. This is an extensive collection of pre–motion picture photographs of the nude human figure in motion. Although the pictures are from the late nineteenth century, this project has not been surpassed. *The Human Figure in Motion* is a vital reference for animators because of the sequential images of figures walking, running, hitting a baseball, and many others. The book is of particular value because accurate and convincing animation of the human form is extremely difficult to do. In fact, one reason why so many animated characters are based on animals is that human-like motions may be applied to animal forms without having to reproduce the human forms accurately.

4. *The Illusion of Life* by Frank Thomas and Ollie Johnston, two master Disney animators. This is a richly illustrated and extremely well written and detailed description of the Disney style of animation. This classic work provides a comprehensive description of the Disney philosophy of animation. A lot can be learned from studying the rich illustrations.

5. *Of Mice and Magic* by Leonard Maltin. This important book deals with the origins and history of studio animation. Although it is not a "how to," it provides an interesting and detailed story of the evolution of character animation. A familiarity with this history provides intellectual and artistic inspiration for the study of character animation in all its styles.

6. *The Animator's Survival Kit* by Richard Williams, the director of animation for *Who Framed Roger Rabbit?* This is a comprehensive manual for animators from classical to computer. This lavishly illustrated book is entertaining and informative.

Though this list is not exhaustive (additional sources are listed at the end of this chapter), it provides more than enough to begin learning about the methods and art of character animation.

Journals
Magazines dedicated to animation provide numerous articles related to processes, developments, and important animators. Two excellent ones are

1. *Animation Magazine* and its online version at www.animationmagazine.net
2. *Animation World* at mag.awn.com.

Organizations for Sharing and Networking
The most active worldwide association that promotes animation as an art form is ASIFA, or L'Association Internationale du Film d'Animation, an international society connecting animators from around the world. Membership includes a quarterly publication in several languages with news about animators, festivals, and related events. Informaton about ASIFA's regional divisions as well as many other subjects of interest to animators or those interested in animation are on the ASIFA web site, http://asifa.net.

Festivals for Watching Animated Movies
Independently produced animated films are rarely available for viewing. However, there are film festivals around the world either dedicated to animation or with an animation category. One of the best places to check for the locations and dates of animated film festivals is on the ASIFA web site, http://asifa.net. Also, many national and local festivals attract independent animated movies. These are worth seeking out because of the underexposed, yet highly original works that are often screened. Independent animators often are ahead of their times artistically and occasionally, because of the recognition from film festivals, attain national and international recognition for their work.

The World Wide Web: Animation Online
A comprehensive search for online animated works will yield many choices because of the growing interest in animation production software designed specifically for creating movies for the World Wide Web. For example, some sites are dedicated specifically to *Flash* animation. Due to the transience of web sites, it would be impractical to list them here. However, even a basic search, for example, in *Yahoo!*, will display hundreds of links to animated movies on the Web.

SUMMARY: HAPPY ANIMATING

As stated earlier in this chapter, perhaps no other multimedia production element has benefited more from technological media production advances than animation. As digital media production tools improve and make their way into the hands of teachers, students, artists, or anyone willing to learn how to use them, the old art form of animation is very much alive.

The exercises in this chapter provide starting points for learning some animation techniques. They have all been field-tested in the real world. They are specific enough to provide step-by-step guides, but they can and should be adapted to fit any number of circumstances. Do not hesitate to interpret them in more creative and challenging ways.

As the tools expand, so do the definitions of what constitutes animation. Is animation simply moving and manipulating graphics and objects, or should the term apply only to using a number of methods to create an illusion of life? In fact, this question could be the first Thought Provoker for this chapter.

THOUGHT PROVOKERS

1. If you have grown up in a culture in which animation in all its styles and manifestations is easily available on television and in the movies, write a personal definition of *animation*. Swap definitions with your classmates and discuss them.

2. Recall your favorite feature-length animated movie, and do research to find the following information: title, producer, release date, animation method(s). Tell why this movie is your favorite. Point out specific qualities that stand out to you. Do the same thing with your favorite animated cartoon short and with your favorite animated television show. Share these with the class and look for differing tastes.

3. Choose at least one of the animation activities described in this chapter. Create the animated product that it describes. Then answer the following:
   a. What did you learn or what insight into the process did you gain?
   b. What surprised you about that activity? That is, what aspect of the project did you find unpredictable?
   c. If and when you do the project again, what would you do differently?
   d. Make some suggestions as to how the directions for the project can be improved or propose a similar, modified, or improved variation of the project.
   e. Share your project with your classmates and have them provide critique and feedback.

4. Identify your favorite animation method or studio or character or animator or any related subject, and conduct a Web search to find out all you can about it. Record and share the URLs. Exchange the information with class members and assign categories. Create an animation reference web site. Create some original animated GIFs for the site.

REFERENCES

Blair, Preston. (1995). *Cartoon Animation*. Tustin, CA: Walter Foster.
Edwards, Betty. (1979). *Drawing on the Right Side of the Brain*. Los Angeles: J. P. Tarcher.
Laybourne, Kit. (1998). *The Animation Book*. New York: Three Rivers Press.

Locke, Lafe. (1992). *Film Animation Techniques: A Beginner's Guide and Handbook.* White Hall, VA: Betterway Publications.

Lutz, E. G., (1920). *Animated Cartoons: How They Are Made, Their Origin and Development.* Bedford, MA: Applewood Books.

Maltin, Leonard. (1987). *Of Mice and Magic.* New York: Penguin Books.

Muybridge, Eadweard. (1955). *The Human Figure in Motion.* New York: Dover.

Nicolaides, K. (1941). *The Natural Way to Draw.* Boston: Houghton Mifflin.

Rubin, Susan. (1984). *Animation: The Art and the Industry.* Upper Saddle River, NJ: Prentice Hall.

Russett, Robert & Starr, Cecile. (1976). *Experimental Animation: Origins of a New Art.* New York: Da Capo.

Thomas, Frank, & Johnston, Ollie. (1995). *The Illusion of Life: Disney Animation.* New York: Hyperion.

Williams, Richard. (2001). *The Animator's Survival Kit: A Manual of Methods, Principles and Formulas.* London: Faber and Faber.

CHAPTER SEVEN

A FINAL PROJECT
AND VERTOV REVISITED

TOPIC OUTLINE

CONSTRUCTING MULTIMEDIA MOUNTAINS

This describes a multimedia classroom project that can be adapted to various audiences and subjects.

VERTOV REVISITED

Here Vertov's visions are applied to the contemporary concept of multimedia.

THOUGHT AND PROJECT PROVOKERS: MULTIMEDIA IDEAS

Five multimedia project ideas are suggested, which use the skills described in this book.

OBJECTIVES

- As a multimedia classroom project, select a shared theme, and create a multimedia exploration of that theme using your choices of the skills and concepts described in previous chapters.

- Based on Vertov's quote, reflect on the perception of multimedia as an activity and process that is driven by ideas and communication.

Students and teachers who produce multimedia works will develop their skills to a point at which they can make informed decisions based on what they want to create. The purpose of this book is to stimulate that development. The acquisition of multimedia skills and concepts is a growth process based on the exploration of a variety of practices, software, and tools. In a practical sense multimedia production decisions also depend on other variables such as available resources and time. The exercises, activities, and projects described in this book were presented with step-by-step instructions with the expectation that these projects and ideas will be adapted and modified to meet the needs of individual students and teachers.

This chapter is presented as a culminating group project that uses many of the multimedia concepts and skills covered in previous chapters. As with all multimedia production ideas in this book, this project can also be adapted to fit numerous teaching and learning goals.

CONSTRUCTING MULTIMEDIA MOUNTAINS

The term *mountain* conjures up many meanings, as does the word *Multimedia.* So what are some results when those two general terms come together? An interesting way to find out is to pose that question to a group or to a class and have each student create a personal interpretation using available multimedia production tools. The following steps describe a process in which a class uses multimedia tools to learn about and share a class-selected topic or theme.

Preproduction and Planning

Concepts
The theoretical concept of having students use multimedia tools to construct their own learning is the basis of this project. Of course, learning while constructing does not happen by accident. The teacher's role of planner, director, motivator, troubleshooter, and evaluator is crucial. In this project, the class selects a topic or theme, and each student produces a project that addresses that theme educationally, creatively, and interactively.

Materials
Software.   Any multimedia software may be used in this project, depending on such variables as skills of the producers, local resources or what is available, or level of sophistication desired. Some software packages that work well for this project include the following:

1. *ClarisWorks* or *AppleWorks.* This integrated software package includes graphic capabilities and a basic slide show function that works well for classroom presentation.
2. *Microsoft PowerPoint* and *HyperStudio.* These easy-to-use, highly versatile, and flexible packages are used for everything from group presentation to online delivery. Both titles provide a high degree of interactivity and work very well with sound, graphics, and movies. For novice multimedia producers, both will require some practice and learning.
3. *Macromedia Dreamweaver.* This very popular and powerful Web design package is used frequently by professional web designers. However, it is not difficult to learn and is also often used by students and teachers on many educational levels.
4. *Macromedia Flash. Flash* is used to create web pages, deliver online instruction, and make movies. That is, *Flash* is highly adaptable to many uses and purposes. Though its basics may be grasped quickly, learning to understand and exploit the enormous creative power of *Flash* does take considerable time and commitment.
5. There are many others, of course, from writing HTML code, creating Java Applets, or using a multitude of HTML editors. However, as crucial as the software is, effective multimedia success is based on criteria such as planning, resourcefulness, originality, and inventiveness.

Multimedia Tools.   In addition to a computer, tools needed include digital cameras, scanners, and Internet access, among others.

A Common Theme, Topic, or Subject.   Because all participants will create a work that addresses a common theme, the students and teacher, as a class, must select that theme. The theme for the project described in this example is "mountains."

Production

The first step for any theme or topic that a class may choose is to discuss the theme. This could be included in preproduction, but because it provides the foundation of the project, it is included as the first production step. A skillfully led discussion will generate some topics, subjects, and perspectives that will provide some direction and specifics related to mountains. Some of these ideas and topics to consider in relation to mountains include the following:

- *Geological and geographical.* Ages of mountain chains vary from very old such as the Appalachian Mountains to the newer Rocky Mountains. Some mountains are covered with soil and some are bare. Elevations vary greatly.
- *Historical and social.* Mountains can isolate societies thus causing distinct cultures to evolve. For example, the tradition of self-sufficiency and fierce independence so often associated with mountain life, whether in the Appalachian region of the United States or the Basque region of Spain and France, is often seen as a result of isolation. For the most part this isolation no longer exists because of technological, economic, and social change.
- *Culture, art, and literature.* Distinctive cultural aspects of mountain life include folk arts and crafts, religion, folklore, storytelling, genealogy, and literature. In particular, the Appalachian region has a long tradition of outstanding writers and literary works from the novelists Harritt Arnow, Jesse Stuart, and Wilma Dykeman to poets Jim Wayne Miller and James Still. Further, musical traditions from Appalachia have influenced popular genres.
- *Animal and plant life.* Mountains provide distinct habitats for animal life and vegetation. For example, the Great Smoky Mountains in the United States have the greatest variety of plant life than anyplace in the country.
- *Natural resources.* Mountains have exploitable resources such as coal and timber, both of which have been subject to significant environmental damage such as strip mining and deforestation.
- *Recreation.* Mountain regions provide popular vacation spots from ski resorts to hiking, white-water rafting, scenic tours, and others. These are so popular in fact that tourism is also a threat to mountain environments.

These categories demonstrate the many perspectives and issues related to the general topic of mountains. Follow the next three major production steps:

1. Each student or small working group selects a topic or issue related to the theme. For example, students in a culturally and internationally diverse course may select topics such as traditional arts of the Carpathian Mountains, life and

death of a Japanese heroic mountain climber, folk structures of Cade's Cove in the Great Smoky Mountains National Park, the spiritual powers of the mountains of Japan, and the religious significance of mountains in Nepal.

2. Select the multimedia software that each student will use to create an interpretation of the theme from the software packages described in the preproduction section.
3. After researching the theme or subject, use a variety of multimedia tools to develop the individual topics. As a short review, consider digital graphics, scanned photos, sounds, digital video, animations, and links to remote web sites. Use the features of the software to make the production interactive. Refer to projects described in previous chapters.

Postproduction

The culmination of this multimedia class endeavor is the creation of a class home page introducing the theme on a title page. From there, the user can link to each of the individual presentations, thus providing an opportunity for all to learn about the theme and observe the many interpretations.

One advantage of a shared multimedia theme is that novice producers are learning the complexities of multimedia production in general or a specific software package in particular as they learn about the theme or subject. That is, beyond learning basic and essential skills, learning to manipulate software without purpose or content is simply learning to manipulate software. The informed use of multimedia authoring software encourages the producer to look for relationships among ideas, content, images, interactivity, words, and other elements. Bringing together all of those elements in such a way that their sum is more than the total of the parts is the educational essence of multimedia as a tool and a concept. The belief was that learning multimedia production skills is enhanced by concentrating on relevant content, subjects, and purposes. Further, the idea was not simply to deliver instruction or dispense information. The idea was to use the expressive and creative powers of the software in motivating, stimulating, and even entertaining ways. To do less is defeating the essence of multimedia as a tool and idea for teaching and learning. On completion of the projects, a class multimedia festival reveals the chosen topic or theme in a remarkable mixture of interpretations, perspectives, and production choices. Not only will the entire class learn about the topic, they will also view diverse uses of multimedia.

VERTOV REVISITED

The Preface of this book quoted Dziga Vertov sharing his vision of the emerging technology of film in 1923. What might he say in the twenty-first century about the electronic digital technologies that are influencing all aspects of our culture from how we learn to how we are entertained to how we express ourselves? Vertov's "mechanical eye" is now the digital eye, the digital ear, and the digital voice, all of which show us the world the way only they can see it. Vertov might suggest that the digital eye, ear, and voice free themselves "for today and forever from human immobility" because they are in constant action, interaction, and movement. The digital eye, ear, and voice "approach and pull away from objects." They "creep under them" and can "move alongside a running horse's mouth" and "fall and rise with the falling and rising bodies." Vertov might tell us that the digital eye, ear, and voice maneuver "in the chaotic movements" revealing and "recording one movement after another in the most complex combinations."

Vertov might also tell us that the digital eye, ear, and voice are "freed from the boundaries of time and space." That they "coordinate any and all points of the universe, wherever I [they] want them to be." Their "way leads towards the creation of a fresh perception of the world." Finally, Vertov might tell us that the digital eye, ear, and voice "explain in new ways the world unknown to you."

THOUGHT AND PROJECT PROVOKERS: MULTIMEDIA IDEAS

The following suggestions are much less specific because each one of them can be created with a variety of multimedia software. That is to say, the following are presented as ideas and concepts that may spark an idea or two.

1. *Multimedia Music Videos.* Music and multimedia are natural complements. The music video is a ubiquitous media production genre in the modern world. Though abstract movies were first combined with music scores in the 1930s, the contemporary music video has become an essential factor of the music business. So, after acquiring some competence and understanding of the complexities of multimedia production, consider experimenting with this potent combination. Create a flow of graphics in time, space, and rhythm. Collaborate with a musician or composer and let the music be the inspiration.

2. *Digital Impressionism.* Create an impressionistic perspective of an interesting location, space, season, or event. Explore the subject with interesting images that reveal its character, mood, and uniqueness. Use digital video or digital still photos. Be especially sensitive to image sequence and transitions and avoid the cliché. That is, reveal the subject in ways viewers many not have considered.

3. *Folktales.* Filmmakers and media producers often look to folktales as inspiration for their work. Animation studios as well as live-action moviemakers seek stories that can be successfully interpreted into entertaining works. Folktales may come from many sources and are often told as the truth. All families have storytellers. One especially rich source is oral tradition, so be on the lookout for those stories as sources of possible digital videos, animated movies, or multimedia productions. The stories need not be very long but they should be entertaining.

4. *Local Resources.* All communities have a history and a sense of place. Local museums and historians may provide suggestions for "local color" productions that use old photos, signs, newspapers, recordings, and appealing personalities. Do not make a travelogue or an economic promotion piece. Do make an informed and sensitive examination of a community and its traditions.

5. *Your Ideas Here.* The ultimate goal of multimedia as an educational tool is to empower individual learners. Based on that principle and referring to the concepts, skills, and projects described in this book, propose some multimedia projects—from digital video to computer animation—that you would like to participate in or create and are based on your personal interests and experiences.

INDEX

Abstract-to-concrete models, 2
Academy of Motion Picture Arts and Sciences, 17, 28
Actionscript, 47
Adams, Ansel, 52, 56, 78
Adobe AfterEffects, 46, 89
Adobe GoLive, 46, 60
Adobe Illustrator, 43, 89
Adobe Photoshop, 42, 59, 60, 89, 139, 185
Adobe Premiere, 43, 86, 89, 105
The Adventures of Prince Achmed, 24, 176
Agee, James, 52
Akira, 28
Analog 8mm, 70
Analog video, 69–70
  editing, 70–71
Animated GIFs, 46, 155–159, 191–192
  postproduction for, 158–159
  preproduction for, 156
  production for, 156–158
Animated movies, festivals for watching, 195
Animation, 21–28. *See also* Digital animation
  cel, 181
  collage, 121, 176–178
  computer, 125–126, 134–137
  creative potential of, 119–120
  cutout, 121, 176–178
  defined, 21, 118, 119
  direct, 134, 159–161
  draw on, 134
  experimental, 125–126, 133
  GIF, 46, 155–159, 191–192
  golden age of, 24–26
  independent, 27–28
  information sources on, 193–195
  international, 27–28
  Japanese, 28
  line, 120
  multiple-cel level, 120–121, 181–183

object, 121–122
  purpose of, 21
  stop motion, 121–122, 179–181
  television, 27
  theories and methods of, 118–126, 133–137
  on World Wide Web, 28
The Animation Book (Laybourne), 184, 194
Animation Magazine, 195
Animation online, 195
Animation stand for a digital camera, 163–166
  postproduction for, 166
  preproduction for, 163–165
  production for, 165–166
Animation World, 195
The Animator's Survival Kit (Williams), 194–195
Anime, 28
AppleWorks, 35, 199
Art, photography as, 58–59
Association for Educational Communications and Technology (AECT), 3
Audio recordings, educational use of, 3
Audio CDs, recording from, 89–90
Audiovisual aids, 2
Audiovisual education, 3, 28–29
Automatic exposure, 60
Automatic exposure meters, 81
Avery, Tex, 26

Bambi, 24
The Battle of San Pietro, 19
Beauty and the Beast, 138, 181
Behaviorism, 2
Betacam digital, 71
BetaSP, 69, 70
Betty Boop, 25
Bimbo, 25
Black-and-white photographs, appeal of, 53
Blackton, J. Stewart, 22

Blair, Preston, 26, 152, 184, 185, 194
Blanc, Mel, 26
Bosustow, Stephen, 26
Bourke-White, Margaret, 56, 57, 78
Bowling for Columbine, 20
Bugs Bunny, 26
Built-in flash, 60
Built-in microphone, 82–83
Burton, Tim, 122

California Raisen Growers, 122
Camera. *See also* Digital camcorders; Digital video camera
  traditional movie, 66–67
Camera-mounted light, 81
Camera-mounted microphone, 89
Cameron, James, 118
Capra, Frank, 19, 69
Cartoon Animation (Blair), 152, 184, 185, 194
CD-ROM, importing effects from, 90
Cel animation, 181
Chaplin, Charlie, 23, 24
A Charlie Brown Christmas, 27
Chicken Run, 122, 179
Clampett, Bob, 25
ClarisWorks, 139, 199
Claris Works Drawing, 91
Claris Works Painting, 91
Claymation, 122–123, 127–133, 179
  characters for, 127–133
  sets for, 132–133
Clip art, 46
Clonky, Art, 122
Close-ups, 78
Cohl, Emil, 22
Collage animation, 121, 176–178
  postproduction for, 178
  preproduction for, 177–178
  production for, 178
Color of multimedia products, 48
Color photography, educational use of, 3

Color process, 24
Communication, 47
Communications technology, evolution of, 8
Composition, 78–81
Computer
  drawing on, 137–144
  as educational tool, vii–viii
Computer animation, 125–126, 134–137
Cone of Experience, 2, 29
Consortium of College and University Media Centers, 40–41
Construction, 4–5
Content in preproduction, 38
Contour drawing, 139–142
Copyright Act (1976), 40
Corel Painter, 43, 139
Corny Concerto, 26
Creativity, 36
Cropping, 80–81
Cunningham, Imogene, 56
Cutout animation, 121, 176–178
  postproduction for, 178
  preproduction for, 177–178
  production for, 178
Cuts, 88
Cutting room floor, 85
Cycle, 147

Daffy Duck, 26
Dale, Edgar, 2, 29
Damuier, Honore, 22
Davis, Peter, 20
Digital 8, 71, 72
Digital animation, 117–195. *See also* Animation
Digital camcorders
  automatic exposure mode for, 73
  battery for, 73
  built-in microphone for, 73
  camera mode for, 71
  camera movement and, 82
  cassette tapes for, 72

Digital camcorders (cont.)
composing and framing with, 78–81
constructing and operating an animation stand for, 163–166
film ratio for, 72
formats and operation of, 69–71
keeping steady, 76–78
overview of, 69
prices of, 71
recording modes for, 72–73
recording sound with, 82–83
in the second language classroom, 54–55
VCR mode for, 71, 73
viewfinders for, 72
Digital doodling, 188–190
postproduction for, 190
preproduction for, 188–189
production for, 189–190
Digital drawing tools, 138–139
Digital editing, 83–87, 105–108
basics in, 86–87
conceptual framework for, 84–85
hardware and software for, 85–86
postproduction for, 107–108
preproduction for, 105
production for, 105–106
software for, 43–44, 192
Digital graphics tablet, 139, 141
Digital movies, 66–90
postproduction, 67
preproduction planning, 67
production, 67
release, critique, and revision of, 40
Digital multimedia technologies, 7
Digital multimedia tools, vii
Digital photography, 60
Digital stills, 51–64
Digital tools, troubleshooting, 34–35
Digital video, advantages of, 71
Digital video camera, crossing index cards with, 166–170
postproduction for, 169–170
preproduction for, 166–168
production for, 168–169

Digital videocassette tape formats, 71
Digital video streaming, 46
Digital video technology, 17
Dipietro, Kathryn, 108
Direct animation, 134, 159–161
postproduction for, 160
preproduction for, 160
production for, 160
Disney, Walt, Studios, animation of, 21, 24, 118
Dissolves, 88
Documentaries
classical view of, 16–17
power of, 13–21
television, 19, 21
in World War II, 18–19
Drawing
on the computer, 137–144
contour, 139–142
digital tools for, 138–139
gesture, 142–144
Draw on animation, 134
Draw programs, 139

Eastman, George, 52
Edison, Thomas, 17, 28, 82, 145
Editing, 7–8, 9. See also Digital editing
analog video, 70–71
digital, 83–87
image, 42–43
music, 39
sound, 87, 89–90, 192–193
sound design, 192–193
sound effects, 39
web software, 55
Education
audiovisual tools in, 28–29
multimedia in, 6–9
Educational media, 3
Eisenstein, Sergei, 17
Evans, Walker, 52, 56, 78
Experimental animation, 125–126, 133
Extreme close-ups, 81

Fade, 88
Fair use guidelines, 40–41
The Family of Man, 52
Fantasia, 24, 26, 126
Fantasia 2000, 24
Farm Security Agency, 52
Feature-length cartoons, 24
Felix in Hollywood, 24
Felix the Cat, 23–24
Filmmaking technology, improvements in, 20
Filmstrips, educational use of, 3, 29

Final Cut Pro, 42, 43–44, 86, 105
Fischinger, Oskar, 126, 133
Flaherty, Frances Hubbard, 17–18
Flaherty, Robert, 13, 16, 17–21
Fleischer, Dave, 24–25, 118
Fleischer, Max, 24–25, 118
Fleischer Studios, 24–25, 187, 191
The Flintstones, 27
Flip book, 153–155
postproduction for, 154–155
preproduction for, 154
production for, 154
Flowers and Trees, 24
Focusing, 73
Foley art, 192
Frame composition, 80–81
Framing, 78–81, 80–81
Frank Film, 121, 176
Fudd, Elmer, 26

Genre in preproduction, 37
Gerald McBoing Boing, 27
Gertie the Dinosaur, 22–23, 28, 120, 135, 154
Gesture drawing, 142–144
Ghost in the Shell, 28
GIF animation, 21, 46, 155–159, 191–192
postproduction for, 158–159
preproduction for, 156
production for, 156–158
Gilliam, Terry, 133, 176
Goldware, 89
The Great Train Robbery, 82
Grierson, John, 17–18
Griffith, D. W., 17
Gulliver's Travels, 25, 191
Gumby, 122, 179

Hanna and Barbera, 27
Harlan County, U.S.A., 20
Harvest of Shame, 19
"Heard It Through the Grapevine," 122
Hearts and Minds, 20
Hen Hop, 159
How the Grinch Stole Christmas, 27
Huckleberry Hound, 27
The Human Figure in Motion (Muybridge), 152, 184, 194
Humanities video, 108–109, 111–116
postproduction for, 114–115
preproduction for, 111–113
production for, 114

Humorous Phases of Funny Faces, 22
Hurd, Earl, 120
Hypercard, 44
HyperStudio, 44, 60, 91, 118, 199
Hyper Text Markup Language (HTML), 39, 47, 60, 188

iFilm, 28
The Illusion of Life (Thomas and Johnston), 194
Illusion of motion, 119
Image editing and creation, software for, 42–43
iMovie, 42, 43–44, 86
Independent animation, 27–28
Instructional communications, 3
Instructional design, 4, 29
Instructional media, 3
Instructional technology, 29
alternative aspects of, 2–5
defined, 3
in teacher education, vii
Interactive testing, 62–63
Interior lighting, 81
International animation, 27–28
Internet, 29
In the Land of the Free: September 11–And After, 53
It's a Wonderful Life, 69

Japanese animation, 28
Java, 47
Java Applets, 199
Javascript, 47
The Jetsons, 27
Johnston, Ollie, 118, 194
Jones, Chuck, 25, 27
JPEG (Joint Photographic Group) file format, 59

Kaufmann, Denis, 16. See also Vertov, Dziga
Kazan, Elia, 19
King Kong, 179
King of the Hill, 27
Koko the Clown, 25
Kopple, Barbara, 20
Koyanisqatsi, 179

Lange, Dorthea, 52
Lantern slides, educational use of, 3, 29
Lascaux, France, cave paintings in, 21–22
L'Association Internationale du Film d' Animation, 195
Lavalier mike, 82–83

Laybourne, Kit, 184, 194
Layout of multimedia
  products, 48
Lighting, 81
Lighting kit, 76, 81
Line animation, 120
Linear portraits, 170–172
  postproduction for, 172
  preproduction for, 170
  production for, 170–172
Line coding, 47
Lip synchronization, 183,
  186–188
Little Nemo, 22
Live-action movies, 192
  making, 118–119
  software for, 46–47
Looney Tunes, 25
Lord, Peter, 179
Lorentz, Pare, 17
Louisiana Story, 17
Luminere, Louis, 16, 17, 145
Lusitana, sinking of, 23

MacDraw, 139
MacPaint, 139
Macromedia Authorware, 45
Macromedia Director, 45,
  60, 185
Macromedia Dreamweaver,
  45–46, 199
Macromedia Flash, 34, 35, 42,
  45, 47, 60, 121, 135–136,
  139, 183, 193, 199
Macromedia Flash Player,
  188
Maltin, Leonaard, 194
Man of Aran, 17
Man with a Movie Camera,
  16
McCay, Winsor, 22–23,
  120, 135, 137, 145, 154,
  193, 194
McLaren, Norman, 27, 119,
  124, 125, 126, 159, 180
McLuhan, Marshall, 8, 29
Media and materials, in
  preproduction, 37
Media creation, steps in,
  36–40
Media production, 5
  language of, 16
  planning, 36–40
Medium shots, 78
Meet John Doe, 69
Melendez, Bill, 27
Memphis Belle, 19
Merrie Melodies, 25
Messmer, Otto, 23–24
Metro Goldwyn Mayer,
  26, 118
Mickey Mouse, 25
Microsoft Front Page, 46, 60
Microsoft Paint, 91, 139
Microsoft Paint Shop Pro, 60

Microsoft PowerPoint, 35,
  44, 60, 91, 118, 199
Mini-DV, 71, 72
Moana, 18
*Monty Python's Flying
  Circus,* 133, 176
Moore, Michael, 20
Moreno, Ruben, 181
Motion, suggestion of, in
  still images, 21–22
Motion Picture code, 25
Motion pictures as
  educational tool, 3, 28–29
Mouris, Frank, 121, 176
Mouse, 139, 141
Movie Clip Symbol, 192
Moving abstractions,
  172–174
  postproduction for, 174
  preproduction for,
    172–173
  production for, 174
Moyers, Bill, 20
Mr. Magoo, 27
*Mr. Smith Goes to
  Washington,* 69
Multimedia, 5
  common design flaws in,
    35
  concept of, vii
  in education, 6–9
  educational purposes of,
    36–40
  fair use guidelines for,
    40–41
  history of, 12–29
  metaphorical language
    of, 12–13
Multimedia mountain,
  199–201
  postproduction for,
    200–201
  preproduction for,
    199–200
  production for, 200–201
Multimedia presentation
  packages, 44
Multimedia production
  graphic design in, 48
  software for, 42–47
Multimedia products
  color of, 48
  design of, 47–48
  layout of, 48
  typeface legibility of, 48
Multimedia software
  learning, 34
  more advanced, 45–47
Multimedia technologies,
  working with, 1–9
Multiplane animation
  camera, 24
Multiple-cel-level
  animation, 120–121,
    181–183

postproduction for, 183
preproduction for, 181–183
production for, 183
Mumford, Louis, 17
Murrow, Edward R., 19
Music editing, 39
Muybridge, Eadweard,
  152, 184, 194
Mystery video, 104
  postproduction for, 104
  preproduction for, 104
  production for, 104

The Name Above the Title, 69
Nannook of the North, 16,
  17–21, 29
National Film Board of
  Canada, 27
Naudet, Gedeon, 20
Naudet, Jules, 20
Neighbors, 124, 125
*The Nightmare Before
  Christmas,* 122
9/11, 20
*Now Let Us Praise Famous
  Men,* 52

Object animation, 121–122
Of Mice and Magic
  (Maltin), 194
Olympia, 17
1-inch video, 69, 70, 71
Online galleries, 53, 55–63
  acquiring basic
    materials, 60
  choosing theme or motif
    for, 56–59
  curating the exhibit, 59
  making and acquiring
    images for, 59–60
  searching and
    evaluating, 56
  selecting, importing,
    arranging, laying out
    images, 61–63
Operant conditioning, 2
Overhead projectors,
  educational use of, 3

Paint, 139
Painter, 42
Paint programs, 139
Pan, 78, 82, 83, 98–99
  postproduction for, 99
  preproduction for, 98–99
  production for, 99
Park, Nick, 122, 123, 179
Pas de Deu, 126
Peace on Earth, 26
People Like Us, 20
Persistence of vision, 68
Phenakistoscope, 22
Photography
  as art, 58–59
  history of, 52–53

Photojournalism, 56–58, 78
Photorealism, 58–59
Pinocchio, 24
Pixar, 193
Pixilated movies, 123–125
Pixilation, 179–180
*The Plow that Broke the
  Plains,* 17
Pokémon, 28
Pokey, 122
Porky Pig, 26
Porter, Edwin, 82
Portraits
  creating video, 110–111
  linear, 170–172
  rotating, 161–163
Postproduction, 36–37,
  39–40, 83–84
  for animated GIFs,
    158–159
  for animation stand for a
    digital camera, 166
  for collage animation, 178
  for crossing index cards
    with, 169–170
  for cutout animation, 178
  for digital doodling, 190
  for digital editing, 107–108
  for digital movies, 67
  for direct animation, 160
  for flip books, 154–155
  for GIF animation,
    158–159
  for humanities video,
    114–115
  for linear portraits, 172
  for moving abstractions,
    174
  for multimedia
    mountain, 200–201
  for multiple-cel-level
    animation, 183
  for mystery video, 104
  for pan, 99
  for rotating portraits,
    162–163, 163
  for rotoscoping, 191–192
  for stop motion
    animation, 181
  for storyboards, 95–97
  for storytelling, 176
  for symbolic shots,
    103–104
  for tilts, 101–102
  for zoetrope, 152
Praxinoscope, 22
Preproduction, 36
  for animation stand for a
    digital camera, 163–165
  for collage animation,
    177–178
  content in, 38
  for crossing index cards
    with digital video
    camera, 166–168

Preproduction (cont.)
for cutout animation, 177–178
for digital doodling, 188–189
for digital editing, 105
for digital movies, 67
for direct animation, 160
for flip books, 154
genre in, 37
for GIF animation, 156
for humanities video, 111–113
for linear portraits, 170
media and materials in, 37
for moving abstractions, 172–173
for multimedia mountain, 199–200
for multiple-cel-level animation, 181–183
for mystery video, 104
for panning, 98–99
for rotating portraits, 161–162
for rotoscoping, 190–191
script in, 39
statement of purpose in, 37
for stop motion animation, 180
for storyboards, 39, 91–92
for symbolic shots, 102
for tilts, 99–100
for zoetrope, 145
Production, 36, 39
for animated GIFs, 156–158
for animation stand for a digital camera, 165–166
for collage animation, 178
for crossing index cards with digital camera, 168–169
for cutout animation, 178
for digital doodling, 189–190
for digital editing, 105–106
for digital movies, 67
for direct animation, 160
for flip books, 154
for GIF animation, 156–158
for humanities video, 114
for linear portraits, 170–172
for moving abstractions, 174
for multimedia mountain, 200–201
for multiple-cel-level animation, 183
for mystery video, 104
for panning, 99

for rotoscoping, 191
for stop motion animation, 180–181
for storyboards, 93–95
for storytelling, 176
for symbolic shots, 102
for tilts, 100–101
for zoetrope, 145–152
Propaganda, 18–19, 20
Public Broadcasting System, 17
Pudovkin, V. I., 85

QuickTime, 46, 188, 189, 190
QuickTime Movie, 106, 191
QuickTime Player, 189, 190
QuickTime Pro, 42, 89, 105, 185, 189, 190, 191
QuickTime VR, 46–47

Ray, Man, 52, 58–59
Real Media, 46
RealNetworks, 46
Real Producer, 89
Red Hot Riding Hood, 26
Reiniger, Lotte, 24
Riefenstalh, Leni, 17
The River, 17
Rocky and Bullwinkle, 27
Roger and Me, 20
Rotating portraits, 161–163
postproduction for, 163
preproduction for, 161–162
production for, 162–163
Rotoscoping, 190–192
postproduction for, 191–192
preproduction for, 190–191
production for, 191
Rough and Ready, 27

Scanning, 59–60
software for, 59
Schickel, Richard, 91
Schildknecht, Ron, 181
Script in preproduction, 39
Second-language classroom, digital camera in, 54–55
See It Now series, 19
Sesame Street, 177
Shockwave, 39
Shrek, 28
The Simpsons, 27
16mm film, 68–69
educational use of, 29
Skinner, B. F., 2
Smith, Eugene, 57, 78
Smith, Webb, 91
Snow White and the Seven Dwarfs, 25
The Sorcerer's Apprentice, 24
Sound, recording, with camcorder, 82–83

Sound cartoons, 24
Sound design, 90, 192–193
Sound editing, 87, 89–90, 192–193
Sound effect libraries, 90
Sound effects editing, 39
South Park, 27
Special effects, 39
Stallings, Carl, 26
Statement of purpose in preproduction, 37
Steamboat Willie, 186–187
Steichen, Edward, 52
Still photography, 53
Stoll, Clifford, vii
Stop motion animation, 121–122, 179–181
postproduction for, 181
preproduction for, 180
production for, 180–181
Storyboards, 91–97, 127, 174–176
postproduction of, 95–97
preproduction for, 39, 91–92
production of, 93–95
Storytelling, 174–176
postproduction for, 176
preproduction for, 175–176
production for, 176
Studio Deluxe, 44, 86
Sullivan, Pat, 24
Super 8mm movie, 69
Symbolic shots, 102–104
postproduction for, 103–104
preproduction for, 102
production for, 102
Systematic instruction, 3, 4

Talking heads, 74–75
Teacher-centered instruction, 2
Technology communications, 8
creative tools of, 7
diffusion of, 8
digital video, 17
filmmaking, 20
instructional, vii, 2–5, 29
Television documentaries on, 19, 21
influence of, 66
Television animation, 27
Television programming, 66
Thaumatrope, 22
Thomas, Frank, 118, 194
Thorndike, E. L., 2
Thumbnails, 56
Tilt, 78, 82, 83, 99–102
postproduction for, 101–102

preproduction for, 99–100
production for, 100–101
Titanic, 118
Toy Story, 137, 138, 180
Transitions, 39, 87–89
Tripods, 76, 78
Triumph of the Will, 17
True Glory, 19
Tweens, 193
Two-frame animation, 119
Typeface, legibility of, in multimedia products, 48

Ulead GIF Animator, 46
Ulman, Doris, 52
Underdog, 27
United Productions of America (UPA), 26–27

VanDerBeek, Stan, 133
Van Dyke, Willard, 17
Vertov, Dziga, vii–viii, 13, 14–16, 66, 201–202
VHS, 69, 70
VHS analog camcorder, 69
Video movies. See Digital movies
VideoWave, 44, 86
Vinton, Will, 122

Walk cycle, 183, 184–186, 188
Wallace and Grommit, 122, 123, 133
Ward, Jay, 27
Warner Brothers, 25–26, 118
Web editing software, 55
What's Opera Doc?, 26
Who Framed Roger Rabbit?, 26, 194
Why We Fight series, 19
Wide shots, 78
A Wild Hare, 26
Williams, Richard, 26, 194
Wireless mike, 82–83
World Trade Center, documentary of terrorist attack on, 19–20, 53
World War II, documentaries in, 18–19
World Wide Web animation on, 28
music and sound on, 90
photographs on, 53, 55
Wyler, William, 19

Zoetrope, 22, 145–153, 193
postproduction for, 152
preproduction for, 145
production for, 145–152
Zoom lenses, 60, 73, 78, 80